The Man in Black

A HISTORY OF THE FOOTBALL REFEREE

ACKNOWLEDGEMENTS

Two truisms about football came up time and time again during the writing of this book. No one trusts referees. And no referee trusts anyone foolish enough to write a book about them. Those kind few League and ex-League referees who answered my calls and letters therefore deserve special mention. In particular, Keith Cooper (Pontypridd), who was frank, fiery but in control at all times. His namesake, Keith Cooper (Swindon), who was animated, vocal and a rigorous time-keeper. Tony Leake (Darwen) made a disciplined contribution on the touchline, as did Jim McMaster (Dalkeith). I am grateful to Barry Davies for an illuminating interview, in which he talked in some detail about issues pertinent to officialdom past and present. Thanks to Jeff King for giving me an expert's insight into the Spanish scene, Jack Bell at the *New York Times* for a highly entertaining resume of American sports umpires. To Colin Miller, Jonathan Berger and Steven Smith – thanks and sorry there wasn't more room. JT for days of heartache at Hampden. Alan Briscoe for the stats. To the *Goal* boys – Hawksbee, Borrows, Ranaldi, Wray, Strickland, and especially, Hodges, Cottrell and Davies – cheers. A big thanks to Kate Beveridge for support and encouragement. An equally big thank you to Andrew Goodfellow for his unfailing patience. Finally, special mention goes to Lydia – thanks for being a star throughout. And to my brother Graeme for his enlightening suggestions, incisive editing and laughing at all the right bits. There are too many others who, for reasons best known to themselves made no attempt to cooperate with the research. Which is a shame because, ultimately this book is about you.

Jeff King's *Bobby Robson: His Year at Barcelona* was invaluable for the chapter on Spanish refereeing. Equally many of the examples used in chapter four are drawn from Tony Mason's *Passion of the People*. *Football Babylon* by Russ Williams was the source of a few of the comical anecdotes in chapter six.

GORDON THOMSON is a freelance print and TV journalist. Born near Glasgow, he now lives and works in London. This is his first book.

The Man in Black

A HISTORY OF THE FOOTBALL REFEREE

Gordon Thomson

First published in 1998 by
Prion Books Limited
32–34 Gordon House Road,
London NW5 1LP

A catalogue record of this book can be obtained from the British Library

ISBN 1-85375-284-3

Cover design by Vivid

Printed and bound in Great Britain
by Creative Print & Design, Wales

PHOTOGRAPH ACKNOWLEDGEMENTS FOR INSERT SECTION

All-Sport 7 (top), 8
Mirror Syndication International 5
Vintage Magazine Co. 3, 4

CONTENTS

PROLOGUE: THE GOOD OLD DAYS 1

TAMING THE GAME
the early regulation of football 5

FROM SIDE LINE TO CENTRE SPOT
the birth of the modern referee 23

RULING THE WORLD
an arbiter's history of the World Cup 47

'SUPER PHLEGM GUYS'
British referees in South America 71

THE STRUTTING PEACOCK
the Spanish refereeing experience 93

THE DARK SIDE
bribes, fixes, violence and the bizarre 105

THE REF ON THE COUCH
the motives of the men in black 131

DOUBTING THOMAS
the life and times of a maverick referee 157

AMONG THE VULTURES
the referee under attack 175

THE FUTURE IS BLACK
bringing the referee into the 21st century 195

'AN ABSOLUTE DISGRACE'
a refereeing diary 1997/8 217

APPENDICES 233

INDEX 245

"I hope it doesn't sound conceited or arrogant, but the top referees make very few mistakes. I'm like a salesman – I'm selling decisions to players and I think I've been a reasonably successful salesman...I feel like I'm the conductor of the orchestra and the orchestra doesn't play as well without a skilled conductor."

Referee George Courtney, 1992

"The referee is available for Christmas pantomime or cabaret."

Keith Valle, tannoy announcer, as Bristol Rovers and Wigan left the pitch after the final whistle, 1989. He thought the microphone was switched off.

PROLOGUE: THE GOOD OLD DAYS

NOSTALGIA is Britain's panacea. In times of uncertainty we take comfort from the past, seek solace in its embrace. Although it can deceive us, cheat us, downright lie to us, it's been a good friend and always will be. If the past is indeed another country, it's more Renaissance Italy than post-war Poland.

In football, nostalgia has become especially seductive; its past is now a commodity with unlimited value. For all the changes rung in by the heavyweights of satellite TV, the Industry – as it has now become – really thrives on the creation of the illusion that we were all there. Football's hard currency is that flourishing artificial environment of collective memory which has spawned numerous halls of fame; long-sleeved cotton replica shirts; kitsch reprints of seventies sticker albums; collectors' issues of magazines plundering the game's heritage to bring us retrospectives; 'original' features on games that time forgot (and matches that we will never be allowed to forget, though most of us have never even seen footage of Real Madrid 7, Eintracht Frankfurt 3); and, most preponderant of all, interview upon interview with the legends of our great national sport. As the unwieldy football juggernaut rumbles towards the millennium, cosmetically more robust and in better condition than ever, it still seeks the approval of the golden generation that spawned the monster. Mostly, it doesn't get it, although the players in question appear more than happy to indulge the industry's interest in them, mindful that at least some of the financial rewards are at last there for the taking. For all concerned, it seems, nostalgia's good for business.

Last year, the former Arsenal star Terry Neill was host to some of the UK's most celebrated ex-players, who had gathered at his Holborn bar to celebrate the announcement of the PFA's International Hall of Fame. The room was crammed with ageing men, sporting the regulation brylcreemed short back and sides of their rank, pointedly ignoring the TV screens showing flickering footage of themselves in action; moments now carved into the national consciousness: Banks's save; Pele's lob; Cruyff's drag back; Hurst's hat-trick, events that nowadays need no more than the briefest introduction and require no further explanation. Journalists – some not even alive when the events took place – pored over the past with the likes of Best and Baxter, Finney and Lofthouse. "I don't think you can really compare the two sides," said Best, ruminating on the topical Ferguson-Busby, Man Utd debate. It was a telling line, serving as a succinct encapsulation of the whole past-present argument; for what he really meant, I sensed, was that football now, for all its glittering garb, could never be as good as it was back then. That for all the vogueish attention and attendant glamour which football now enjoys, something has been irretrievably lost along the way. Mind you, historical perspective never has had much truck with grey areas; it serves merely to greaten the good, vilify the bad and make the mediocre mass disappear. The further back into the mists we go, the more cursory those delineations are wont to become. It's easier that way.

PROLOGUE

So now, for spectacle and a sense of occasion we have Sky's Saturday morning and Sunday evening kickoffs and multi-angled television replays; for chirpy chatter and 'playing for the shirt' we instead get bitter post-match rantings and contractual get-out clauses; 'Mr Finney' and 'Sir Stanley' have become 'Mary Poppins' and 'The Spice Boys'. Respect and sportsmanship, goes the argument, are no longer the cornerstones of football. Nowhere, it continues, is this unwanted transformation of the game more evident than in adherence to the Laws of the Game. Where once a dubious penalty decision would be met with shrugs of masculine resignation from the offending team, a full-scale media enquiry is now the norm. Referee-bashing is the new national pastime.

Of course, in the halcyon days of the 'white horse final' and the Wembley wizards, players didn't call for the introduction of professional officials and electronic eyes. They didn't turn the air blue voicing imaginary grievances, or attempt that two-footed hospital tackle when no one was looking. They were gentlemen; they just got on with it didn't they, mindful that their conscience would always be the ultimate arbiter?

Well, no – not exactly. What was that about nostalgia again…

TAMING THE GAME

the early regulation of football

BLAME the Romans. While the Chinese and Greeks undoubtedly meddled with a rudimentary form of the game of football during breaks from backgammon, metaphysics and empire-building, it was the Italians who gave the man in black his first walk-on part in football. Around the mid-1500s Giovanni Bardi, football's first administrator, drew up a set of rules for the ancient game of *calcio storico*, which by the 17th century had become all the rage in Northern Italy and Eastern France. Visit Florence in mid-June and you will still see it being played. The Lyonese, who took up calcio during the reign of Henry III, even organised a clash with their Italian rivals as part of the recent World Cup 98 celebrations in the city.

Cunningly disguised as football, the game is more like a bastard hybrid of rugby and Greco-Roman wrestling. Four teams of 27 men – each team representing a medieval *rione* (district) of the city – do battle for honour, not to mention a cow – the victors' prize. It takes place on a *five-a-side size* sand pit with the Harlequin-clad players pinned in by waist-high wooden hoardings and a bloodthirsty crowd occupying the kind of makeshift stands that are knocked up every June to sate groups of middle-aged Cliff Richard fans during the opening rounds of Wimbledon. Not that there was, or indeed is, anything remotely effete about calcio. Imagine British Bulldog played by the cast of *Goodfellas* and you're close – anything goes. So Joe Pesci harries midfielder Ray Liotta into touch, punching him repeatedly in the face as he does so? Play on. Maybe De Niro takes exception to a taunting fan in the crowd and wades in with some piano-wire to request silence? It just means his team's one short on the park for a while. There's little talk of 4-4-2 or zonal marking here, and you get the sense that putting 'a man in the hole' has a somewhat more literal significance. There are moments of skill, but never at the expense of a good scrap. Yet somewhere amidst this colourful mêlée of hands, feet and heads, a semblance of order is restored: by a man wearing a black ruff-necked tunic and brandishing a four-foot ceremonial sword.

This *maestro de campo* (master-of-the-field) was probably the world's first 'football' arbiter. He certainly existed as early as 1688, the year in which *Memore del Calcio Fiorentina* was published, believed to be the first book entirely dedicated to the game. In it, the first primitive guidelines for refereeing are laid out: "The master of the field is responsible for keeping the peace and passing judgements on disputes…" Note the order in which the author prioritises the maestro's dual function. Here, first and foremost, is a pacifier; a policeman. Like the game itself, he is unskilled and brutish, prone to bouts of wilful violence. But when called upon he is also the judge.

The maestro's very presence at early games of calcio highlights the basic tensions and contradictions that still surround the referee today. Disliked, unwanted, unsung, he was ultimately essential – the mother of necessary evils. Nonetheless, the Italians seemed to hold their maestros in higher regard than football does the referee today. Indeed, from a modern perspective he looks more like a latter-day Caesar – deciding the fate of the assembled gladiators with a delicate twist of his thumb – than today's much maligned interloper. And if he held a sword, then it was because either pomp or the nature of the game dictated it. Besides, no one had ever heard of anybody trying to separate grown men using coloured cards and a whistle.

Almost 200 years later, minus the dandy with the scabbard and the neck-ruff, a not dissimilar game to calcio was being played in Britain. Foolishly thinking they could regulate themselves, the men who participated shunned the referee. It took them years to learn that in the heat of competition a vague code of conduct and a gentleman's sensibilities were no substitutes for a man in the middle. Or on the touchline. Before long, they would need the referee too.

Prototype football was being played behind the walls of Britain's public schools as early as the mid-18th century or, more accurately, it was being played wherever the ball led the two teams. Mob games, of the kind still ritually played each New Year in The Orkneys, thundered noisily across the countryside. Up and down cobbled lanes, dozens of men chased a single 'ball' like a pack of witless sheep. The game had one easy-to-grasp governing rule: to get the ball in to the opposition's 'goal' by any means necessary. Hands, feet, elbows and any other part of the anatomy that happened to be closest to it, were deployed to this end and used frequently to assault members of the other team. It certainly wasn't a spectator sport, if only because bystanders were often drawn into the mêlée. Hours could elapse before anything meaningful took place. Games only finished once one 'team' finally reached the others 'goal', which invariably lay miles in the opposite direction. Mercifully, there were never any scoreless draws.

Once coaxed into a more modest playing area things improved, but only slightly. Teams were pared down, pitches designated, times arranged for games. Yet, the central tenets remained the same. Players still rushed thirstily after the ball like hounds in pursuit of the fox; no quarter was given, nor expected. No limit was placed on the number of players and nobody was asked, nor – unsurprisingly – did they volunteer, to take charge of this ill-tempered, artless eyesore.

By the time the schools and universities of England had adopted a form of football as part of their wider sporting curriculum, many of the more primitive features of the mob game had been eradicated, apparently in the interest of pupil safety and discipline. Still, by the 1840s the game remained at best a dangerous cocktail of modern-day rugby and freestyle kickboxing, with unsporting behaviour seemingly encouraged by rival school authorities – by men like the Reverend Samuel Sands, a Rugby School 'Old boy'. "The custom of the big boys at the beginning of the term", he said, without explicit reference to any of Vinnie Jones' male ancestors, "is to take a pair of boots to the shoemakers to have thick soles put on them, sharpened at the toes so as to cut into the shins of the enemy". Nice. Sands was once asked after watching a particularly nasty encounter at which point he had decided to interfere with the contest. "Short of manslaughter," he replied. Like many of his public school peers who witnessed these early contests, Sands wasn't a referee in the modern form. His actions were more akin to those of a boxing official, stepping in to stop a bout when it had gone well beyond the realms of fairness or safety. Aside from that, he left them to it.

Before meaningful competition between universities and schools necessitated the introduction of a neutral official to control proceedings, the captain of a team governed his side, and was responsible for ensuring that his players did nothing contrary to the perceived 'spirit' of the game. Rules, which from the early 1800s began to appear sporadically on school noticeboards, were arbitrarily drawn up by headmasters who urged players to adhere to their every letter. Rule 16, Harrow School Football: "The rules should be put up conspicuously in every House at the beginning of every football quarter, and new boys should be required to make themselves thoroughly acquainted with them."

Knowledge of the rules was one thing. Their application was another entirely. Ostensibly, the two captains were the referees, although their status as match adjudicators was never officially recognised. But it was the captains who were responsible for the 'regularity' of the play and for acting if any of his players did anything to contravene the accepted 'laws' of the game. The overwhelming desire to kick your opponent into an adjoining field had inevitably dominated early mob football and, as such, the formative years of inter-school competition necessarily walked the tightrope between acceptable aggression and wilful harm; so while the vigour and bodily contact always associated with the game was tolerated, and the possibility of damage or even casual injury manfully accepted, intentional foul play was totally unacceptable. Worse, it was deemed – horror of horrors – 'ungentlemanly'.

The venerable J R Witty, in a short essay published in vol. 1 of *Association Football*, puts us in the picture. "It was never thought that a player would intentionally do anything to hurt an opponent. Such conduct would be ungentlemanly, and that was an unpardonable offence; accidents were within reason, but the lowering of self-control to the depths of ungentlemanly conduct was something which could not be overlooked. An excess of enthusiasm or lack of skill, or even a momentary reaction might be checked or censured, but any recurrence, due to ill-temper or spite, would receive short shrift and captain's orders to 'Leave the field'." Impossible as it seemed, the captain sent his own players off. Indeed, in theory, he could send himself off. As is the practice nowadays, a player guilty of misconduct was warned (booked) and then asked to take an early bath if he repeated the misdemeanour. Much as now a referee must decide for himself if an act merits a red card, then it was down to the captain to interpret the ruling on 'ungentlemanly behaviour'. It's hard to reconcile the tendency in the modern game for players to fake injury in order to get an opponent sent off with the picture postcard impression of self-regulated gentlemanly combat. Although contemporary accounts suggest that the Victorians did not shrink from the aggressive (and occasionally brutal) side of football, the behaviour of these early players still stopped some way short of the sophisticated and theatrical gamesmanship employed by the likes of Bilic and Klinsmann.

One fundamental problem that emerged once competition between schools and universities became more common was the lack of a uniform set of rules. To begin with the laws of the game were rarely written down at all. But more of a sticking point was the very nature of the game itself, which varied wildly from school to school. From the size of the pitch to the shape of the ball, schools adopted different laws. Indeed the physical layout of a school's games pitch was often crucial in determining the codes of practice adopted, and subsequently handed down, from generation to generation. At Rugby, where radical change was imminent, boys could handle the ball but could not run with it in their hands. At Charterhouse no hand-to-ball contact was permitted. Instead the players became adept at dribbling with the ball across the stony surface of the cloisters, surely dispelling the myth that Hughie Gallagher was the first man on this island to be crowned 'Jinky'. With 20-a-side the norm, football at Charterhouse resembled a school-yard jamboree, a poignant evocation of the rites of passage game still played by children after school and into twilight during the long British summer holidays. At Harrow it was less idyllic but much more 'conventional': 11-a-side in the thick mud at the bottom of the school's hill. The ball could be caught with the hands, but then had to be kicked from the same spot (rather like 'calling the mark' in modern Rugby Union. This, until the 1870s, was what was meant by the term 'free kick'. It bore no relation to our modern-day equivalent.) Eton, of course, had the Wall Game, the most peculiar form of football to be found at the time. The goals were a small door and a tree at either end of a 120-yard-long dyke, and the pitch was 6 yards wide. The game, clearly a real visual treat for the spectator, still averages one goal every two years. Still, at least Eton recognised the need for goals. At Winchester the game existed without any recognisable target, points being awarded when the ball was kicked over the 'goal line'.

The type of challenges allowed by teams also differed. Most agreed that 'hacking' (a sharp kick to the shins) was ungentlemanly, but still some schools permitted it. One contemporary observer described a group of football players as 'a set of harmless lunatics, who amused themselves by kicking one another's shins, but did no great harm to the public at large'.

Eton and Harrow – in their own distinct ways – both subscribed to the beautiful game, but couldn't agree on the finer details. "No player may hit with his hands or arms, or use them in any way to push or hold one of the opposite party" (Eton rule 17). "All charging is fair...but no tripping, shinning or backshinning is allowed" (Harrow rule 11). The minutiae of the foul could be resolved before a game began, but often early teams must have found themselves playing a game totally alien to each other.

"So long as football was played purely for recreation between friends who had no intention of breaking any accepted rule wilfully, or of deliberately injuring an opponent – even though he was then termed an 'adversary' – the onus of control rested on the players," mused J R Witty of this early period in football. He had a point, but it was one born of naivety. The game had now passed that point. Growing competitiveness allied with the lack of a recognisable rulebook paved the way for the introduction of an arbiter. A gentleman arbiter, of course.

Honours such as the Cock House trophy for football (a kind of early League Cup) were provided by wealthy benefactors, often Old Boys, giving the schools and universities an impetus to win something tangible. Once football rivalry became a focus for meaningful competition and not just an extension of 'crest warfare', players and teams began to take the whole thing a bit more seriously. Aside from the obvious problems presented by teams playing different games with different rules, football, at least in its general concept, was rapidly becoming an institution – and a rowdy one at that. Genial captains increasingly struggled for impartiality, and petty squabbles amongst players very quickly turned into violent debates on points of dispute. One onlooker described a game from 1846, a year before the first 'umpires' came onto the scene, as 'completely chaotic'; and by now this was probably the rule rather than the exception: "Shortly before the end [of the game] three or four players entered into an extremely heated dispute...over what I could not tell. The two captains tried to separate them but it was fully five minutes before the game was continued." Blissfully unaware that 140 years of football with officials would do very little to prevent these kind of scenes, the powers-that-be nevertheless resolved to find a scapegoat willing to be a receptacle for disgruntled public schoolboys' outpourings on the pitch. In their hour of need they turned to what they knew best. Cricket, the gentleman's game.

FA Archives do not give any clear indication that the cricketing umpire was the inspiration behind officialdom in football.

Indeed, any rational soul would argue that cricket and football were entrenched opposites. One, a leisurely non-contact sport where controversy was rare and sportsmanship common (this was 140 years ago); the other, a muddy maelstrom of fists and feet inclined to prolonged physical exertion and pronounced bad-temperedness. One had a recognised tradition and a well-observed set of rules; the other neither. Cricket remained a gent's sport, while football, although initially a pastime of public school boys, never really convinced as a genteel recreation. Despite some early good intentions, the game was never going to be one for the faint-hearted. Whatever restrictive ideas schools might have had about 'hacking' or 'tripping', football was a contact sport. And with contact there is inevitably confrontation. However cricket was the long established summer game of universities and schools across England and it is likely that in football the authorities saw the future of winter sport – if only it could come to be as well-behaved as its elder sibling.

The first game to use the putative 'umpire' is not known. But by 1847 it was common practice to enlist the services of 'neutrals' for important matches. Generally two umpires were selected, but this was not a hard and fast rule. On many occasions only one was present, but sometimes there were no neutrals at all in attendance. Still, as early on as this, the powers of the umpire were considerable, as excerpts from the earliest school football rules to mention them serve to illustrate.

ETON c.1847

Two umpires must be chosen, one by each party [team]; their position is to be at the goals of their respective parties (Rule 3)

If the umpire is unable to give a decision, a 'bully' shall be formed one yard in front of the line (Rule 7)

Should a player fall on the ball, or crawl on his hands and

knees with the ball between his legs, the umpire must, if possible, force him to rise. (Rule 15)

The latter ruling – a primitive version of the 'ruck' in rugby – highlights the random evolution of football's laws. If a player chose to do something unprecedented but not condemned by the existing school statutes it would often evolve into law. William Webb Ellis – widely credited with 'inventing' modern rugby – did exactly that in 1823 when he picked the ball up and ran toward the opposition goal-line. In doing so he was not contravening any accepted law of the game, and within twenty years it became an accepted – indeed a defining – feature of football at Rugby.

WINCHESTER 1847
Two umpires are to be chosen before the commencement of the game. They must stand at opposite ends and sides of the ground, commanding a view of the side and also of the line of the goal nearest him.

The duty of the umpires is to score [record] the goals, and in all cases of doubt in which they are referred to, to give their decision, which is final

One of the umpires must have a watch, to call the time of beginning the game, changing sides and ending.

Winchester was one of the first schools to grasp the idea that the umpire should be both adjudicator and time-keeper. He was also to keep the score, which he did from memory. Despite these duties, the umpire was still a marginal figure, running the line furthest from the middle of the pitch and referred to by a team only at the discretion of the two captains. Captains 'appealed' to the umpires for scores and fouls – much as modern-day cricket etiquette still elicits cries of 'howzat!' from players calling for a wicket, or in the way players barrack modern referees – and they would signal to show agreement. How the umpires did this seemed to vary. Most sources suggest he waved a handkerchief, but several early paintings and photographs clearly show the umpire brandishing a walking stick which he may have raised to indicate an infringement. 'Appeals' apart, the umpires remained subordinate to the captains, though manners were still at a premium. This excerpt from the first *Referees' Chart* published by W Pickford in 1896 as a handbook for both players and officials, illustrates the protocol expected from players when appealing to an official. "Play a gentlemanly game. Don't allow yourself to lose your temper; keep a still tongue in your head. When you do claim, say what for and do not shout out 'foul' which may mean one of a dozen offences. If 'hands' say 'hands' and so on. The referee then knows what you want. 'How's that' cannot in any way be taken as an appeal."

By the time this passage had been written the referee ruled the roost. But the principles were equally relevant during the ascendancy of the umpire.

Incidentally, note the use of cricketing vernacular. The links between football and cricket, where 'appealing' is still a part of the rule book, remained strong up until the early 20th century when both games used Kennington Oval for their most important events; many leading figures in the FA were also keen County cricketers, most famously Charles Alcock who was secretary for Surrey County.

HARROW 1847

There must always be two umpires in a House Match, and if possible in School Matches. Their decision shall be final in matters of fact, but they are at liberty to refer to any question of law to the

Committee, if they feel unable to decide it at the time (Rule 13).

It shall be the duty of the umpire in all football matches to take away a goal obtained by unfair means, and in House Matches to put out of the game any player wilfully breaking any of the football rules (Rule 14).

Harrow, unusually, took away the powers of the captain and gave them to the umpire. Armed with the authority to dismiss players for the first time, Harrow's intrepid umpires must have been among the first to experience verbal recriminations from football players. They would not be the last. In a game with wildly varying regulations, however, this was by no means the norm. The umpire could certainly disallow goals – mainly for 'hacking' and 'tripping' (flooring the goalkeeper off the ball, known as 'charging', was still fair game) and refer to a committee of the schools' football administrators when he felt unsure of a decision he had made during the game, but he had very little authority other than that. Modern-day punishments like penalties or free kicks did not yet exist, and as such the umpire – if not at Harrow – generally relied upon the integrity of the captains to provide the only discipline possible: to caution the offender and, if he persisted in blatant disregard to the spirit of the game, to 'request' that he leave the field of play.

Furthermore, these umpires were not trained in the laws of the game and therefore often liable to make basic errors of judgement. Bias, a rather predictable result of the selection process, was rife, and led to widespread accusations of preferential treatment. The committee was the 19th century's answer to the fourth official. But it offered scant solace for the lonely umpire.

If, and it is undeniable from these sources, the referee was given his first role in football by the public schools and universities of England, then it is equally true that the 'Old Boy' network built the barriers that impeded his advance in the game. Teams chose umpires from their rank-and-file, just as school rugby teams now rely on willing pupils to run the line with a flag or a discarded jersey. But as long as there remained little uniformity of rules, the mediators would struggle to perform to any level of consistency. It was bad enough pleading ignorance to the laws governing their own school game without lacking the added nous required to handle the heat of a big school derby, with its conflicting rules and maze of discrepancies. Often they relied on the players to inform them of what was going on, or rather, of what was about to take place. Before a game kicked off, captains could minimise the damage bound to be inflicted on their teams by these befuddled officials with a quick clarification of aims: shall we allow running with the ball? How long shall we play for? Next goal wins, that kind of thing. But ultimately the contest would likely as not degenerate into a free-for-all. The umpires must have felt like they had been party to a conversation between two diplomats, each one stoically persevering in their mother tongue without the aid of a translator.

Something had to change. Not only were umpires poorly trained, ignorant of the laws and generally ill-equipped to mediate in football matches, they were constantly at loggerheads with one another. As if the battles between rival players wasn't enough for them to contend with, umpires added to the pandemonium by quarrelling over their respective involvement in games. Despite being employed at opposite ends of the pitch, precisely to ensure the greater part of the game was covered, umpires would often stray from their stoop in the quieter moments of matches and impinge on the territory of their counterpart. At controversial moments this could result in umpires arguing over a decision while the players did the same. The mediators – barely capable of controlling the game, never mind their own egos or tempers – were badly in need of a calming influence themselves. Luckily, an anonymous schoolmaster from Cheltenham – no doubt among others – noticed this need. Tentatively, the referee ambled into view.

CHELTENHAM c.1849
Two umpires and the referee shall be the sole arbiters of all disputes. In every important match there shall be (a) an umpire for each side (each captain to chose his own) and (b) a referee to be chosen by these umpires. Any point on which the umpires cannot agree shall be decided by the referee.

So the referee replaced the umpire as the final court of appeal, operating on the fringes of the game as the last point of reference (the word 'referee' deriving from the verb 'to refer'). He was a walking rule book – at least in principle – available to the umpires when they had extinguished all hope of reaching a mutually acceptable decision. Committees still sat, but the referee was their advance party, sent out to pace the touchline in his deerstalker hat and school blazer in the hope that he would sort out what the umpires couldn't.

But even if the umpires now had their baby-sitter, it remained a far from ideal arrangement. The referee was part of the same Old Boy network that had spawned the umpire. He was his friend before he became his colleague. With the two captains still choosing the umpires, and they in turn nominating a referee to oversee points of dispute, it could be argued that the circle of bias and favouritism that had plagued the evolution of the official thus far had only been widened; that self-interest still governed the game. Furthermore, it was a convoluted process: between two captains, two umpires, a referee and a committee, there could be little hope of anything but confusion.

There is no real suggestion that the referee was better qualified to mediate than the umpire. Like the umpire he was called upon to resolve a situation he could see unfolding before him. He was also working from a half-formed and constantly evolving rule book which rather than aiding must have seriously hindered his judgement. If the players were confused, imagine the befuddlement of the officials. A typical school game didn't exist, but if it had done it must have been hellish to referee. The pitch was a muddy, divot-strewn expanse with few markings and no flags. The players still indulged their herd instincts as they pursued the ball (it was years before the canny Scots pioneered the passing game). Throw-ins, set-pieces and the offside rule lay on the distant horizon. There was no 'goalkeeper' in the modern sense. There was no goalkeeper's area, or goalkeeper's shirt. One simple rule, still common in kickabouts, governed the last line of defence: whoever was nearest the goal guarded it. The goal itself was at best two wooden sticks with a piece of string as the crossbar. (The tape or string was finally made compulsory in 1866 after a goal had been scored at Reigate '...from a balloon kick which had passed quite 90 feet in the air between the posts' according to the FA Chairman). Decision-making was fraught with danger. If the umpires disagreed on the validity of a captain's appeal, for example, they did so on the basis of the testimony of one man standing near the action and the opinion of another marooned up-field. The referee was not obliged to keep up with play nor was he permitted to enter onto the pitch. Clearly, the adjudicator was in no position to adjudicate.

By the 1850s, football's growing network of unofficial marshals and administrators had set about remedying these problems. Perhaps mindful that their name derived from the old French *nomper*, meaning 'the man without equal', the umpires were released from their restrictive vantage points on the goal-line and given carte blanche to patrol the two halves of the pitch; one half each. While the referee sat impassive yet alert on the sideline, waiting for his invitation to join in the fun, the umpire's powers increased. But the lack of a consistent set of rules remained a hindrance. Football would have to secure its identity before the officials could come into their own.

In 1848, 14 representatives from a number of England's leading public schools drew up what they hoped would become the first nationally recognised Rules of Football – the Cambridge Rules. Oxford, Cambridge and several other of England's foremost universities certainly used the new code, which was the first to lay out some of the principle rules of the modern game. Significantly, Rule 7 decreed that 'a goal is when the ball is kicked through the flag-posts and under the string'. That idea at least was a winner. Handling the ball was permitted, but sparingly, and players were barred from running with it. 'Grabbing', 'tripping' or 'holding' a player was disallowed. Rudimentary throw-ins and goal-kicks were written in. These laws helped colleagues compete with one another, but didn't in any way clarify the roles of the umpires and the referees.

Significantly, the game was also beginning to shift away from its exclusive existence in academic institutions. Sheffield's professional and middle-class males were the first to adopt the game purely as a leisure pursuit, and by 1854 a group of cricketers and budding footballers had formed the first non-university club there. In 1857 they shunned the Cambridge oligarchy by drawing up their own set of rules and subsequently the game took off, with as many as fifteen clubs formed in the city by 1860. Still, although these two prototype codes – Cambridge and Sheffield – adopted similar stances, there were enough differences of opinion on points of law to prevent a single rule book – and therefore a single recognisable game – being introduced.

During this period of transition, umpires and referees continued to adhere to whatever code their school, college or club adopted. But the officials themselves remained an afterthought. Although we have seen that earlier school rule books recognised the need for arbiters, neither Cambridge's or Sheffield's did so. By 1860 these codes, or slight variations on them, were being used in the majority of games and had largely superseded the disciplinary efforts of their forebears. It seemed the official was in danger of being marginalised.

Nevertheless, referees and umpires adapted as best they could to the two predominant rule books that were foisted upon them. Unfortunately for them, however, another school tossed its top hat into the ring in 1862, complicating matters further. Edward Thring, Headmaster of Uppingham School, and his younger brother, the enigmatic J C, formalised their game in a rule book entitled, without a hint of irony, *The Simplest Game*. Their view of football was almost puritanical: no kicking ("kicks to be aimed only at the ball"), no tripping, in truth football with barely a hint of physical contact. Instead the emphasis was placed on scoring goals. And with the target areas made up of two sticks joined by tape, stretching the entire width of the pitch at either end, there was no shortage of takers. Andy Cole – not to say FIFA's modern day tinkerers – would have been in paradise. Everybody could score, and mostly they did.

With Cambridge, Sheffield and even goal-festive Uppingham all claiming to be the true pioneers of football, there was a desperate need for a consensus on how the game should be played. Among umpires and referees confusion reigned supreme. Then in 1863 a decisive moment came. A fourth group calling themselves, with some authority, The Football Association (the implied emphasis falling unequivocally on 'the') arrived with the aim of laying down the definitive law. This was make or break time for the nompers and his henchmen. Official recognition had yet to materialise and if it didn't soon the match official would almost certainly have warranted no more than a cursory footnote in the history of the game.

FROM SIDE LINE TO CENTRE SPOT

the birth of the modern referee

THE Football Association was formed by a group of ex-public school boys meeting in London on 26 October 1863. That it changed football from a disparate but popular game into a sport is undeniable, though its initial impact was negligible – the news of its creation merited just three column inches in *The Times*. So what great plans did the world's first footballing body have for the referee? In truth, not a lot. Officials weren't anywhere near the top of their list of priorities when the FA first met, as a trawl through their early minutes makes abundantly clear. The historic code of law they drew up for a unified game in November 1863 didn't even give the umpire or referee a cursory mention. Not until the inception of the FA Challenge Cup in 1871 are they deemed worthy of inclusion in the procedural minutes.

Nonetheless, 1863 marked a watershed in the search to find a unifying set of rules, culminating in 1877 when the stoical pioneers of Sheffield finally gave in to the FA's way of thinking. With the laws it laid down in 1863, the FA's game grew in stature and started to become more easily distinguishable from rugby football (the first 8 of its original 14 laws closely resembled the present-day laws of Rugby Union). Indeed, by 1884 many of the fundamental features of the modern-day game had tentatively appeared: the penalty; the free kick; proper goal posts; one recognised goalkeeper; the offside rule, and so on. And with many clubs, in the South at least, quickly adopting the unified rule book, there was considerably less confusion and aggression on the pitch too.

Despite all this, it would be wrong to overemphasise the unity of the game during this period. Clubs in many areas still adhered to their own traditional guidelines, and as such there were several teething problems which beset the new regulations. Despite the undeniable influence of the FA, in truth it was fully twenty years before the whole country was playing to an accepted set of rules. Even as late as the 1884 Cup Final there were bitter disputes over basic interpretations.

For umpires and referees there remained fundamental problems with the new FA rules, like the continuing lack of provision for a set number of players. When Sheffield met Nottingham on 2 Jan 1865 they won with an 18-man team. FA minutes recall that for the Surrey v Kent match in February 1868 "the 25 players assembled…at 3.15". It took until 1870 for most clubs to accept 11-a-side as the norm, and even then there were still no free kicks or penalties in the modern-day footballing sense. (Referees remain prone to the occasional mathematical error. In 1983 Clive Thomas started the second half of a league match between Arsenal and Luton with goalkeeper Pat Jennings still in the dressing room.) Before the mid-1880s, the umpire and referee had to struggle with a whole host of additional restrictions and allowances that remained outside FA auspices (i.e. outside the rule book), and which still fell to the discretion of the competing captains. Admittedly many officials were accustomed to the practice of ironing out conflicting interpretations of the laws before a game commenced – and there was nothing particularly novel about any of the 14 laws laid down by the FA, so most umpires and referees would have recognised them – but it was hardly a step forward. In short, the early FA games were still fairly chaotic. The original off side ruling (which survives, almost unchanged, in present day Rugby Union) led to considerable confusion, particularly as no one – least of all the invidiously positioned umpire – seemed to know whether heading the ball forward prevented a player from placing his team-mate offside. "Some men seemed certain they could [while] some complained that heading and kicking were the same...", noted a head-scratching umpire in 1866. Luckily, the ruling was soon changed to what had been the Cambridge version, under which an attacker was onside unless there were fewer than three defenders (including the goalkeeper) between himself and the goal.

One man who had perhaps more reason than most to study the laws of the game at the time was Charles W Alcock. On 31 March 1866 during a match between the FA and Sheffield, Alcock had the distinction of being the first man ruled offside in an official Football Association fixture. The match report doesn't recall the umpire responsible for ratifying the infringement but then Alcock – a notable nomper himself – probably knew he was in the wrong anyway.

Born in Sunderland, but educated at Harrow, Alcock joined the FA committee three years after its formation and went on to become arguably the single most influential figure in British footballing history. He was secretary of the association, founder of the famous FA Cup, instigator of the first ever international and captain of the imperious Wanderers team. And he was an umpire too. Honorary Harrovian David Elleray – the premiership referee is a teacher at the school – clearly has much to do before he retires if he wants to emulate the master administrator of football. Alcock was in many ways a pioneer, and arguably the founding father of football officials. With a wider, more sweeping vision than most of his contemporaries, he was instrumental in waking the game from its slumber and dragging it into the modern, professional era. Significantly, he chose to bring the referee along for the ride.

While performing surely the most audacious juggling act in footballing history, Alcock and his colleagues at the FA slowly chiselled away at the rule book until they had produced a more robust model, one most of us would certainly recognise today. Out went the majority of the archaic rugby laws which had previously permitted handling of the ball, and caused so much dissension between different schools. In their place came rulings devised by Alcock to ease the confusion on the pitch, with a substantial emphasis on making life easier for the officials. The goalkeeper was introduced in 1870, distinguishable by his cap, and he alone was given the right to handle the ball. Goal-kicks first appeared in 1869, corners three years later. By 1874 umpires could award free kicks – which by now resembled the modern set piece – and send players off:

"The umpire shall in all cases declare an infringement…with an appeal made to him by the captain, and it shall then be the option of the opposite team to claim the free kick…in the event of any persistent infringement the umpire, upon an appeal by the captain of the opposite side, shall rule the player so offending out of play…"

So although the umpire had the authority to send a player off, he was still bound by the will of the captains. Alcock had pushed for the total abolition of the archaic 'appeal' system, effectively trying to wrest power from the captains and give it to the umpires, but was vetoed by the rest of the FA when he tabled the motion on 10 February, 1874. In the end, Alcock had to wait until 1894 before his plans came to fruition.

It took one highly contentious game in particular to convince his peers that the time was ripe for change. Queen's Park of Glasgow (founders of the SFA and the Scottish Cup) played Blackburn Rovers in the Final of the FA Cup in 1884. Rovers won 2-1, but the referee Major Francis Marindin later admitted the scoreline could have been quite different. According to Queen's Park's official history, Marindin visited the team the following day and told them that Rovers first goal had been offside and that Queen's Park had not been awarded one perfectly good goal because, in both cases, they did not appeal. Furthermore, he had ruled two Queen's Park 'goals' offside – on appeal from Rovers – because they didn't conform to the English offside ruling, which had only been conceded theoretically as law by the joint home associations two years previously. The Scots favoured the 'two men including the goalkeeper' offside ruling, but it was ignored by Marindin and the English version of 'two men plus the goalkeeper' enforced instead. Losing an FA Cup Final on the vagaries of an as yet imperfect rule book was tough luck. However the real kick in the teeth for the Scots was knowing Major Marindin was President of the English FA.

By 1886 the size of the ball had been fixed and the rather flimsy 'stick and tape' goal replaced by wooden posts and a cross-bar – goal-nets had to wait until 1890. For the referee, one of the more interesting, and at this stage unresolved aspects of the game, was the problem of telling players apart. The goalkeeper by now had his own set of rules and occupied a relatively fixed area, although he could still handle outside the 'circle'. But the rest of the players were more of a problem. They did not wear numbered shirts, but instead were identified by a frankly bizarre – and inexplicable – system of coloured socks and caps which must have made life particularly problematic for officials during a goal-mouth scramble. Sartorially, the participants in the 1875 Hampden encounter between Wanderers and Queen's Park were the brave spiritual forefathers of Quentin Crisp. Hubert Heron, Wanderers' left-winger, wore grey stockings and an 'orange, violet and black cap'. Unorthodox, but – in this company – not too outrageous. J Kenrick cut a dashing figure on the right wing in his 'cerise and French grey cap' whilst centre H S Otter wore a simple pink affair atop his head. Bear in mind, this was in Glasgow. The Scots themselves were not to be outdone, however. Queens Park's R W Neil took to the field in a fetching 'heather mixture stocking'. All this must have been frankly eye-popping for a referee merely trying to establish who's who; but other, more major modifications, didn't run altogether smoothly either.

The alteration of the humble throw-in caused a surprising amount of disharmony. The Scots, who by now had forged ahead with their innovative and soon-to-be much copied short passing game, used the throw roughly as it is today, though at right angles, like a rugby line-out. The English, however, preferred a single arm hurl which could carry the ball considerably further up the pitch. Before the 1880 Scotland v. England International, the English refused to take the field unless the referee – a Mr Hamilton – agreed to let them take throws as they liked. Though he promised he would, Hamilton lapsed into a strange state of selective amnesia as soon as the game kicked off, which led him to penalise all English attempts at throws. William Gunn – contemporary England and Notts County cricketer, creator of the 'Gunn and Moore' cricket bat and footballer – was largely blamed for the subsequent demise of the one-handed throw. Like a one-man Norwegian XI, in his heyday he would frequently hurl the ball right to the other end of the pitch, circumnavigating any real need for a midfield. Still it was several years before the Scottish version was nationally accepted.

The penalty kick was finally introduced in 1891, on appeal to the referee – not the umpire – following a lengthy and troubled trial period. After a series of unsavoury incidents, matters came to a head in fairly comical fashion during a 1890-1 FA Cup Quarter-Final between Notts County and Stoke at Trent Bridge. During the match a shot was punched off the line by the County left-back Hendry, with his goalkeeper, Thraves, helplessly stranded. As the laws made no mention of 'penalties', the referee awarded Stoke a free kick right on the goal-line which Thraves, wrapped around the ball in the foetal position, simply smothered. County won the match 1-0 and went on to the Final. Largely as a result of the heated comment the incident provoked (and on recommendation of the Irish FA), penalties from the spot were introduced by the combined home associations (who by 1883 had adopted a uniform rule book) from September 1891. Ironically, it only led to further confusion. The referee who took charge of the league game between Stoke and Aston Villa in 1891 must have questioned his sanity as he watched the home team, 1-0 down, prepare to take a penalty in the final minutes of the match. Realising how close his team were to victory, the Villa keeper picked up the ball before it could be placed on the spot and booted it out of the ground. By the time the original one had been retrieved the referee had blown for full-time. Before word had spread about this new and perfectly legal way to scupper the opposition, the laws had changed to allow referees to add on time, specifically for taking penalties and generally for hold-ups during a game.

But the contentious issue of penalties didn't end there. The law had to be updated again to prevent players touching the ball twice in succession and simply dribbling the ball into the net, then changed a further time to stop penalty-takers knocking the ball back to a colleague in a better position – a ruling still in force today. In fact it was not until 1929 that the law we accept today came into being. Up until then the goalkeeper was permitted to move where he liked along the line (a rule recently re-instated), and anywhere else he cared to once the whistle had been blown. Several keepers took to charging from the back of the net toward the penalty-taker, as if trying to unnerve a predatory bullock. One of the last players to get away with such off-putting tactics was Cardiff goalkeeper Farquharson, whose penalty save during an FA Cup Quarter-Final against Chelsea in 1927 proved crucial to the Welsh side's successful pursuit of the Cup that year. His crazed dash toward the spot-kick was legal, but consequently deemed 'against the spirit of the laws'.

How the tremulous official handled such seismic changes in the game is difficult to discern. Hardly any match reports from the late nineteenth century acknowledged the presence of officials at games, save to list the names and clubs (or job title, as was the practice then) of the two umpires and referee.

Those writers who dared attempt more comprehensive coverage hardly set the critical world alight. However *The Times* was often quite insightful, as this extract describing the problems of selecting impartial officials for the second FA Cup Final in 1873 serves to illustrate.

"Owing to the laws framed for the competition preventing the appointment of umpires connected with either of the clubs interested [in this case, the two finalists, Wanderers and Oxford University], some difficulty was experienced in the selection… eventually it was resolved that Messrs J R Dasent and J H Clark should officiate, one man chosen from each side, with Mr A Stair, Assistant Honorary Secretary of the FA, acting as referee." This selection obviously contravened the rulings laid down to govern the new Challenge Cup which stated: "The committee shall appoint two umpires and a referee to act at each of the matches in the final ties. Neither the umpires nor the referee shall be members of either of the contending Clubs..." [FA Minutes, 29 November 1871]. The problem was a lack of 'qualified', impartial officials. The Referees' Association wasn't formed until 1893, and no equivalent body existed, so the FA had no real way of knowing where to find new recruits, let alone men who were already officiating. And although the appointment of officials was increasingly becoming regulated by the FA, it didn't prevent teams lapsing into dubious old habits, picking their own friends and colleagues to take charge of games. In many ways, the problem and the solution to it lay with the FA itself.

The Association had been providing the top tier of the game – and remember there were really very few meaningful games at all – with the bulk of its officials since its inception. We have seen already that Alcock, the FA's master-builder, was an umpire and referee. As well as paving the way for the first ever International between Scotland and England in his position as Honorary Secretary of the FA, Alcock also umpired the match which took place in Partick in November 1872. Indeed, he was one of the umpires at the return match, which England won 4-2 at the Kennington Oval four months later. Alcock umpired more important Cup and club games during his time at the FA than any other official. Major Marindin, the man responsible for the Queen's Park Cup Final debacle, was also an official and 'top' player, as well as being President of the FA during the 1880s. He refereed eight FA Cup Finals and was the inspiration behind the great Royal Engineers team which introduced the passing game into England. Finally, to complete the triumvirate of all-rounders, there was Lord Arthur Kinnaird. A great bear of a man, with a beard which bore the mark of lifelong dedication, Kinnaird was Marindin's successor at the Association in 1890, winner of five FA Cup medals with Wanderers, future High

Commissioner of the Church of Scotland and yes, an umpire. It might come as a surprise to learn that the three most important figures in the establishment of the modern game were all officials, but really it shouldn't. They were all ex-public school men, and individually responsible for the initial flourishing of the game at this level in the 1850s. They shared a common vision of football, especially in the way they envisaged the game being played, and each of them was an able administrator. If clichéd football parlance had existed at the time it would have coined them 'students of the game'. Having taken charge of matches from early on, and witnessed first-hand the steady rise of indiscipline and intolerance in the game, they finally found themselves in a position where they were able to do something about it. As each man, and in particular Alcock, became concerned with updating the FA rule book, it made sense that they too should oversee its subsequent development at close quarters. So when they no longer played in games, they took charge of them. In a time of extreme change, who better to show players and watching officials the ropes? A little like the three tenors guiding you through the rudiments of yodelling, it must have been somewhat reassuring to have them around.

Of course, there was an element of nepotism at play here, as well as a hefty dose of egotism. Nobody could prevent any of the public school network at the FA picking themselves or friends to umpire and, when it became a more prestigious honour, referee a match. And so they did. The latter part of the century is littered with examples of the game's power-brokers officiating at the kind of high profile matches they had established and often previously played in. Alcock umpired the Finals of 1875 and 1879, having won the Cup himself with Wanderers in 1872. W S Rawson, a member of the victorious Oxford University team of 1874 and prominent football administrator, officiated the Final of 1876. Marindin, as well as taking charge of eight finals, was runner-up in two. He was also at Oxford with Rawson and had played for the University side during spells away from Royal Engineers. J C Clegg – later Sir Charles Clegg – was President of the Sheffield Association when he refereed the Final in 1886. Only six men have ever 'refereed' three or more Cup Finals, in only one instance after 1900 (A Kingscott in 1901), and all without exception were leading lights in the world of football administration and raised in the public school system.

The current crop of FA big-wigs may not spend their Saturdays running the line at Anfield or Highbury, but several could – at least in theory. Chief executive Graham Kelly is a qualified referee, though quite what authority a man with the fixed gaze of a perpetually frightened rabbit would bring to a game is mystifying. The most famous player-cum-(self-professed-revolutionary)-administrator-referee was, of course, Jimmy Hill.

Hill was pulled out of his commentary position by referee Pat Partridge to run the line in an old first division match between Liverpool and Arsenal in 1972 after an official had injured himself. It was the one and only time the omniscient Hill so smugly imparts from his privileged vantage point was put to the test. By all accounts he had a suprisingly good game. "He was an FA coach, knew the laws of the game, and I had no worries in pushing him on…I got the flag when I needed one and in no way did he try to steal any thunder," reported Partridge. And the most famous chin in British football even took time to praise his fellow officials: "I appreciated on the day after the match what it must feel like for a linesman to have his performance pulled to pieces. It must be bad enough to have a decision challenged by someone with a knowledge of the laws of the game, but to have to read the next day that you are at fault with a decision when you know you were right, must make linesmen feel like gunning down the press boxes and television studios." A rare armistice between pundit and official.

Alcock and his Victorian cohorts' meddling with football was not entirely motivated by self-interest. They had all been skilled players and were genuine 'fans' of the game, so they naturally wanted to be around football as much as possible. There is every reason to suggest that but for the enthusiasm of these men football might have evolved very differently. More significantly, the referee might never have existed in his present-day guise if Alcock and his colleagues had not convinced football of the need to accept a figure of authority. Interestingly, the motives that Alcock, Mandarin and Kinnaird appeared to have had for officiating are still recognisable today. Most of today's referees were footballers (though markedly less successful than Alcock and co.) and many are control freaks (though the majority would never admit it).

There was no easy solution to the problem created by the FA's rather blinkered selection process. While Alcock, Kinnaird, Marindin et al were apparently competent umpires – though again, the lack of commentary and competition makes rational judgement difficult – there was a limit to how much their DIY school of officiating could teach anyone. They were busy men. But until later measures designed solely to educate the aspiring official were introduced, (*The Referees' Handbook* and their own Association) it was really the only option. On the other hand, tentative protection for officials was provided for in the form of the FA committee. If the FA today is resolved to stand unequivocally by the referee – however invidious the task – then they have Alcock to blame. Certainly, at times he may have been protecting himself or his friends, but the principle was an admirable and undeniably durable one. During an FA meeting in February 1875 Alcock outlined, for the first time ever, FA policy on post-match appeals.

"The question of the appeal by Maidenhead against the decision of the umpires in their recent match with the Old Etonians was discussed, but as the committee were unanimous in holding that the decision of the umpires is final, and could not be in any way reviewed by them, the subject matter of the appeal was not gone into." The message was resoundingly clear.

By setting in motion a national game, with a unified code, these three men ensured that the referee would eventually have his day. And in creating the FA Cup in 1871 Alcock provided the official with a vital catalyst for change. The world's most celebrated knock-out tournament started life as an exclusive prize for a select number of teams. In its first 12 years the competition was dominated by four teams – Old Etonians, Wanderers, Royal Engineers and Oxford University – largely because contemplating another set of rules, not to mention an expensive trip south, was more than most other clubs could bear. But the tournament very quickly began to grow in stature and repute, its organisers aided by the knowledge that, until the formation of the Football League in 1888, the Cup was the only regular and meaningful guide to domestic form. There was a trophy (although derided by northern objectors as a 'tin pot') and growing prestige too. With more teams seeking admission it followed that they were forced to adopt FA rules – though as we have seen this was not without its problems. For umpires and referees the growth of a tournament of real consequence meant regular work. More than that, it meant working with a consistent rule book, although consistent rulings didn't – indeed still don't – always follow. But this was a major step forward. Alcock, as a former pupil of Harrow, had played in the school's 'Cock-House' Cup and therefore knew that the promise of spoils at the end of a competition lifted the temperature of the game, making it more exciting, yet undeniably more raucous. Although based unashamedly on this knock-out tournament, the FA Cup had exactly the same effect – only on a larger scale. The greater numbers of games and players added a combative edge, more people came to watch and, as a natural consequence of all these factors, more officials were needed. Finding these men was now the task that lay ahead.

By this time, with the FA Cup becoming more than just an annual excuse for an old-boys convention, old father football was preparing to spawn his second son. The arrival of the Football League in 1888 intensified even further the need for willing and able officials, governed by a distinct set of laws. Much like the Cup, the new League took years to establish itself, but once it had it quickly forged its own separate and distinguished identity, becoming even more popular and important than the Cup.

By 1890, with the introduction of the Scottish League (which remained amateur until 1893) complementing the already existing Scottish Cup, Britain had four burgeoning football tournaments, not to mention a host of other home nation competitions. It also had a fiercely contested international fixture which became loaded with even more significance once Scottish players began joining English clubs in search of higher wages. The onerous task of finding a way to regulate these events was left with the two leading associations, but there was never any question of officialdom being left out in the cold. With 12 clubs admitted to the new Football League and 22 Saturdays set aside for the first ever football 'season', the match official's day of reckoning was looming fast. The men in black were given provisional invites to the party; they just had to go away and sort themselves out first. It took them two years to do it.

By 1891 the law relating to the powers of umpires and referees had been irrevocably amended. The former was given a particularly rough ride out of town. On 2 June 1891, when a seven-man board met at Glasgow's Alexandra Hotel to decide the future of the football official, it was unanimously agreed to abolish the umpire in favour of a single referee. The referee would now operate on the field of play as the game's lawyer, arbitrator and, although he couldn't have known it at the time, its favourite whipping boy. The umpire, however, was not cast into football oblivion solely on the basis of one day's deliberation. His luck had been slowly running out for years. The referee had already been granted the power to award penalties and free kicks, the latter without appeal, presumably much to the annoyance of the umpire. In 1889 he was given several additional responsibilities, all of which pointed towards an imminent and significant shift of power. The right to send off a player once he had already been 'cautioned' by the umpire and then re-offended was handed to the referee, who could also issue dismissals for a single act of 'violent conduct', without recourse to either of his colleagues. As well as maintaining his role as time-keeper and official 'recorder of the game', the referee was now empowered to 'stop the game whenever, by reason of darkness, interference by spectators, or other cause, he shall think fit…and report to the Association …who have full power to deal with the matter'. Having started out as a pawn, the referee – with the muscle of the Association now on his side – had simply been picking his moment to call 'check mate' on his beleaguered rival. The umpire had no moves left.

With dual control consigned to the Association scrapheap in June 1891, the umpire was finally gone – in name at least. Banished to the touchline and given the brutally precise title of 'linesman', the umpire's descent through football's expanding hierarchy was humiliatingly navigable: he simply plodded off the pitch.

Linesmen had none of the authority vested in the umpire. The name itself sounded more like a derogatory afterthought than a job-description, and yet it defined his role with resounding clarity. Linesmen, like Johnny Cash, walked the line. They signalled to the referee if the ball crossed their line, and later they even helped him with offside rulings – from their line. But these former umpires had been consigned to the territory of the old referee – they were strictly off-pitch.

The small print, however, revealed one concessionary upgrade. Where umpires had carried handkerchiefs and sticks to approve 'appeals', linesmen were to be given flags, as yet of no discernible colour, to wave about on their line. It didn't alter the fact that they had become, in essence, powerless touch-judges. Around a hundred years later, they were accorded their final indignity, branded with the unpalatable sobriquet their station proclaimed: the referee's assistant.

The arrival of the referee's whistle – now such a potent symbol of his authority – is clouded in contradiction. The popular assertion is that the whistle was first used in 1878 in a game between Nottingham Forest and Sheffield. This, however, was 11 years before the referee was given the power to award free kicks and make the call on penalty appeals. His job in 1878 was still mainly to cast the decisive vote when umpires couldn't reach a decision between themselves. It seems unlikely he would have needed a whistle for this. Moreover, and rather more conclusively, records show that Nottingham and Sheffield didn't even play one another in 1878. The most viable explanation is that the referee was not given a whistle until he moved on to the field of play in 1891, by which time he was regularly required to stop play without appeal, and often from some distance. Before this time, it seems, he would have utilised one of three things to attract the umpire's attention: a handkerchief, a stick, or his throat.

The changes instigated between 1888 and 1891 were crucial to the long-term development of the game, as well as being obviously beneficial to the referee. But what appeared to be a betrayal of their own by the FA was in fact just sheer common sense. Previously, Alcock and his cronies had been happy to dominate as umpires, but now that the tables had been turned they simply chose to champion the referee. Nonetheless, the switch wasn't as simple as this implies. Certainly, some umpires with less experience – and perhaps with age no longer on their side – were happy to take a step backwards as linesmen while others, notably the men who had dominated officialdom previously, continued as referees – now something of a misnomer, as they were no longer to be 'referred' to in any way. This aside, there was no real pattern to the transition. It seems that no preconceived grooming of referees had taken place during the countdown to systematic change, other than the logical step of employing the men who had enjoyed greater responsibility during the final days of the old regime. Similarly it seemed sensible to continue with old umpires acting as new referees – and inevitable, given that they still held the reins of power and right of selection. Although armed with a more substantial rule book, the new-look referee still had to perform the same basic task of the now obsolete umpire – maintaining order on the pitch. The difference was that he now had to do it alone.

In August 1891 the first referees and linesmen took their places. With only two months to find, educate and train officials for the daunting job that lay ahead, the FA were clearly up against it. Even so, they didn't exactly pull out all the stops. No formal physical or 'legal' training was provided. Most referees were simply given a brief reminder of their duties, handed a copy of the (still-evolving) FA rules and told to get on with it. Sartorially, they were still a dreary looking lot. No uniform was imposed, so most officials just stuck to their favoured wardrobe: old woollen caps, riding hitches and blazers. It was *de rigueur* really, though nobody ever said as much. The Football League clubs were also issued with instructions on the new referees and their powers, and players quickly set about exploiting the tyro officials before they had time to settle, knowing as well as the referees did that without a partner on the pitch, and lacking sufficiently empowered colleagues on the touchline, they could probably get away with murder. With the officials' lack of preparation palpably evident, it was no surprise that they often did.

Still, the decision to switch to a single neutral referee was resolutely defended by the FA. They all agreed that the two-umpire system was outdated and corrupting, arguing that the element of bias resulting from the way in which officials were selected had fatally undermined it. This was a startlingly honest appraisal given that in many cases it was tantamount to an admission of personal fallibility. Yet with the old network of teams – Wanderers, Royal Engineers, the university sides and many others – slowly being dismantled in the wake of professionalism, this problem soon took care of itself. The arrival of what we would now term 'modern' football clubs – Preston, Stoke, Aston Villa – and their domination of football's new tournaments and leagues, meant the inevitable erosion of nepotism in officialdom. The old clubs, as we have seen, were a breeding ground for the games' administrators and, more importantly, its umpires and referees. The urban, non-school-based clubs were obliged by their league to provide a list of referees they wished the FA to consider for games, with the caveat that these men could not officiate games involving their 'team'. To this day, of course, officials' purported allegiances remain a contentious issue throughout the world.

Having one neutral referee instead of two was reckoned to be advantageous. In the past, the constant bickering between umpires as they sought to reach a consensus on an appeal had bordered on the tedious. It was also extremely time-consuming, not to mention detrimental to the flow of the game. Even worse were the delays and confusion caused when the old-style referee was then called upon to mediate between his squabbling colleagues. Having one official in charge of the proceedings might test his fitness levels and powers of restraint, but it was still preferable to all that. Experiments with two referees, something Arsenal's Arsene Wenger has recently called for, were tried again in 1935 first in Czechoslovakia and then in England. Dr A W Barton, a public schoolmaster, and Mr E Wood, who had refereed the 1933 Cup Final, took charge of two trial games at the Hawthorns – England v The Rest and the FA v West Brom – without the assistance of linesmen. It proved an unsatisfactory arrangement on both occasions, and when put to the vote, the idea was vetoed. More recently in 1995, an experiment with two referees was conducted in a Sunday League Cup match in Co. Durham between Spennymour Voltigeur and Highland Laddie (no joke). Jimmy Handley oversaw one half of the pitch while Gordon McMillan patrolled the other. The game went reasonably well, although a major disciplinary discrepancy somewhat ruined things: Handley booked nine players while McMillan cautioned no one.

Applying basic logic, having one official halved the problem and, though there is no primary evidence, one suspects that the old adage about 'cooks' and 'broth' may have been firmly pinned on the FA noticeboard around this time. Finally, the old 'appeal' system left too much room for interpretation, and gave a disproportionate amount of power to the players, or even bystanders, as this 1885 memorandum for officials made clear:

"Umpires should bear in mind that it is entirely against the spirit of the Laws to give advice or to make any claim on behalf of either side, and they should be careful to ascertain that a claim is made by one of the players and not by a spectator..."

Despite such apparent urgency, it was 1895 before the FA actually got round to doing anything about the 'appeal' rule. That the crowd were already attempting to influence, and willing to challenge match officials' decisions, indicate that the umpire and referee had already become folk devils of the British game. It signalled the start of a tempestuous relationship, one which was soon regarded by many as an integral part of the spectacle of football. Packed northern terraces would soon be calling into question the eyesight and birthright of the men in black.

The first few years after going solo were the worst for the referee, as J R Witty noted: "It was obvious that much greater attention would have to be paid to [the referee's] quality as the sole arbitrator. His very loneliness invited criticism and sometimes blame for defeat. Clubs employing professional players threw much of the onus of maintaining discipline amongst their employed men upon the referee. He was expected to control their intentions as well as their actions, and by his demeanour and methods to compel players to act properly." Witty, though not exactly revelling in the promise of his name, had a valid point. The referee was no longer just an inconsequential sideshow to the main event, he had become the circus's friendless ringleader. The new guidelines indicated that the referee should be not just a policeman, but a bogeyman who could inspire fear alongside respect, and an able adversary in a battle of wits. Much the same as today, the referee had to demonstrate his authority to stand any chance of survival. The weak officials in 1890, like 1990, didn't tend to last long.

The FA now delegated the right to appoint officials to the various professional leagues (many others had formed by 1892), who in turn selected men to referee and run the line from lists provided by the clubs. But there was no quality control of this system. With growing complaints about levels of competence, and a scarcity of officials willing to submit themselves to the weekly ordeal on the pitch, the time was ripe for a concerted show of support. It came, finally, in March 1893, when the Referees' Association was formed by W Pickford on the initiative of the future FA secretary F J Wall.

It was a master stroke, combining as it did the twin incentives of training and money. The Association appointed district councils in several football centres in the South of England to test referees on their knowledge of the laws, to give guidance to those being tested and to appoint them, on request, to matches, for which they would now be paid a fee. The practice of giving small remuneration to match officials had started in 1883 when, in FA Cup ties where the FA appointed referees, "Second-class railway fares, together with cab expenses where necessary, should be allowed for umpires and referees, and 5s. for sundry expenses if travelling 30 miles from home or 10s, if unavoidably absent from home for the night". This provided a professional structure – official expense forms were distributed – for the referee to work within.

The Referees' Association was a small organisation at first but nevertheless an important one. It offered the referee sanctuary, and in this way was as influential in the development of officialdom as the FA had been for the nation's players and clubs. Advice on the minutiae of law was regulated three years later when the Association published *The Referees' Chart*. In 1885, the FA had issued a code of rules for the guidance of umpires and referees – the very first of its kind – but that skeletal memorandum was hardly what was required. It took another 11 years for this next set of instructions to arrive. Luckily, the *Chart* was a good deal more substantial and informative. It was initially produced to inform referees of the FA council's decision to finally abolish the 'appeal' law, which was made on 16 January, 1895:

"A referee had absolute power to award a free kick for every breach of the Laws…the penalty kick excepted, whether there be an appeal from a player or not…he must wait for an appeal before awarding a penalty kick, and even here he must award [one], with or without appeal, for a wilful trip."

This was big news. Short of one piece of legislation (and the penalty 'appeal' wouldn't last much longer), the referee was now in sole charge of the game. Both he and the umpire had been included in the new FA Laws, which in 1894 reached the modern number of 17. Finally, they were an intrinsic part of the game of football.

The first *Referees' Chart* is kept at Lancaster Gate in London. It is a curious pamphlet, each page divided into three columns – one for the player, one for the official, and one for 'advice to the referee', giving a blow by blow account of the 17 laws. Official announcements of the FA and other Leagues and boards are published too. It was the referee's bible: his rule book, newsletter and critical companion rolled into one. Its value cannot be challenged and its format and contents were copied by practically every fledgling football nation. It is still published annually, though now as 'Laws of Association Football', and remains the basis of all referee instruction. Every candidate for examination as a qualified referee must pass a test, orally and in writing, on the theory of the laws of the game as published in the *Chart*. The pamphlet even made it into the laws of the game, and it is still the case that every footballer has the following extract printed in his contract:

"A copy of the Laws of Association Football [i.e. the *Chart*] must be kept by the club for the use of the players upon application."

FROM SIDE LINE TO CENTRE SPOT

The referee was now much better equipped to deal with the machinations of the game going into the 20th century. Other changes to the laws of football over the following 30 years would continue to be executed with the referee in mind. FIFA formed in Paris in 1904, and the organisation provided an international Referees' Association from the start, doing for the world's officials what Pickford's prototype had done for England's. The introduction of something closely resembling the modern penalty box in 1902 eased the continuing confusion over penalties, as did new goalkeeping legislation in 1912, which confined his handling to this area. The arrival of the 10-yard rule for free kicks a year later must have been a boon at the time, though officials would not have been able to predict the practical problems it would come to cause. By 1938 the present laws were in place, although innovations continued within the framework of the Referees' Association. In 1934 Sir Stanley Rous, a prominent international referee and future President of FIFA, devised the first system of refereeing – the first of its kind – called the 'diagonal run method', which essentially maximised the area of play in the referee's field of view, while designating the residual areas to his linesmen (it still holds sway today). Such changes reflected the growing popularity of the game and ensured that the standards of refereeing gradually improved, although in truth, with crowds reaching record levels and competition following suit, they had little option but to keep up. And with the first World Cup almost upon them, referees were in for their biggest test yet.

RULING THE WORLD

an arbiter's history of the World Cup

FOOTBALL and the referee had changed by 1950. For the first time in their relationship, the referee stopped playing the stately but neglected butler to the footballer's cheeky aristocrat: he was no longer subservient. Many factors contributed to this shift in roles. Since emerging from the shadows onto the pitch in the late nineteenth century the referee had steadily grown in presence and stature. They had become a footballing 'body' in their own right, rather than just a disparate group of individuals, and were protected by two increasingly influential organisations: the FA (in Britain), which had also provided officials with their own Association, and FIFA. Football's world-governing body did not, of course, 'represent' referees from different countries in the way their home associations did; instead it attempted to streamline officialdom in preparation for the coming of the international era, heralded by the first ever World Cup.

The World Cup was an opportunity for referees to demonstrate how far they had come, and for those left behind – considering it was a 13-team event, this meant the vast majority – it became their goal. The FA Management Committee (which from 1912 was responsible for the appointment of referees) already separated the great from the good, and the hopeless, when it allocated officials for big Cup, League and international games. This unspoken hierarchy was nevertheless reflected in a classification system that provided every referee – from the lowliest county official to the Class One (later Grade One) veteran – with an incentive to improve. It also introduced an element of competitiveness into the referees' workplace, which had hitherto been lacking. This was magnified when the process of selecting referees for the first World Cup begun. For the first time in his unmomentous history, the official had a chance to really shine outside his native land, on the world stage: it was the pursuit of this dream that changed the way in which the referee, and the rest of the footballing hierarchy, perceived his role.

Most referees were not highly regarded by FIFA, at least initially. Although considerable effort was put into ensuring officials made the trip to Uruguay in 1930 for the first World Cup, no provision was made by the Federation to guarantee the presence of the best. The financial incentive they offered was negligible, and foisted onto the host nation. Still it was proposed that the referee receive preferential treatment, as Rodolfe Seeldrayers, the FIFA vice-president, outlined. "The country staging the event", he said, "should make funds available for, in the following order of priority, transport and accommodation expenses for referees first, then FIFA members, and lastly the teams." In the end the plan didn't coax many able referees to South America, but FIFA's willing was nevertheless admirable. To British referees in particular, the World Cup was to become a home from home, but not until after the Second World War. Between 1928 and 1946 the British Associations had frequently boycotted FIFA, mainly on the grounds that it wasn't really on to play football against countries you had lately been to war against. Whatever Paul

McCartney had to say on the matter. Nor did they particularly want to belong to the same 'club' as them. So it was not until the 1950 tournament in Brazil that the first Brits refereed matches in the great tournament. By then, 73 countries were affiliated to FIFA, so the home countries faced years playing third rate nations in meaningless matches if they continued to operate independently. Moreover, FIFA soon came to the realisation that they could scarcely afford to continue without the membership of the home nations. This was brought home to them in 1947 when 135,000 paying customers watched Great Britain play the Rest of Europe at Hampden Park. FIFA's share of the gate receipts meant that for the first time in its history the organisation had a financially sound base. British football had pulling power and as a consequence British officials soon found they had it too. No other country provided more officials for football's premier event between 1950 and 1978. It was hardly surprising given the often calamitous efforts of referees from other countries during the three pre-war World Cups.

In 1930, during the first stages of the inaugural tournament in Uruguay, Brazilian referee Almeida Rego became the first World Cup official to experience the hateful backlash a man in black was capable of inciting. Argentina had scored with six minutes remaining of their Pool 1 game, giving them a 1-0 lead over France. A minute later, as the French play-maker Marcel Langiller dribbled his way into a shooting position in the Argentine box, Rego, perplexingly, blew for time. Chaos ensued. While Argentine fans invaded the pitch to congratulate their heroes, the entire French team assailed the referee, furious that the game had ended long before the 90 minutes were up. Mounted police then made their World Cup début to some effect. What happened next, however, was perhaps unique in the history of refereeing. Having consulted first his watch and then linesmen to try and clear up the confusion, Segnor Rego lifted his head and raised his arms to the skies before crying that he had made a mistake, but in good faith. Cierro, the Argentinean inside-left, fainted, the game resumed, and the remaining minutes ticked away without incident. Nothing further was said of the matter, and the idea of the referee admitting human culpability during a match was – with Stalinist efficiency – never heard of again. That the referee's admission of a genuine error was seemingly recompense enough for the French, who had almost certainly been robbed of an equaliser, takes some believing. On the behalf of both parties.

The same tournament had its fair share of Ron Harris figures, who caused weak officials no end of hardship. Romania versus Peru, in particular, was a referee's (and physio's) nightmare. The Chilean referee Alberto Warken started the game like a frightened school child, giving free kicks at random while pointedly ignoring the assailants, the most brutal and persistent of which was Peru's Captian De Las Casas. At some point in the game Warken finally found his courage, only to send off the wrong Peruvian for breaking the leg of the Romanian right-back Steiner. De Las Casas who, for once, was nowhere near the victim was dismissed and went into the history books as the first man to be sent off in a World Cup. Warken, found guilty in the tournament's first (but by no means last) case of mistaken identity, left the match as a walking endorsement for the introduction of numbers on players' shirts. It was nine farcical years before FIFA took any notice. The Belgian Jean Langenus, one of the more famous, and certainly more capable referees at the tournament, was involved in a truly bizarre incident during Argentina's 6-1 thrashing of the USA in the Semi-finals. Langenus blew for a foul against an American, which had brought the US bench to their feet. The US medical attendant rushed onto the field in protest at the decision, threw down his box of medicines in front of the referee, smashed a bottle of chloroform, and was very swiftly overcome by the fumes. He had to be helped off the field. The rumour was Mel Brooks later stole the idea for a film.

Langenus, a highly colourful figure, also refereed the final between Uruguay and Argentina, which the hosts won 4-2, taking to the world's greatest stage in plus fours, a red striped tie and a dinner jacket. A regular dandy. It wasn't until 1950 that referees and linesmen wore a recognisable uniform – black socks, long black shorts, a white shirt and black blazer with a FIFA badge – at the World Cup. Incidently, black was not chosen as the predominant colour for the referee's uniform solely on the basis of its neutral qualities, but rather on economic grounds – with a huge surplus of cheap black material left over from the war. Until the 1950s, all sorts of inappropriate clobber was worn by the world's officials. When French referee George Capdeville took charge of the 1938 Final between Italy and Hungary he wore a dark blue shirt with so few buttons that a chunk of his Gallic chest was on show for the whole match. Langenus's first concern of the 1930 final was the match ball. Each team had insisted on using its own, an eventuality the organisers hadn't prepared themselves for. The matter was finally resolved with the toss of a coin – it's not recorded whose – which Argentina won. The game itself passed without incident, although Langenus had questioned his own safety before kick-off, fearing a pitch-invasion from the 100,000 fans crammed into the newly constructed Centenary Stadium.

In 1934 the Italian players weren't the only ones to feel the life-threatening pressure of playing at home in the presence of Mussolini. The feared Fascist dictator, smirking under a yachting cap, appeared at Rome's Stadio Torino to watch the games and 'playfully' encourage his men to do their best, offering the option 'win or die' in a letter sent to the team's dressing room before the opening game. Referees also came in for widespread criticism, amid allegations that the '34 tournament was fixed, or at least in some way 'pre-ordained', for the Italians to win. Langenus, ever present, made a pertinent summing up of the situation when he said: "Italy wanted to win…it was natural, but they made it far too obvious." Some of the refereeing decisions were somewhat suspect too.

Langenus's Belgian compatriot Louis Baert was accused of favouring the home nation during their second round match against the capable Spanish. Zamora, Spain's goalkeeper, was subjected to some horrendous treatment from the bruising Italian forwards, but at no point in the match did he receive a free kick. Baert then compounded the goalkeeper's sense of injustice when he allowed a highly contentious equaliser for the Italians to stand after Schiavio had pushed Zamora out of the way for Ferrari to score. Another broken leg in the same game added to the legacy of weak and neglectful refereeing. The match was replayed and duly provided another flashpoint. Referee Rene Mercet from Switzerland had been chosen to replace Baert, although his performance betrayed none of the country's famed love of neutrality. Italy won 1-0 thanks to the absence of Zamora and the obvious difficulty Mercet had understanding the offside rule. Spain had two goals wiped off the scoresheet as a result of this, and Mercet was subsequently suspended by the Swiss FA.

Mercet and Baert were among the first referees to be subjected to the merciless jibes and taunts of such a huge and expectant crowd. (Referees from smaller competing nations continue to be overawed by the World Cup, where the relentless scrutiny of fans, commentators and the media far exceeds the scale of their workaday experiences.) Mercet and Baert were not the only ones to be affected by the fierce partisanship. Almost every referee who took charge of an Italian game in 1934 fell foul of Mussolini and his 'win-at-all-costs' manifesto. That Vittorio Pozzo's team did emerge victorious was hardly surprising: with *il Duce*'s gentle encouragement and *il arbitro* seemingly in their pocket they could hardly have failed.

The often volatile reactions to refereeing decisions at early World Cups was in many ways a reflection of how far match officials had come. And a clear indication of how far they had to go. The criticisms elicited from players, managers, fans and journalists alike – fuelled by a state media intent on hyping up the political and military significance of some contests – proved the referee now had an overpowering influence on the outcome of matches, though many officials certainly failed to live up to the magnitude of this responsibility. The World Cup was an overwhelming experience for referees, even in the tournament's formative years. With record crowds and the passion of rival fans and competing nations, the sense of disorientation caused by a new experience in a new country made the task a thoroughly unenviable one.

Furthermore, the language barrier between the referee and his linesmen, not to mention the players, didn't help matters, as the Italian referee Rinaldo Barlassini found out much to his amazement during the 1934 tournament. "When I tried to talk to my two linesmen before the game, it was hopeless. When I tried to talk to the players before kick-off, to wish them luck, and so on, it was as if I was speaking only to myself. I have never felt so alone walking out onto the pitch..." Barlassini refereed the first round game between Hungary and Egypt. His linesmen for the day were Swedish and Brazilian. 'Pissing in the wind' doesn't really do the poor man's plight sufficient justice. Today, communication problems on the pitch are largely confined to working out the intent of muttered expletives from disgruntled players.

Modern referees may not possess much in the way of linguistic dexterity, but a permanent body of FIFA and UEFA translators are now installed for all international fixtures to introduce and relay preparitory information between referees and their assistants. Most referees take time to discuss a mutually agreeable system (usually involving a series of internationally recognisable hand and flag signals) with their assistants long before kick-off.

Apart from weakness, ineptitude, intimidation and an apparent lack of TEFL qualifications however, there was little excuse for not getting it right on the pitch. Since British *émigrés* had effectively introduced football to all of the countries competing in the World Cup, FIFA experienced few problems introducing a rule book that referees from all nationalities would instantly recognise. Essentially, countries just copied the FA Laws and translated them. Few changes had occurred to the rule book since pitch markings had been modernised in 1902, save for minor tinkerings with the goalkeeper's 'penalty' rights and the alteration which allowed a goal to be scored directly from a corner-kick. Certainly nothing had been added to the referee's arsenal; and nothing major to the laws which he wouldn't have had at least 30 years to get to grips with.

However there were other factors conspiring against the referee. Unruly players dominated the early tournaments more than the skilful ones, adding to the woes of the inexperienced referee. Most officials didn't have the faintest idea how to control them. The fabled 'Battle of Bordeaux' in the French-hosted tournament of 1938 was the classic case of a World Cup match reduced to farce by the combination of player brutality and refereeing naivety, though it's hard to lay too much blame at the feet of match official Paul Van Hertzka. It was easily the most violent game of World Cup history. Three players received their marching orders. Brazil's wing-half Zeze Procopio was sent off for a savage challenge on the Czech inside-forward Nejedly – an innocent party as 'pure as Bohemian crystal' according to a French journalist – who suffered a broken leg. Two other assailants were sent packing for becoming involved in a fist fight, and the Czech keeper Planicka played most of the game with a broken arm. The referee could neither contain nor clearly cope with the bloody battle. The punishment of a red card (or rather a dismissal, cards were not introduced until 1974) was a stick wielded by the referee, but it failed resoundingly to beat any sense of fair play into Brazil or Czechoslovakia.

With few exceptions – one being Langenus – though even he was fallible, the referees selected for World Cups before the war were woefully incompetent. It's hardly surprising given the rather random manner in which they were chosen. FIFA, as we have seen, was prevented from head-hunting many officials because their country was either not a member of the Federation (only 41 were in 1930) or had simply not 'qualified' (the 1930 Finals were invite only) for the tournament. Thus, referees were not selected from any country not competing in the Finals. The predominance of South American officials in 1930 was particularly striking. Only three referees from Europe – two from Belgium and one from France – were present, whereas 10 had been picked from the Americas. A singularly odd, and slightly suspicious proviso was made for the home nation's officials: they had four referees at the first ever Finals, all of them hopeless. Although no referee ever officiated a World Cup game involving his own country, the ramifications of four Uruguayan officials in a tournament involving only 13 teams were glaringly obvious. Yet it took until June 1950, on the eve of the fourth Finals, before the International Board decided officials for all international matches must be from a neutral country.

A basic pattern of nepotism emerged in the first 20 years of the tournament. FIFA tended to pick referees from countries who had strong and influential figureheads on the board of the Federation. Quality, despite early pronouncements to the contrary, was really only a minor consideration, and in any case, something in very short supply. Both statements are borne out by the facts. Langenus refereed more games in the first three World Cups than any other official, including the inaugural Final. Henri Cristophe and Louis Baert, fellow low country men, also handled several games each between 1930 and 1938. Similarly, France were the only other European nation with representation in 1930 and their officials virtually dominated the 1938 home event. Both Belgium and France were founder members of the Federation. The French could boast the man who helped realise FIFA – Robert Guerin, as well as Jules Rimet, the president who gave his name to the World Cup trophy. Belgium too had several leading lights in the organisation, including one L Muhlinghaus, who was FIFA general secretary in the first two years of its existence. Finally, as well as the French and the Belgians, the Swiss, Dutch, Swedish and Spanish influence on the board was as overwhelming: as it was on the pitch, where each country was disproportionately represented by officials between 1934-38. Although no South American country joined FIFA until the 1920s, the rapid rise in the quality and popularity of the game on the continent combined with the Federation's desire to see their tournament become a truly global one (an ambition not realised until after the war) meant the organisers were keen to attract as many of the continent's top teams – especially the 'big three' of Brazil, Argentina and Uruguay – to the early Finals. It is unlikely, however, that they expected, or indeed wanted quite so many of the continent's referees to join the party.

That they did so in 1930 was more as a result of convenience than any passionate desire from FIFA to witness first hand the highly idiosyncratic Brazilian and Bolivian whistleblowers in action. Given the kind of life-threatening situations South American referees were inclined to fall into, it was inconceivable that FIFA would have invited so many if not for the fact that it was going to cost much less to get them there in the first place. The Federation had already neatly shifted the financial burden of the tournament onto the host nation, which had to pick up the referees' tab and travelling expenses. It was therefore no coincidence that the host country fell into the habit of employing as many 'local' officials as possible, an equally neat manoeuvre that meant a minimal outlay on potentially crippling boat fares for the Europeans. The relative absence of South American officials from the 1934 and 1938 World Cups held in Italy and France confirmed these practical problems while also suggesting that they hadn't exactly set the world on fire in 1930. The FIFA policy of selecting referees from the competing countries tied in nicely with the intentions of the Uruguayan FA: six of the 13 finalists in 1930 were South American nations; the seventh was Mexico.

The quality of refereeing was low on the list of FIFA priorities in the pre-war years of the World Cup; it was a rare characteristic of most referees anyway. The nations that competed for the trophy between 1930-38 simply had a shortage of good match officials. The South American FAs didn't even have regulated Referees' Associations to aid the training of their men in black. The non-competing countries were not even given the option of proposing theirs at all – although in Britain's case it was becoming rather obvious to the footballing world – if not to FIFA – that they possessed the finest on offer. The reputation of Britain's officials, cemented during trips abroad and based largely on the theory that they should be good after all these years of practice, was enough to ensure that when England sailed to Brazil for the

Finals in 1950, the nation's referees were on the boat too. And it didn't stop with England. Scottish referee Bobby Mitchell and Welshman Mervyn Griffiths were invited too, becoming the first men to referee in a World Cup minus their national team.

The previous three World Cups had produced a total of six red cards, which, especially in 1938, didn't really do justice to the prevalent atmosphere of ill-temper. The 1950 World Cup, by now known officially as the Jules Rimet trophy, was notable for producing no sendings off and indeed barely one tackle worthy of a caution today. It is unlikely that this relative tranquillity was unconnected to the presence of so many British officials. The British Associations had five representatives in Brazil, FIFA having finally realised that their policy of hanging with the home boys was perhaps not the best way to ensure a trouble-free, and impartially handled World Cup. Three were English – George Reader, Reg Leafe and Arthur Ellis. Griffiths and Mitchell represented Wales and Scotland respectively. Of the 22 games played in the tournament, 10 were handled by the British whistleblowers, including the first game between Brazil and Mexico and the shock Final, won by Uruguay against an overconfident Brazil, and ably refereed by Reader. The organisation of the tournament itself was a bit of a farce, even down to the group arrangements (incredibly, there were two groups of four, one group of three and one group comprising only the lucky Uruguayans and the luckless Bolivians), yet Britain's intrepid officials emerged as unlikely, yet modest heroes at the end of it all; which is more than can be said for the English team – disgraced and effectively knocked out by an inexperienced USA side, who beat Billy Wright's men 1-0 in Belo Horizonte during the first stages.

All of Britain's refereeing representatives were well received in Brazil, by players and fans alike; indeed, not one criticism was reckoned to have been levelled at them during the entire three-week event. George Reader, in particular, came in for rich praise following his admirable handling of one of the tournament's rougher games – the final pool match between Uruguay and Spain. Colonel Volpe of the Uruguayan delegation – a man who was more inclined to a fit of pique than any gesture of gratitude – said of Reader's performance: "The referee was very good today…he was fair, decisive and above all competent. We would be happy if Mr Reader takes charge of the Final, which is our aim…" Whether Volpe's remarkably kind words had been overheard by FIFA's referee selectors, or indeed intended for their ears, was irrelevant: Reader got the nod and became the first British official to referee a World Cup Final. Four years later, amid scenes of chaos, Arthur Ellis would be remembered for entirely different reasons. Indeed, by 1954 the referee was starting to become as famous as the game itself. At least in his own mind.

Ellis proved the dictum that a book should never be judged by its cover, unless it's about art history, of course. The handful of out of print referee biographies that lie gathering dust, but mercifully not value, in London bookshops, paint an idyllic picture of the British referee in post-war international football, which is at once factual and gravely misleading. To suggest that by 1950 the referee was becoming a popular source of post-match conversation is certainly beyond doubt. Newspaper reports of matches and contemporary radio programmes confirmed the growing interest in the behaviour of the man in black. But to imply that he was responsible for the spectacle of the match in the first place – which perhaps unwittingly is nevertheless what referee biographies often do – is stretching it a bit.

Ellis more or less started the trend for referee books in 1962. An avuncular man, he was nevertheless seemingly so consumed by his own worth that he compiled a footballing *weltenschaung* – *The Final Whistle* – as a bookend to his glorious international career. Ellis is best known for his part in The 'Battle of Berne', the infamous 1954 World Cup Quarter-Final between Brazil and Hungary. In the course of that game Ellis controversially dismissed three players resulting in mini-riots in the tunnel and Hungarian dressing room after the final whistle. The scene culminated in the podgy Hungarian hero Ferenc Puskas (who was injured and hadn't even played in the game) bottling the Brazilian centre-half, Anheiro, with a glass soda siphon. Ah, the good old days. Ellis, you may recall, ended his 'glorious career' on another field of play, as Stuart Hall's prancing sidekick on *It's A Knockout*. It was Ellis, indeed, who coined the phrase 'They're playing their joker'. But *The Final Whistle* – 'as told to Steve Richards' – is no joke; it's pure unashamed hagiography. On the cover Ellis, resplendent in a cufflinked shirt and stiff starched white collars – half Errol Flynn, half Frankie Howard – stands on the centre spot smiling a knowing smile. The sun lights his large face, and around him two national team captains and a balding linesman follow the flight of a flipped coin. Here, clearly, is a significant figure. His book confirms this. "The most famous international referee of all time has retired after thirty years with the whistle," the sleevenotes gravely intone. "His career abounds in excitement, drama and danger," they continue, "His full and exciting life makes a remarkable story…this book recaptures all the thrills." This, we are by now beginning to suspect, is an important book. And one festooned with insert pictures confirming the international repute of its protagonist: Ellis enjoys fun and games with a bushy-haired Bruce Forsyth. Ellis receives a bunch of flowers from the captain of the Russian national team in 1954. Ellis chats pitchside to a young German man in a wheelchair. Ellis poses with a Central American beauty Queen. Ellis relaxes on board President Peron's yacht. In one picture, the phantomlike Ellis appears on the shoulder of the King of Sweden as the monarch meets the German national team, his beaming face eerily recalling one of Stalin's more bizarre revisionist exercises. Woody Allen's *Zelig* and its pale imitator *Forrest Gump* were still decades away.

Britain's post-war referees saw in the game's rapidly expanding boundaries the opportunity to become stars in their own right; and they seized it with gusto. With financial rewards scant and regular televised football still a distant dream, the referee turned to the world stage in his quest for recognition. The referee became a personality, although he was rarely treated with the gravitas he felt his position merited.

Ellis was undeniably an extremely capable referee, who officiated in three consecutive World Cup Finals between 1950 and 1958. He claims, however, that the "wonderful" experience of being involved was continually dampened by FIFA's blatant disregard for the referee in general, and his wallet in particular. "Financially, the tournaments were a dead loss for the referee," he says, "I'll give you the figures. The daily allowance was £4 18s. plus hotel and travelling expenses – it should have been £10 – and we were not paid a penny for handling a match, even if it was the final of the World Cup." It nearly prompted Ellis to take drastic action: "If, like some of the referees, I had had wages stopped back home for time off...I might have been compelled to send my wife back to work". This was the 1950s.

Bitterness at not being given enough respect is clearly Ellis's abiding memory of the World Cup. "The referee, who becomes the prominent figure of the match if he makes a vital...decision, is just an insignificant minnow, it seems, when FIFA get down to sharing the spoils. In the showpiece of world soccer, staged only every four years, he is surely entitled to a reasonable financial return for his service, even if he isn't there to entertain." But entertain he did. If recognition was what Ellis craved, then he certainly got a bundle of it in 1954 following his part in the 'Battle of Berne' fiasco. Mostly, it must be said, from Brazilians threatening to have him shot. In fact, the Brazilian team were largely to blame for the whole incident.

They took the field that day in a state of collective hysteria. Geraldo Jorge de Almeida, the best known commentator at the time, visited the team in their dressing room before kick-off to call on them to avenge the deaths of the many Brazilians killed in Italy during the war. Quite what this had to do with Hungary wasn't clear. The head of the Brazilian delegation then launched into a protracted speech about patriotism and miracles. Suffice to say, the team – and its entourage – were being deliberately and successfully cranked up for action: they knew they were about to face the best team in the world. That the game was actually completed at all was down to Ellis. Although he sent off three players, and was later accused of favouring the mighty Magyars, his severe actions were certainly warranted. One of several neutral commentators to praise him at the final whistle was an Italian journalist, who called his performance "magisterial", adding that Ellis's slightly dictatorial refereeing had been "necessary and legitimate". The Brazilians, of course, fabricated a conspiracy theory to suit their needs. One of the country's leading referees, Mario Vianna, approached Ellis at the end of the battle, wielding a huge microphone he had snatched from a reporter, and accused the poor man of being a Communist agent. Later the Brazilian delegation made an official complaint to FIFA, insisting that Ellis had refereed the game "in the interests of International Communism against Western Civilisation and Christ". This was a tad harsh, although Ellis's name remains a profanity in Brazil even today.

Ellis clearly enjoyed the powers refereeing afforded him, even if on occasion they didn't amount to more than the ability to control violent conduct on the pitch. In particular Ellis did not like linesmen who questioned his supreme control of a game. "Some men" – and we are left in no doubt as to which man in particular he is referring to – "are at their best when they are in full command, but they are unable to play second fiddle." Having thus exempted himself from their lowly rank, Ellis goes on to explain how to be a good little linesman. "The first duty of a linesman should be to ensure he arrives early. The referee will want to give his instructions and explain his methods of control." In Ellis's case, the 'method of control' was probably inspired by the absolute monarchy of Louis XIV. "A good linesman will follow instructions carefully. Some don't!...Linesmen should appreciate that the signal they give are indications to the referee of some incident they have observed, but they should also appreciate that they do not give overriding decisions. A linesman should be an assistant referee and not an insistent linesman." Despite his queasy stab at wordplay, there is no suggestion whatsoever from Ellis that this might merely be a playful reminder of who's boss, a verbal nudge and wink. Instead, the dressing down of football's flag-waving minnows continues apace with a stern lecture on etiquette. "A linesman should never carry his flag unfurled or raise it just halfway. As a signal, the flag should be raised high and waved smartly." Should there be any lingering doubts as to Mr Ellis's regard for his 'assistants', one of the chapters in his book is called simply 'Linesmen I Don't Like'. Those Brazilians never stood a chance.

While Ellis may not have been a prominent figure on most South American players' Christmas card lists, he was certainly a firm favourite with the big-wigs of FIFA. However, many favoured officials were not nearly so capable. Refereeing standards – particularly in Britain – had certainly improved since the war, but football's world-governing body was still guilty of overlooking ability when picking their referees. Indeed, throughout the 60s and into the 70s, the overtly political nature of FIFA's selection process became increasingly discernible.

In 1974, with the experienced Jack Taylor, Scotland's Bob Davidson (officiating in his fourth consecutive Finals) and the Welshman Clive Thomas all selected, standards were reasonably high, and levels of nepotism negligible. Still, variable levels of competence and the constant bickering between officials over game allocation somewhat sullied the experience. A combination of both factors led to one of the most farcical sendings-off in World Cup history. The Welshman was chosen as reserve linesman for the first round game between Australia and Chile, with a friend of his, Jafar Namdar from Iran, as referee. Namdar, a nervy, inexperienced official, took to the field in a highly apprehensive state, his Belgian and Dutch linesmen having blanked the poor man during his pre-match 'team talk', then refused to check the goalnets for him. During the second half, in a fit of pique prompted by the lack of protection being offered to his team by Namdar and his unsupportive linesmen, Australia's no.6 Ray Richards, felled a Chilean player and was promptly booked. As Thomas organised a stretcher for the upended Chilean, an official interpreter informed him that Richards had already been booked in the first half for kicking the ball away after the referee had blown for an infringement. Namdar, lost and alone on the pitch, hadn't a clue. Thomas called his friend to the touchline and told him the offender had to go. Namdar tried to send off Richards, but was engulfed by a group of his team-mates trying to persuade him that they should be booked instead. "It was me!", "No, It was me", they could almost be seen to cry as they pointed to the back of their shirts, and pleaded with Namdar to caution them. Eventually, Richards, who seemed quite happy to skulk in the background as his team-mates sought to take the blame for his thuggery, was singled out and guided off the pitch by the fourth official. All in all, the whole episode was not exactly a glowing testament to competent international refereeing.

At half-time in another match between Holland and Sweden, one linesman ran into the officials' dressing room furious that his Canadian referee Werner Winsemann had over-ruled his calls on a number of crucial occasions. "Do you want me or not?" he shouted. The reply was unequivocal: "Tonight, you are the linesman, I am the referee and you will do exactly as you are told." Such clashes of ego persisted throughout the tournament, and even pervaded the British camp. Several accounts of the story surrounding the appointment of the referee for the Final in 1974 suggest that FIFA were guilty of playing off Jack Taylor and Bob Davidson against one another in the days leading up to the big match. Davidson claims that Ken Aston, FIFA's British referee supremo, and the man at the centre of controversy during the infamous Battle of Santiago between Chile and Italy in 1962, told him "on the train from Frankfurt to Munich" that he had been selected to referee the Final, despite a poor performance running the line in one of the Semi-finals. The next day, on the eve of the game, Jack Taylor received a call giving him the appointment. While Clive Thomas congratulated Taylor, Davidson, who refused to even shake his hand, was heard to say "It's a mistake...I've got it," before leaving the room muttering about FIFA's treachery, deception and bare-faced lying.

The '74 World Cup was also notable for squabbles over payment of officials. The 30 referees were paid nothing for matches and given a ridiculously low subsistence allowance of about £20 a day. One European referee was close to returning home before the tournament had even begun because he claimed he could not afford to feed his family. Referees were forced to pay for their own taxis, pick up their own laundry bills and, in some cases, share hotel rooms. FIFA's reply to the criticism was that referees were 'the only amateurs left in the game'.

The referees brought to the brink of poverty in '74 would have choked on their whistles had they known then that FIFA would pay referees and assistants £16,000 and £12,000 respectively just for appearing at France '98. This temporary promotion to the rank of professionals, however, failed to make them any less fallible than their poorly remunerated predecessors.

By the time the next World Cup had swung around in 1978, political considerations were even more pronounced. Once again, some referees and linesmen were excluded from matches and others promoted to prestigious appointments on the relative strengths of their relationships with the decision-makers in the World Cup refereeing committee. For the final of a tournament that had been awash with rumours of match-rigging tactics from the Argentine junta, the highly inept Italian official Sergio Gonella was chosen, mainly on the casting vote of his fellow countryman Dr Artemio Franchi – one of the most influential figures on the international referees' committee. After an abysmal performance in the game between Argentina and Holland, Gonella never refereed again, either in Europe or in his own country. Throughout the tournament referees who had failed fitness tests were allowed to officiate matches while others, such as Britain's Pat Partridge, were given no further matches after complaining about levels of communication between officials (the language barrier was still a problem, but less so than the animosity between officials on good terms with the selection committee and those disliked by the authorities) or the appalling travelling arrangements for referees. Referees who had not run the line for 10 or more years were selected as linesmen for high profile games. From a referee's perspective, the whole tournament was a chaotic mess, running crookedly and precariously along the lines of nepotism and ineptitude.

In 1992 FIFA addressed this particular problem by announcing that, at the world's top football tournaments, officials must be either linesmen or referees; no longer would they be permitted to combine these roles. This directive has radically improved the general standard of officiating across the world. Since 1992 UEFA have also operated a highly efficient 'team' system in their major club and international tournaments (European Championship, Champions League, etc.) where it is common – although not mandatory – for a group of three officials from the same country to be selected for any one match. The days of the jack-of-all-trades are long gone.

Although things appear to have improved since then, there remain clear discrepancies in competence among officials at the world's flagship football tournament. Indeed, during France '98, several referees were clearly not up to the task. The Hungarian referee Laszlo Vagner conspired to send the luckless Cameroon team out of the competition by disallowing three perfectly good goals during their deciding first round match with Chile. Any one of the trio of strikes wrongly called offside by Vagner would have seen the African side through to the second phase. Chile also suffered at the hands of an inexperienced official – the Nigerian referee Bouchardeau – but were fortunate that the penalty he awarded Italy for deliberate handball (there was clearly no intent) did not hinder the team's progress to the next stage of the tournament. The referee was not so lucky. He was the first official to be sent home from France '98 by FIFA; the pressure of performing on the world stage got to him in the end. "I may never referee again," he said.

FIFA's often contradictory directives on 'the tackle from behind' hardly aided the World Cup's referees. In the month leading up to France '98 much was made of the new ruling. It stipulated that any tackle from behind that endangered a player and could be described as 'ferocious' or 'brutal' was now automatically punishable with a red card. In the early stages of the tournament the rash of reds that had been predicted in the wake of the directive completely failed to materialise (much to the relief of players, managers and fans alike). Common sense had prevailed. It didn't last long. Eight days into the tournament FIFA President, Sepp Blatter, backed by the figurehead of France '98, Michel Platini, announced to the press that too many players were being allowed to get away with dangerous play. The referees were subsequently gathered together and told in no uncertain terms that they 'must' enforce the red card directive. It was, of course, a veiled threat. Almost immediately Blatter got what he wanted. The day after he had issued his statement five players were sent off in two unexceptional matches. (The irony of French libero Zinadine Zidane becoming one of the first players to suffer as a result of the clamp down, was presumably lost on Platini.) The deluge continued unabated marring several crucial matches en route. The tournament's weaker officials buckled under the weight of the restated directive, but in many instances this acquiescence was rewarded not punished. Scotland's Hugh Dallas, for example, was handed a place in the second stage of the tournament despite his wilfully harsh handling of the Belgium-Mexico game in which two players were given their marching orders.

Ultimately it was FIFA's heavy-handed tactics that provoked the inconsistency among the World Cup's referees. After 18 June no definitive reading of the red card ruling seemed to exist. While David Beckham and Laurent Blanc were sent off for relatively innocuous 'taps', Dennis Bergkamp escaped despite trampling on Sinisa Mihajlovic and Stephane Guivarc'h survived elbowing Fabio Cannavaro. In short, referees deserted their instinct and judgement to become FIFA automatons. In many ways it was understandable. As ever, defiance was never going to win any referee the favour of FIFA's powerbrokers.

FIFA's policy of employing referees from many different countries was the main reason for the inconsistency of performance during France '98. "It's impossible to achieve consistency when you have referees in charge of top games with little experience at that level," says ex-World Cup official and the Premiership's first ever referees' officer Philip Don. Former French manager Michel Hidalgo agrees, pointing out that the explicit political nature of FIFA's selection process has hindered the game for far too long. "Take the match between Morocco and Scotland," he says, "it should never have been refereed by a man from the United Arab Emirates. Being at the World Cup should be about merit not about favours. We need the best." Michel Platini, too, is all too aware of the need for better quality control. His one chance at reaching a World Cup Final in '82 was denied him by a weak ref who refused to send off Harold Schumacher for a horrific assault on Patrick Battiston: "It is necessary to get the best referees, even if that means penalising certain countries." This, indeed, appears to be the way forward for the World Cup. "I'm glad Sepp Blatter has said he might opperate with an elite group of officials from now on," says Don, refereing to FIFA's plan to recruit four or more referees from each of the major European football nations. One thing is certain. The officials charged with travelling to the Far East in 2002 will be under more pressure than ever to perform.

'SUPER PHLEGM GUYS'

British referees in South America

STRANGE as it may seem, the British are largely responsible for the existence today of football in South America, if not for its undoubted quality. In the 1860s Argentina began building her railways under the expertise of British labourers and engineers. These men brought the basic requirements for a game – the ball – with them, and rudimentary matches (what must have been the first ever internationals) were played out at twilight on the mud flats and plains of the South Pacific. Precisely what skills the British brought to the Argentinians remains unclear, but it seems unlikely that a country – not to say a continent – with such a rich footballing lineage owes too much to these early pioneers. The newly emancipated locals, paying little heed to rules laid down by the FA in 1863, quickly forged a game for themselves. One that was unquestionably cultured; improbably skilful; but which often embraced the etiquette of the battlefield rather than the football pitch. Referees, those who dared offer their services, were never going to have it easy here.

Standards of refereeing in South America were poor from the start. The ever-present threat of violence did little to encourage new recruits or increase the competence of established officials. Tony Mason's excellent *Passion of the People* charts the formative years of the game in South America, when the combination of flair and disorder was at its most volatile. Most games were accidents waiting to happen. "Footballers in South America could rise to heights which others could rarely match," says Mason. "Here was a grace under pressure, with individual ball control of an almost magical kind and passing more like a caress than a kick. But there was another side to the passion for football in South America. If the play was more flamboyant and the crowd more colourful, then both could erupt into a violence that seemed particularly out of place in an arena of pleasure."

Increasingly, heightened levels of tension were exacerbated by a population which was suddenly taking an unprecedented interest in the game. Never before had the continent seen such startling levels of support for a competitive sport. "Matches often failed to start on time because the field was occupied by more than just the players and the officials," says Mason. "Trams and buses would be over-run by fans clinging to poles and ledges, dangling from roofs, grasping anything that might ensure some kind of passage to the ground. Surviving newsreels show lorry-loads of supporters heading for the stadiums, looking more like an invading army than a travelling fan-base. During games the crowd were noisy and excitable when their team was attacking, silent and anxious when they were on the retreat. Confetti, powder and rice were thrown, flags unfurled. Fireworks filled the stadiums with a 'magical cloud-like mist'." Samba bands – an institution in Brazil now – first played at Flamengo in 1941, and soon became widely imitated by other clubs. These were the beginnings of football mania in South America, scenes that every fan can immediately associate with modern-day Latin American football. When a goal was scored by the home team celebrations washed over the ground like a prolonged and very public orgasm. "I shall never forget the sight we saw when the only goal of the match was scored," remembered one British player attending a local game. "The 50,000 people present waved their handkerchiefs for a full five minutes. They seemed to go mad."

Other visitors, such as the French author Albert Camus, were equally overwhelmed by South America's unconditional love for football and its alumni. "When I ask to see a soccer game," he recollects of an early visit to the country, "Guests get very excited, and when I mention that I had a long career as a soccer player, I provoke a general delirium. Unwittingly, I have stumbled upon their principle passion." Twenty years later, a staff writer from a Brazilian newspaper advising the cancellation of a British tour echoed Camus's incredulity. "It appears that football in this country arouses passions that can only be compared to the factions of the Green and Blue in Byzantium." Mason recalls an apocryphal tale which nevertheless serves to illustrate the widespread fervour aroused by football in South America during its first flowering. "A match was being played in Rio in the national championship. Many of the audience at a local theatre had brought transistors to listen to the game during the play. When a goal was scored the audience stirred so audibly that the male lead stopped, looked out into the galleries and asked, 'What's the score?'" More significant was Eva Peron's decision to postpone the Sunday football fixtures during her vice-presidential rally in Argentina during 1951. It was the only way she could guarantee an audience.

Despite rising levels of hysteria surrounding football in Latin America by 1950, a thin veneer of sportsmanship and camaraderie existed between opposing teams. This development was in some ways inspired by the arrival of the famous British amateur side The Corinthians in 1910. Although not the first team to be invited to the Americas (Southern League leaders Southampton beat them to it in 1904 when the Argentine Hippic club extended a welcoming hand), the fabled Corinthians made a lasting impact on the Brazilian towns they toured. "Well into the 1920s", says Mason, "Brazilian teams would still enter the field and raise their right arms with closed fists shouting hip hip hurrah, three times, in the fashion of the English Corinthians. It meant spectators were guaranteed an honest match." And a laugh. Football missionaries since their secession from the FA in 1907 (a move provoked by the team's oppostion to professionalism and the unsporting cynicism that they felt lay therein), the Corinthians were more or less forced to look abroad for more meaningful competition than could be offered by England's struggling amateur sides. Unsurprisingly, with Latin America still learning to crawl on the football pitch, they didn't get it. The handful of teams from Rio and São Paulo who took up the British challenge offered very little in the way of resistance – Fluminese of Rio capitulated 10-1 in the opening game of the tour. But by 1913, when a Rio combination side containing two English players defeated Corinthians 2-1, the roving amateurs were forced to concede that 'a brilliant future is in store for Brazilian football'. Nostradamus couldn't have nailed it any better.

Around the same time in Argentina, the Alumni team – a side with a strong British migrant presence – were busy extolling Corinthian values on the pitch. They aimed to 'play well without passion', and to avoid ungentlemanly conduct during their games. Once, during a match with Estudiantes, Alumni player Watson Hutton persuaded the referee to reverse a dubious penalty decision given in favour of his own team, who were losing 2-1 at the time. Justice was done when Alumni later equalised. Eighty-five years on, the spirit of Hutton was rekindled by

Liverpool's Robbie Fowler, though with less success. Alumni disbanded in 1912, without ever having played their spiritual founding fathers. "It's a pity," reflects Mason, "a match between Alumni and Corinthians would have been a real gentlemen's Cup Final."

While brilliance undeniably lay ahead, and efforts to maintain acceptable levels of restraint on the field appeared to be of genuine concern to the continent's pre-war administrators (at least in Brazil if not elsewhere), South American football struggled from its popular inception with the ominous spectre of crowd control. Early 'international' matches (something of a misnomer – the historic meeting of Exeter City and a Brazilian select XI in 1914 being a case in point) created a tangible friction, as witnessed by Swindon Town's diplomat, Sam Allen. "Partisanship must be encountered wherever football is really known," he observed with some caution in 1912. "It is proof of interest in the game." It was also proof of differing interpretations of the rules, especially regarding the sanctity of the goalkeeper. "An Argentine goalkeeper is untouchable," wrote a Buenos Aires official. "As soon as he gets the ball into his hands he is entitled to a free kick. Argentine players and spectators are very excitable and the sight of a 12-stone Arsenal forward charging one of their goalkeepers with the ball into the net might start a battle." Luckily, Ian Wright never did make it to Buenos Aires.

Crowds too formed their own set of highly distinctive 'rules', which the noble Corinthians would certainly have balked at. Eschewing conventional football etiquette, a band of supporters from the Province of Buenos Aires flooded the pitch during a match between a local select team and a touring Scottish Eleven in 1923. A corner had been given to the visitors and so galled were the home fans by the referee's decision that they instinctively lined up to form a wall in front of the Scots, preventing them from taking the free kick. Eventually one of the touring side kicked the ball into touch so the game could continue.

If football provided a focus for national pride throughout the countries of South America, it certainly didn't do much to quell burgeoning regional rivalries. On the contrary, it gave them an edge they had previously lacked. Inter-city clubs formed pairs and became bitter antagonists. In Uruguay it was Nacional and Penarol of Montevideo; in Brazil, Flamengo and Fluminese, Botafogo and Vasco de Gama of Rio; Corinthians and Palmeiras of São Paulo; in Buenos Aires, five teams became locked in inextricable opposition: Racing, Independiente, San Lorenzo, Boca and River Plate. By the 1930s, when professional football finally took off in the major cities of South America, the cauldron of national and international rivalries had become red hot. It was only a matter of time before it boiled over.

It was into these powder-keg arenas that the tremulous football referee was hurled, sometimes literally, swiftly becoming the prime source of – and target for – crowd discontent. In Brazil, a 1904 post-match report filed by the Journal do Comercio correspondent barely hinted at the kind of seething resentment that would soon typify the relationship between spectator and referee. "[The fans] shouted at the players and the referee when they did something that did not please them," noted the anonymous observer, who continues with genteel naiveté, "And what most annoys us to say Oh! Shame! is that even young men from other clubs, interested only in the victory of one team or another to benefit their own team, also over-reacted in a very rude and undignified way." The reality – if not at first in Brazil, where the game remained for some time in the hands of an elite who strove to uphold the conciliatory virtues of the English Corinthians – was in fact altogether more disturbing.

In June 1910, during the Argentinian Second Division clash

between Boca Juniors and the Western Railway club, a full-scale pitch invasion occurred. Boca, the away team, quickly sided with the throng, and two of their players were seen to assault the referee and the 'home' linesman. The Boca captain stood by impassively as the officials felt the wrath of his team-mates. Retribution from the Argentinian FA was swift: the guilty Boca players were suspended for a year, and the home side were handed a hefty fine for failing to provide a police presence at the Caballito Stadium. The fact that officials were still frequently being accused of harbouring grudges against certain individuals and teams didn't exactly help matters much. Crowds were frenzied enough as it was without the knowledge that a man reportedly affiliated to the opposition had just given a decision against their team. Pre-match anxiety, inexperience and a justifiable fear of the supporters massed behind him, combined to make the linesman a nervous wreck, prone to regular and potentially life-threatening errors of judgement. The lack of protection at grounds (fences didn't go up in Argentina until 1924) left him horribly exposed. Both referees and linesmen were, as a result, easily intimidated by the home support who regarded them as little more than the lepers of the game. Clearly, it wasn't a job for the faint-hearted. Or, some might add, the sane.

In the circumstances, to question why attacks on officials occurred is somewhat naive; it would be more pertinent to ask why it didn't happen more often. The answer is easy: it did. As the stature of football grew, referees and linesmen were continually the victims of premeditated assaults and threats from the continent's rapidly growing network of players, supporters and club administrators. At half-time, during Exeter City's 2-0 defeat at Racing in 1914, the referee was allegedly threatened at gunpoint by a disgruntled home team official. His leniency toward Racing in the second half was undeniable, yet hardly surprising, given the rather limited long-term options an away win would have presented. Following the Argentine First Division match between Racing and Huracan on 12 June 1932 Senore Bruzzone, the match official was severely beaten up by Huracan fans. Their team had lost narrowly, 1-0. Other match officials with first hand experience of what a South American crowd was capable of simply ran for cover at the merest hint of confrontation. One such gentleman, Senor De Angelis, had already been molested by fans of Ferrocarril Oeste when he was picked to referee River Plate against Estudiantes at La Plata in August 1932. It was a game that taught him a valuable lesson in the art of South American football: you can run, you can hide, but ultimately you will have to give the goal. De Angelis disallowed a disputed goal for Estudiantes early in the second half, when they were 1-0 down. As soon as the aggrieved home team players began to surround him in protest at the decision he panicked and bolted for the sanctuary of the dressing room. On re-emerging 15 minutes later he explained that he had been mistaken – the goal would stand. It was strongly rumoured the President of Estudiantes had pulled a gun on him during his brief break from the game.

With the arrival of professionalism and the attendant pressures it placed on clubs to be successful, the referee was never going to find life in South America anything less than torturous. To train officials was a rarity; textbooks simply didn't exist and besides, nobody knew who or what these mediators should be aspiring to. In 1926, in a state of disarray, the Amateur League of São Paulo called for professional referees to come to the aid of its teams. Their plea fell on deaf ears. The fact that touring teams were often permitted to bring their own match officials with them (Notts Forest did in 1905, Plymouth in 1924) can't have done much for the confidence of the continent's home-grown referees and linesmen. There was no association or governing body guiding the referees of Argentina and Brazil. And it took the South American Football Confederation until 1929 to organise a meeting of referees from its member countries. Just what they discussed isn't clear – stricter gun laws, perhaps – but the situation on the pitch didn't improve. It simply got worse.

The growing wealth of teams, and the resulting increase in the significance of each game, meant that the referee was no longer just an object of hatred and ridicule; he became a genuine threat, a man who, with the blast of a whistle or the raising of an arm, could influence the long-term success of a side – both on and off the pitch. Much as it is now the practice for managers and players to publicly criticise the performance of referees, club directors and chairmen in Argentina and Brazil began to pour scorn on the hapless man in black. The River Plate club were particularly derogatory in their comments. They had earned the nickname Los Millionarios in 1932 as a result of their record spending on new players, and as such were in no hurry to lose their new-found status on the whim of a referee. Moreover, although it seems that violence was a far more widely used (and successful) deterrent to an ambitious official than extortion or bribery, River Plate undeniably had the financial clout to influence the world of officialdom. Heavy-handed tactics certainly seemed to work on the increasingly jumpy referee: he became a pawn to the most popular sides, blowing for the smallest infringement and generally favouring the most powerful and popular teams for fear of retribution.

Newspapers – initially merely wary of the man with the whistle – were becoming increasingly critical too. Papers in Argentina and across South America had begun their infatuation with the game as early as the first visit of the Corinthians, dedicating pages to match reports and colourful features. It was only a matter of time before the darker underbelly of the game caught their attention. In 1912 the *Buenos Aires Herald* complained about the 'chronic rowdyism' prevalent at football grounds. In 1929, after Chelsea's almost comically violent game against Capital, the same paper calmly conceded that, yes, there had been an 'unruly element in the crowd', which caused the contest to end amidst 'disorderly scenes'. Aside from admonishing Maradona for being a naughty little boy all these years, it's hard to imagine a more misleadingly understated example of observational journalism. The match cannot be said to have been played in the most generous of spirits, and had descended to the level of a particularly violent Brian Rix farce long before the end. A Chelsea defender's tackle injured a Capital forward early in the first half. This in itself was enough to provoke a minor insurrection by a group of the home support, one of whom ran straight up to the Chelsea captain and punched him in the face. Luis Monti, the Argentine internationals took this as a signal to kick Rodger, the Chelsea centre-half, in the groin, which resulted in 'a happy shout of acclamation' from the Capital supporters. When the same player fainted and was removed from the field 'the public cheered'. More fighting then broke out between the two teams. At the end another Argentine player put his foot through a glass panel in the visitors dressing room door. "The Argentine player", concluded the report in an implicitly moral tone, "must learn to lose as well as win. Any player can win gracefully. But it takes a better man to lose gracefully. Locally, they lose disgracefully." Capital won the match 3-2, and Chelsea – no doubt to their eternal regret – never got to see the locals really upset. And the referee? Not mentioned in the report, presumably he just turned the other cheek. It was the safest thing, perhaps the only thing, he could do.

Those lucky enough to escape physical assault could always rely on the press to give them a verbal battering, thus ensuring the wider immortalisation of their infamy. Gimnasia y Esgrima were heading the Championship challenge in 1933 when they visited their closest rivals Boca in September of that year. Leading 2-1 at half-time the away side eventually went down 3-2, the result of a highly dubious penalty and an even more suspect off-side decision. The League suspended the referee and then teed him up nicely for the magazine *La Cancha* ('The Football Ground') to have a swipe: "For Blowing his whistle so well/On that mad evening/They nominated Little Angel/As volunteer spy for Boca".

Even in broken verse (it sounds much better in Spanish) journalists never strayed far from their favoured theme of bribery and favouritism. Argentine fans too betrayed their growing sense of paranoia when they started screaming the word '*bombero*' – meaning 'spy' – at referees. 'Bombero' also means 'fireman', a peculiar form of insult, and one no doubt entirely lost on the officials it was aimed at.

Gimnasia were to suffer further before the season's denouement. At home, against San Lorenzo (the eventual League winners), the referee awarded an equalising goal to the travelling team, though the goalkeeper had clearly kept the ball from crossing his line. The enraged Gimnasia players staged a sit-down protest on the pitch, which did little to allay the situation. Once play had been allowed to restart San Lorenzo quickly notched up four more goals against their prostrate opponents before the match was abandoned. With referees in the pocket of the five Argentinian super clubs there was little hope of the general farce coming to an end.

When the situation in Argentina became so untenable that it threatened the very future of the game, the AFA acted. In October 1937, seeking to find a way to ensure the impartiality of officialdom, they invited a Labour councillor and former League referee from Blackburn to Buenos Aires. His name was Isaac

Caswell, and during the following three years he would attempt to bring some order to the fundamentally chaotic state of Argentine football; a state which, indeed, characterised the game throughout most of the continent.

Caswell was initially only an observer, and presumably a nervous one given that his arrival coincided with a renewed campaign of intolerance against referees in Argentina (bribery was thought to be on the increase again). Still, by attending League games it was hoped he could find a way to bring the essence of the gentleman's game back to South America.

The AFA saw Caswell as their saviour. He would, they hoped, be an educator, a leveller, someone who epitomised the British ideals of fairness and sportsmanship on the field of conflict, and who could help them draw up a template along these lines for their ill-tempered game. In short, he was their Equaliser, Edward Woodward without the patent leather gloves: a man who could get you out of a scrape, restore some order. Of course, he was also a referee and, at some point, he was going to have to get out onto the pitch and show them how it was supposed to be done. That was the hard bit.

Caswell was an able and firm referee, but the relative tranquility of the English League could hardly have prepared him for what Argentina had to offer. After all, being threatened at gunpoint, stoned or spat upon wasn't exactly common practice at Molineux or Ewood Park in the 1930s. Still, he coped reasonably well with the constant barrackings, despite admitting that the first six months were pretty unbearable. As it transpired, most of his time was spent on the pitch and he barely had time to lay out his spare whistle and stopwatch the night before a game, let alone a detailed plan for the wholesale restructuring of officialdom in Argentina. But the AFA's experiment with Caswell was nevertheless deemed a success, something the referee himself hinted at following a particularly nasty incident in a game between Boca and Racing in 1938. Caswell had sent off a favoured – and famous – Argentine player for repeatedly arguing with him. For his troubles, Caswell was ritually stoned at the end of the match. The player was given a one month suspension. Nothing new there. But in a radio interview following the debacle, the disgraced player made clear his respect for the English referee, something which Caswell, perhaps conceitedly, heralded as a step in the right direction. "My firmness in this match, and the fact that I showed I was out for discipline and was not to be deterred either by the fame of the players or by the clubs, made an impression and changed the situation." He had a point. Where his predecessors had frequently bowed to the wealth, power and the accompanying heavy-handed tactics of the super-clubs, Caswell refused to play the game. The fact that he wasn't shot for his pains does seem rather miraculous, but even more surprising is that the bullies appeared to get some kind of sadistic pleasure out of tasting their own medicine.

Caswell refereed the only way he knew how: with authority and fairness. It worked in England, and, when the time had come for him to head home, it had begun to work in Argentina. In the short term at least, he had left a blueprint for successful refereeing in South America.

As Tony Mason says: "The Caswell experiment probably influenced the AFA to recruit eight referees from Britain to take charge of all the First Division matches in 1948." While some stuck to the unenviable task at hand, others quickly turned on their heels and fled. By 1950 their were 12 British referees in Argentina, contracted to officiate all top flight games, financially supported by the footballing authorities to the handsome tune of £100 a month, and aided by translators who accompanied them to matches and helped them write their match reports.

Many of the British referees were able to find extra work as teachers in Buenos Aires' British schools. Slowly, a social infrastructure for referees was being constructed in the hope and expectation that referees would repay the AFA by ridding their game of its worst excesses and replacing them with improved guidelines to carry into the future. The rewards for braving the war zones of Argentinian football were enough to ensure that some of the original 12 stayed as long as nine years.

Initially however, Caswell's crusade was a one-man affair, and in this sense he was always swimming against the tide. He was, of course, well looked after, but the compatriots who followed in his wake enjoyed many more benefits, both on the pitch and off it. Firstly, they were given the opportunity to oversee the instruction of local referees. Recognising the need to entice and then train fledgling officials in the wily ways of the British referee, the AFA gave each of the 12 a team of three 'apprentice' linesmen who would take charge at the reserve team match which preceded the first team fixture on Sunday afternoon before running the line in the big game. No formal training as such was given to the Argentine charges by their British mentors, although *The Referees' Handbook* was by now an annual (not to say slightly anal) publication and was most probably carried by the itinerant officials. The new boys would have learnt mainly by adhering to the age-old principle of 'Do as I do Son, and you'll be alright' – arguably a risky approach considering the average Argentine player was unlikely to take so kindly to one of his own countrymen 'doing a Caswell' during a match. The outsider status of the English officials undoubtly gave them much of their authority.

Undeniably, levels of competence and confidence did improve among the ranks of the apprentices as a result of this system. However, it came more out of necessity than choice that these men began to be given first class games to officiate by the AFA.

By 1954, one First Division match a week was being refereed by an Argentine. Unfortunately, this new-found power went straight to their heads, and almost even before they had wearily negotiated their first top level stoning, the Argentine referees betrayed the British officials, beginning a campaign of non-co-operation with the very men who had ushered them onto the big stage in the first place. It was a predictable betrayal. Regardless of ability, Argentine referees were never going to have an easy time of it on home soil. Accusations of favouritism and bribery began again. The British, with no affiliation to club or colour, escaped the brunt of these onslaughts, and were in fact well received by most clubs outside the Buenos Aires coterie, being looked upon by the smaller teams as the arch angels of equality and impartiality. Despite the obvious fact that they were 'aliens', the official's birthplace was never going to be a justifiable provocation for assault when the ref hailed from Blackburn. It most definitely was, however, if you were an Argentine official from the capital giving a penalty against Boca or Independiente. That, in essence, was all it took.

In truth, British referees were much better equipped to deal with Argentine football than their inexperienced sidekicks. They were organised, more resilient and less likely to be lured into conflict against men they could never hope to beat. That is not to say that all Argentinean referees were bad, but the handful of technically sound local officials who made the grade were severely undermined by the knowledge of what had happened to some of their predecessors. They were terrified that the same fate may befall them too. The 'alien', unconstrained by the baggage of Argentina's distinctly messy footballing heritage, arrived with only the burden of duty to weigh him down. He had a job to do, and like any self-respecting Brit, he was determined to do it well. And, in the end, he had a clear advantage – he had ignorance on his side.

Not that British referees were spared the lash completely. South America's insatiable media decreed that most officials – regardless of background or allegiance – came in for uncomfortable scrutiny at some time or other. Ignorance didn't always pay. During a match between Racing and Platense one English referee, Bob Turner, fell foul of a much loved Argentine footballing by-law: never award a penalty in the dying moments of a game. He gave not one but two, split evenly between the teams in the – with hindsight foolish – presumption that the second would balance things out nicely and leave everybody happy. Not so. He had to be smuggled out of the ground in a police van after a deluge of stones and other sharp objects heralded his departure from the pitch. He no doubt considered himself immeasurably fortunate that the match had only been drawn – otherwise things might just have turned nasty. The local press turned on the hapless Turner too, although one paper blew a potentially stinging critique by apparently nabbing its pay-off line from Stanley Unwin. "Get out Mr Turner and bad lucky (sic)" didn't quite land the required sucker punch, somehow.

Insults fired by the press were generally not so lacklustre. Journalists could be, and often were, personally vindictive, using the paper to issue sinister threats quite openly. One English referee, who had sent off a much loved Boca player during a home game with local rivals River Plate in 1955, was the next day informed by the local paper that if he didn't leave the country immediately his wife would be killed. Threats like this – although idle – nevertheless beat many an able and, more importantly, impartial referee into submission, and presumably didn't do much for their spouses sense of social integration either. This naturally helped the big clubs, who gained from corrupt and corruptible officials, but it did little to aid the minnows. Unsurprisingly, club magazines, in particular those run by the

Buenos Aires sides, were the worst culprits. They adopted a firm policy of non-toleration against referees who sullied the good name of their team with biased – in other words fair – refereeing. Any defeat meant that the man in the middle got it in the neck. Rough justice indeed.

A firm rebuke was the best most referees could hope for in the form of post-match appraisal although, in the circumstances, some fared remarkably well. Always passionate, South American football writers could sometimes be surprisingly euphoric in their approbation when they weren't too busy condemning referees to a lifetime in Hades. Bob Turner saw the more forgiving side of the press in 1957, when he was selected to take charge of the South American Championship match between Peru and Ecuador. Worth quoting in its entirety, the 'review' makes for an illuminating read.

"Turner brought to the task all the phlegm of the islands. To arrive in a strange country, a Latin American country, which has a reputation for violence; to begin by actually controlling a game in which the local team [Peru played at home] takes on a country to which it is traditionally antagonistic – Ecuador – and to disallow, in fifteen minutes, two goals for the local team, is a spectacular case of British phlegm...Mr Turner, without worrying what they might say, disallowed the goals, not just one but two, one after the other and for no reason at all! If it had been in my country, commented a Uruguayan, the smell of fried referee would have been in the air, or if it had been in Buenos Aires, we added. Happily for Mr Turner, we were in Lima and here, up to now, the custom of eating referees has not been developed...Mr Turner will be able to carry on with his contract, and carry on disallowing goals which is where this super phlegm is shown to best effect – super phlegm, personified in the referee called Turner."

The author's unhinged, incredulous tone masks a definite air of respect. The passage shows the extent to which some dangerously stubborn British referees were resolved to go in their efforts to combat favouritism and champion impartiality. Even if 'Super-phlegm guy' had got it wrong (and there's no telling whether he did or not) Turner showed he was prepared to stand by a decision even with the threat of death – or worse, being served up as a local delicacy – hanging over him. Turner's critics seemed less inclined to laugh off his misdemeanour. They wanted to fry him.

British referees could never really do much about the press they received in South America – they didn't deal with the press, the press dealt with them. However partial the fourth estate may have been to the occasional dose of British phlegm, it fiercely protected its role of the dominatrix. But as long as the referee knew he was there to be fired at by the press, he developed an immunity to the bullets. South American supporters, of course, had a much more immediate and dangerous arsenal at their disposal. But controlling the crowd, or at least limiting its capacity for unrest, was an impossibility for the British referee abroad. Anyway he recognised, no doubt with some relief, that it was outside his remit.

The 22 players, of course, were expected to behave in a manner which would distinguish them from the crowd. In Britain, the referee was proud of his ability to harness players to the rule book and keep them from the path of 'ungentlemanly conduct'. But controlling South American players proved far more difficult than many referees could have imagined. It was an onerous task. Restraint, resilience and even ability may have shown the British referees to be a cut above the rest when dealing with the press and the continent's footballing heavyweights, but to the players it didn't mark them out for any preferential treatment. Frequently the referee ended up as arbiter and peacekeeper, the players often becoming involved in more than just the odd heated exchange during the course of a game. If fighting the referee was fair game – and we have seen that it was – then attacking each other was almost *de rigueur*.

Referee John Meade discovered this early in his tenure when, in 1950, an apparently trivial foul five minutes from the end of a match between Huracan and Velez Sarsfield led to a fight in which all 22 players were soon eagerly engaged. Fortunately for the hapless man in the middle, police intervention was swift and incisive. The match was abandoned and the players were arrested and detained for two days in the local gaol. On release they were each handed lengthy suspensions. This was no isolated incident. Racing had already secured the Championship in 1957, but still seven players were sent off for continual fouling and fighting in what should have been an exhibition match with Indepeniente. A Division Two match between Riestra and Los Andes was abandoned, also in 1957, after nine home players and seven visitors had been sent off for their involvement in a mass brawl. Clearly, there was still a real problem.

British referees certainly didn't balk at dismissing players for fighting or persistent fouling, but nothing could have prepared them for the situations they would have to face in South America. One official admitted that the 1958 contest between Argentina and Uruguay had been easily the hardest of his long career as a referee. He sent off three Uruguayans and two Argentines.

While British officials seem to have been a lot less tolerant than the continent's own referees, the problem of violent conduct on the pitch had no real solution. Leniency meant the cheats prospered. Firmness simply resulted in retaliation which in turn often led to abandonment or worse, pitch invasion. In total, 82 players were sent off in First Division matches in Argentina in 1964. By 1977 in the Campeonato Metropolitano the figure had reached 186, compared with only 96 in the whole of the four English football leagues in the same year. The helplessness of the situation was tacitly acknowledged by the AFA. Despite their efforts to curb violence on the terraces – an extensive police presence with tear gas and fences was provided at most games, as well as moats and firemen at the larger stadiums – they could do very little to stop the constant threat of insurrections occurring on the pitch. Games were disrupted so often that football's governing bodies stopped trying to explain the reasons. Instead, reports simply noted that an 'incident' resulted in the match ending prematurely. Everybody got the drift.

Around this time, an outbreak of relative civility seemed poised to threaten these traditional and all-pervasive disciplinary problems: newspapers began grading referees' performances, giving them marks out of 10 for their efforts. Common enough practice for today's Monday morning sports editors perhaps, but something entirely new – and presumably welcome – for the South American official wearily accustomed to somewhat more direct action. Naturally, the introduction of ratings didn't completely eradicate the stonings or the death threats – these were, after all, the long-standing staples of the disgruntled football fan/player/chairman in these parts and could not be so easily swept under the carpet. But the genesis of a decidedly less Old Testament style of criticism at least signalled the way forward. As we've seen, the sharpened poison pens of the club magazine scribes and football editors could be brutal. Yet if a one out of 10 character assassination hurt, it hurt a lot less than the force of a brick or the crack of a fist. Or the tell-tale spit of oil in the frying pan.

The combination of on-the-pitch violence and off-the-pitch

hack criticism in South America was a fiery and unpredictable coupling which the British officials had to just learn to accept. Harsh words and easy violence remain an occupational hazard for South American officials, and even a second imperialist sortie by Britain's referees would be unlikely to significantly alter the basic yet durable tenets of the game there.

Despite failing to overhaul the image and standing of the referee in Argentina, Britain's missionary officials achieved enough during their bumpy sabbatical on the continent to attract the attention of a number of football associations. "During the 1950s, British referees were in demand throughout South America," says Mason. Indeed, during this period, British officials were to be found officiating at club matches and Internationals in Chile, Brazil and Peru as well as in Argentina. Some were even invited by clubs to accompany players and coaching staff on summer tours of the continent. During these excursions, the referee would be urged to help teach the team about rule changes and advise unruly players on acceptable disciplinary etiquette. When Paul Durkin joined the England squad at Bisham Abbey before France '98 to brief players on the implications of FIFA's new tackling missives, he was merely continuing a long and worthy refereeing tradition.

One of the most popular and successful British referees to follow in the footsteps of Caswell was Jack Barrick from Northampton, who had retired in 1948 after taking charge of the FA Cup Final. He refereed 12 out of the 29 games played during the South American Championship of 1949. He also refereed six of Arsenal's seven games in Brazil in the same year. In eight and a half months abroad he took charge of 91 games in total, including some of the most prestigious and dangerous. He claims to have enjoyed the experience.

The Brazilians, or at least their press, seemed to derive great pleasure from his skills too. If Barrick did indeed have real prestige as a referee in Brazil he was nevertheless forced to adopt the local rule book when officiating in the country. In 23 years in the English league he had sent off just six players. In eight and a half months in Brazil he sent off 19, including nine in internationals and four during a match between Brazil and Peru.

Barrick, like those before him, couldn't significantly change the way in which South Americans treated the humble referee. But his stay did prove that even if the players couldn't be won over to the benefits of good old-fashioned British refereeing, others grew to appreciate its positive impact on the game. When Barrick left Porto Alegre in 1950, a local paper lamented:

"Mr Barrick's leaving opens a curtain on a black panorama for our football, which he has nearly retrieved from chaos. We shall be like the man who delighted in Shakespeare plays for several weeks, has to turn back to clown jesters..."

Now that's a send off.

THE STRUTTING PEACOCK

the Spanish refereeing experience

BRITISH players who accuse domestic officials of arrogance and self-importance should really look more closely at the Spanish experience before bemoaning their lot. From the persecutions of the Inquisitors to the opulent heyday of Phillip II, Europe's Iberian peninsula has a long and proud history of opposition to autocratic pretenders.

And in a country where footballers wear their aristocratic pretensions firmly on their sleeves, someone has to give them a run for their money. Suffice it to say, Spanish football referees have some of the most impressively inflated egos this side of the Atlantic; the lazy 'hot blooded' tag doesn't tell the half of it. Whole games can pass in a blur of red and yellow; black books are filled with merciless ease; indeed, given the prevailing activity on the pitch, it's a wonder the Spanish game hasn't been re-christened 'Whistle'. Spanish 'jueces' consider themselves part of the spectacle, not merely the mediators of it. Take the 1996-7 season. Spain's 10 First Division referees averaged nearly five cards a game (as opposed to under three in the English Premiership). One Spanish magazine printed its own table of shame: half of the country's officials were shown to have sent off a player every other game. Arturo Dauden Ibanez – Spain's answer to David Elleray – seems to be from the nothing-exceeds-like-excess school of arbitration. In 59 career games the Professor of Biology from Aragon has sent off 37 players and booked 324. Most Spanish football fans could reel off similarly detailed facts about other match officials. A subculture has developed around the referee. Newspapers and football shows are filled with vitriolic columns and editorials dedicated solely to the referee. At live matches, retired referees sit on the jury with the obligatory panelists, the former ever-keen to pick over their erstwhile colleague's errors as the game unfolds. Afterwards, they crow about the players and the manager, in an eerie role reversal of the British model. In short, Spanish referees are jumped up prima donnas, perhaps as much responsible for the demise of 'flowing football' on the continent as George Graham has been off it. Jeff King, a leading observer of the Spanish game agrees. "The referees over here want to be the protagonist," he says. "They're like strutting peacocks, desperate to play an integral part of the whole event. If they don't get the attention of the players and the press they seem to act like spoilt kids. But instead of going off in a sulk they just start booking players." Therein, perhaps, lies an implicit warning to the prevailing trend in Britain: the more fuss we make of referees, the more attention they will crave.

King spent 1996/7 documenting Bobby Robson's one season as Barcelona coach. Much of his time was occupied trying to keep pace with the refereeing merry-go-round, onto which Robson – somewhat inevitably – was the latest in a long line of esteemed managers to jump. In contrast to most Englishmen abroad, Robson initially kept his views on the local types unaired, and was generally not inclined to pass the kind of judgement that would have resulted in a Monday morning appointment with the head honchos at Lancaster Gate had he been in England. He soon learned, however, that post-match comments on referees from his Spanish managerial adversaries were spoken by altogether less forgiving tongues. He assimilated admirably.

"I try to avoid criticising referees," claimed Robson following a 2-0 defeat by Espanyol, in which he saw the youngest referee in the Premier League – Megia Davila – gift a penalty to the home team before sending off Barca's Figo, "but that penalty was as dubious as Madrid's on Thursday, and it changed the course of the game."

Robson soon got his teeth into the subject of another traditional Spanish pastime – the dive: "All the rolling over after you get fouled. It's the same as in Portugal – all the diving. You don't get those theatrics in Northern European leagues. Spanish players get bumped and immediately go down. They're too willing to go down here; if you're really hurt you don't roll over four or five times; refs should know that to start with. Cheating players get the crowd going, too. That puts referees under pressure, makes their job difficult."

Robson had clearly witnessed enough of the Spanish way by then to realise that the scrutiny of refereeing and the seemingly endemic corruption of Spain's officials was as much part of the country's footballing heritage as the famed Barca/Real Madrid rivalry. He wouldn't be the first to express horror at the spectacle of grossly 'misjudged' penalty decisions, and he certainly wouldn't be the last. But he was never going to change anything in a season. During his first month in charge at the Nou Camp, Robson witnessed school janitor-cum-linesman Rafael Guerrero cajoling referee Mejuto Gonzalez into dismissing a completely innocent Real Zaragoza player in a case of mistaken identity during Barca's 5-3 away defeat in September 1996. The result? A 10-minute delay caused by Zaragoza's Gustavo Poyet's attempts to incite a mass walk-off. For the linesman the hiatus was more prolonged, and less easily forgotten. He was forced to endure a volley of colourful expletives from Mejuto once the referee had realised the implications of what his assistant had signalled for; the dressing down was subsequently repeated ad nauseam on Spanish TV and then adopted as a terrace chant for the benefit of the hapless official on his visits to other league grounds. By comparison, the telephone threats and graffiti at his school must have seemed like manna from heaven.

Robson in fact discovered the whistle-happy and highly erratic nature of Spanish referees during his first game in charge. Nine yellow cards were dished out in what, for Spanish standards, was a fairly well-tempered encounter between Oviedo and Barca. Luis Enrique was booked on his début – not for any of the eight fouls he committed – but for celebrating the first of his two goals with a quick strip-tease. Three weeks later Robson would see Vallodolid's club doctor being dismissed at Rayo Vallencano whilst attending an injured player. 'I didn't like the way he looked at me,' shrugged the referee in reply to his critics. Poor bedside manner, obviously.

In a country where cab drivers and shop assistants can rattle off the names of top referees as if they were former pin-ups of the national game, there is one debate that never ends: the supposed allegiance of referees to the two giants of Spanish football – Barcelona and Real Madrid, and because discretion has never served the fame-seeking Spanish referee too well down the years, the theory is difficult, nay impossible to ignore. If history and the TV cameras are to be believed, Spanish officialdom is awash with corruption, bribery and unabashed favouritism for these two teams. Madrid's referees have long been accused of favouring the capital's premier team, most often to the detriment of their hated Catalan rivals. Emilio Guruceta – the referee at the centre of bribery accusations following Anderlecht's UEFA Semi-final win over Nottingham Forest in 1984 – confirmed what most had suspected during a 50-year reign of 'persecution at the hands of referees in cohorts with Real Madrid', when he was picked to take charge of the 1970 Spanish Cup Final, played between Barca and Real at the Nou Camp stadium. Guruceta awarded a penalty to the visitors – which in the end proved to be all decisive – on the basis of a foul committed a full two yards outside the required area. The Barca fans took this as a cue to instigate the infamous 'Cushions Riot', in which they hurled plastic hire cushions from the stands onto the pitch. Guruceta was suspended for six months and blacklisted from all Barcelona games for 14 years. Presumably feeling a little neglected after such a long lay-off, he was more than ready for the attention he duly received when he accepted a back-hander from Anderlecht officials in the run up to the Nottingham Forest debacle. Controversy followed him to the grave three years later, when a fatal car crash secured his place at the high altar of Spanish refereeing martyrs. Unsurprisingly Guruceta is still worshipped in some quarters of central Spain. In many ways, he set the standards, and fledging jueces have struggled valiantly to emulate the 'great one's' astonishing commitment to the honourable cause of Barca-bashing ever since.

More recently, Madrid referee Jose Nunez Manrique stole the limelight during Barcelona's 2-0 defeat at the hands of Real Sociedad in February 1997 with a remarkably creative display of refereeing. 'Misconstruing' an accidental first half collision between Craioveana and Abelardo as a vicious assault, Manrique gave a penalty to Real, handing them a 1-0 lead. In the second half, amid a series of errors, he waved play on when Real's Fuentes halted a dazzling run into the penalty area by Ronaldo – with his hands. Guruceta, you feel sure, would have been proud of the boy. Robson, now fluent in Spanish anti-ref vernacular, wasn't so enamoured: "The first penalty was ridiculous and then there's a clear handball in the area and he ignores it. If the guy makes the right decisions we're looking at a totally different game." Asked whether he thought Manrique was biased toward Real Robson replied "no". There was a hint of uncertainty in his voice as he continued, "Well, I don't think so...at least I hope not. What people have said or done previously [referring to Real's constant accusations of a refereeing bias against them] should make no difference."

It shouldn't make a difference, but, of course, it does. King insists that Spain's men in black are rather easily swayed, despite their rampant egos. "They're basically not of the highest quality ...they aspire to the model of the British referee...I'm not suggesting they always favour Real or Barca, but if the past is anything to go by, there are some who have more than just a passing interest in 'their team', be it Madrid or Barcelona. They're an odd bunch really – they never act in the way they do here [i.e. full of pomp and arrogance] when they get selected for a European match or a World Cup."

Still, back home, the referees can't escape from the allegations of favouritism, which swing back and forth like a pendulum between the two factions. Manuel Diaz Vega is the undisputed king of referees in Spain. He is also not a big Barcelona fan. During Johan Cruyff's tenure at the Nou Camp Diaz Vega set remarkable new standards in partiality. Cruyff twice went to the Bernabeu to play Real with the man dubbed 'Darth Vader' in charge. He lost twice, both times by the odd goal courtesy of a dubious penalty. Diaz Vega could have built a small cottage out of all the cards he flashed at Barca players during the former Dutch hero's time at Nou Camp. Not that he ever tried to hide his hatred of the man. The ref-cum-bank manager once claimed that "Cruyff is only fit to coach kids". He followed this putdown with the stunningly visual allegation that Barca's most celebrated coach "pisses his pants every time he visits the Bernabeu". When Cruyff was sacked, a clearly flustered Diaz Vega was reduced to picking on his gormless son, Jordi, giving him the only sending-off of his professional career.

During Robson's spell at Barca Diaz Vega proved there was nothing personal about his dislike of the Cruyff's – he hated all Barca managers. Softened up by the Real players in the run-up to the big game with Barca – Mijatovic and Suker insisting in the press that Vader was 'a great referee' – Diaz Vega promptly awarded the Madrid side a shocking penalty in the dying minutes to even up the scores.

The help of just one referee isn't normally enough to satisfy Real's ferocious President Lorenz Sanz however, or even the club's ever-diving Yugoslav striker Mijatovic for that matter. The latter blamed the 'down and outs' (referees) for launching a campaign against his 'tactics' during a 1-0 defeat at home to Rayo Vallencano, adding somewhat threateningly "either he didn't want to give them or else he was scared to". Time for Barca's referees to get a hammering. Sanz, a man who would sell his grandmother for the right result, had his say on the penalty 'controversy': "What do our players have to do to get a penalty – get shot? We haven't had a penalty since October [this was February]; maybe we should just retire now and let Barca play on their own. Gaspart [Barca's president] has got what he was after, though now I suppose he'll say we're making excuses." Surely not. Anyway, Gaspart quickly dispatched Sanz's volley with an effortless smash. "If I had the clout with the media and referees that he says I do, Madrid would be in the Second Division by now."

And so the accusations fly back and forth, the ever-present referee adding fuel to the two clubs' escalating paranoia. Sanz was at it again following his team's 3-0 capitulation against Barca at the Nou Camp in March 1998. Referee Senor Redondo from Aragon got it in the neck this time. "He was Barca's best player ...if he hadn't made us play with 10 men for most of the second half then it would have been a completely different story." With this defeat went Real's chances of retaining the title. By the time Barca wrapped up the Championship a few weeks later the clubs and officials had virtually ceased to comment on referees and their hatred of all things Catalan. Now there's a surprise.

The seething animosity towards referees in Spain is shared by fans, players and managers alike. Most don't see any reason to justify their hatred – it is inherited like a gene, from generation to generation – and normally the officials have no option but to try and withstand the onslaught. Occasionally, however, they reach breaking point. In November 1997, precipitated by a League match in which referee Pino Zamorano had to send off a player and cautioned 11 others, Spain's top officials simply went on strike. Or rather they withdrew their labour from the League programme, insisting that their industrial action was, in fact, a 'day of reflection'. In other words, they had had enough of it all. The strike went ahead – without, incidentally, the backing of Referees' Association Chairman Victoriano Sanchez Armino, the officials deciding after an emergency meeting in Madrid that to call off the strike once they had made their intentions clear would be tantamount to losing face. They'd already lost enough. In the end, the Premier referees were joined by colleagues from Segunda A, and so the black-leg labour of Segunda B leapt into the breach. The players found the whole strike rather amusing, and were sorely disappointed when the Federation went ahead with recruitment of officials from the Spanish Second Division. Presumably they would have preferred no referees at all, but the Federation decided that letting these kind of men out onto the pitch without their favourite punch-bag didn't really bear consideration. The public shared the players' mirth and spent the weekend chortling over the headlines in the papers – the Spanish word for whistle (*pito*) doubles for willy so there was no end of *double entendres* on the 'down tools' theme. The referees, however, were genuinely fed up with the situation. And they had every reason to be so. Pilloried by every man, woman and donkey, lambasted by the newspapers and radio, criticised by former friends and colleagues – the majority of whom earn their retirment crust by appearing on Spanish TV to pick over the failings of referees – the jueces are forced to exist in what amounts to sniper's alley. One ex-league referee currently employed with the onerous task of slaughtering his former associates on TV is Joaquin Ramos Marcos. 'Joky', as he is known, appears every Monday on a show presented by the former Liverpool player Michael Robinson, a celebrity himself in Spain since he finished his playing career in the country. The avuncular Joky is by no means the only ex-referee on the payroll of Spain's myriad terrestrial TV stations and broadsheets – they're all at it – but he appears to take more pleasure out of his work than most. Joky presents a regular feature of the show called *lo que el arbitro no ve* (what the referee didn't see), in which he gleefully picks the bones from a collection of the week's worst refereeing blunders, using an on-screen graphic to indicate where the unfortunate official has gone wrong. If Joky flashes a red light it means the decision was a poor one; something, one suspects, the crowd and players are quite likely to have succinctly pointed out to the referee already. A rare green light and Joky gives the 'ref the thumbs up on a contested offside ruling or disputed caution. And although this may seem a late and unnecessary admonishment, similar tactics are used in South American and French TV shows. Somehow – mercifully – it's hard to see Paul Durkin cracking jokes with Des Lynam about Uriah Rennie, even 10 years down the line.

Of all the reasons for the referees' 'day of reflection', one of the more prominent ones was the insufferable and persistent play-acting in which players continue to indulge. The fans dusted off the old Spanish proverb – 'baby no cry, baby get no milk' – during the strike; this didn't impress the already disgruntled referees. The referee's union leader, Antonio Lopez Nieto – the ref who scuppered Dynamo Kiev's bribery attempt – made his thoughts on every Spaniard's favourite tactic perfectly clear: it was high time the clubs grew up and stopped their bawling.

Unusually, money was not at the root of this problem. Unlike in Britain, where top officials are unlikely to earn more than £450 (including expenses) from a Premiership match, Spain's whistleblowers are extremely well compensated for the hazards of their employment – though some would say the peseta was scant reward for the pain. Graham Turner, a British football journalist working in Spain, explains. "The country's Premier League referees receive a retainer of just over £700 a month for all but two months of the year and are paid £670 a match, plus expenses. But what they really want is respect, and the introduction of suitably harsh deterrents (longer suspensions and larger fines) to ensure they get it. The problem is, any legislative punishment drawn up for inclusion in the football rule book has to go through the Superior Sports Council and possibly even the Spanish parliament before it can be written in." Unfortunately, the referees don't have these bodies on their side. Tellingly, the strike was described by the Minister for Sport as "a hasty, inappropriate and untimely decision" – nobody in Spain likes their football season disrupted.

So the referees were rather roughly shaken from their reflections to face the reality that in Spain, as in most countries, football officials have to earn the right to respect. Judging by the treatment most received on returning to their stoop, they faced another long hot spell on the ropes before they were likely to achieve it.

The welcome back party was a rowdy one. Real Madrid's president claimed the referee in his match "demonstrated faults of ability and personality". He was being nice. In lower divisions over the same weekend one official was concussed by a bottle of water, one was stoned by home fans, one was punched in the stomach and a linesman had to be taken to hospital after being hit over the head by a plastic seat. Reflect on that seemed to be the message.

The Spanish referees' 'day of reflection' wasn't a first. In 1989 Greek referees went on strike in protest against the rising tide of violence against match officials. The straw that broke the camel's back was the beating up of referee Nikos Hrysanis by both players and spectators after a Cup tie in Crete. Hrysanis described the incident: "More than a dozen fans started kicking and punching me about the head and face. Fans had blocked the entrance to the dressing room and tunnel and my linesman and I didn't know which way to turn…the punches and kicks and blows were coming from all directions. I don't know how we managed to get to the dressing room." They had the police to thank for that. Non-league referees have been known to put down tools too. During the Christmas period of 1995 Halifax officials went on strike after a referee was knocked unconscious after merely cautioning a player. It was the sixth attack on a Halifax official in just four seasons.

THE DARK SIDE

bribes, fixes, violence and the bizarre

WHERE there is a referee, then, there is inevitably a good story. From the foot of the Dr Marten's League to the dizzy heights of the Premiership; from Steinhousmuir to Seville; Barry Town to Buenos Aires, the common denominator is the referee and his generally unenviable plight. Whether being bribed by the gift of a hooker (or a horse, for that matter) threatened by the barrel of a gun; whisked into the skies to avoid evisceration, or boozing on the job, the world's officials are certain never to be far from trouble.

MATCH-FIXING, BRIBERY AND CHEATING

"Madrid are the most consistent side in Spain," goes the joke, according to Jeff King. "Every week they persuade the referee to do them a favour." Maybe so, but allegations of favouritism, despite frequently being accompanied by pretty damning evidence, usually go unpunished. Referees who become embroiled in systematic match-fixing, however, play a much more dangerous game. In some countries, failing to follow well-connected advice and show 'favouritism' during a match is the biggest crime of all; occasionally it is deemed a capital offence.

In January 1990 the Colombian league was suspended and the title declared null and void after referee Alvaro Ortega was shot dead by gunmen as he was entering his hotel following a match between Independiente Medellin and America. He was 27. Medellin, home to the drugs Cartel that has caused the country and its football teams years of unceasing heartache, failed to qualify for the Championship Finals as a result of the match, which had been refereed honestly. Newspapers reported that the Mafia had lost substantial amounts of money on the game, and one served as a conduit for the Mafia's message that other referees failing to take a bribe would be put on a hit list and face a similar fate. The Mafia's threat led directly to the resignation of a number of the country's leading officials, but the violence didn't end there. Two days after Ortega's murder another top League referee was kidnapped. He was released a few hours later, semi-drugged, yet fully aware that his ordeal would not have such a happy ending the next time.

In the wake of the horror, the Colombian government restated its policy: the use of stadiums would not be permitted unless clubs voluntarily vowed that they were under no outside pressure from drug cartels and betting syndicates. They also threatened to suspend all Leagues and Cups if clubs complained in any way of being bullied, bribed or blackmailed.

There were no discernible good guys either. A year prior to the murder of Ortega, Colombian football had been in uproar over another referee kidnapping, this time by a group claiming to uphold the values of impartial officials. Armondo Perez was captured by a group who had sworn to "rub out" referees who bowed to match-fixing or "were incapable of controlling games properly", and was allegedly only set free once he had given his captors a list of officials (as well as players and managers) he knew to be involved in rigging results. Presumably, their first target was the referee who, later the same month, added twelve minutes of injury-time onto the match between Armenia Quindio and Independiente Sante Fe, during which the visitors scored a vital winner. The Quindio fans stormed the pitch to attack the referee and the Sante Fe players, seven of whom were badly injured.

Colombian football was suffering from the various ill effects of corruption, violence and bribery as early as 1981. In an eerie modern-day equivalent of the Argentine experiment with British referees in the 1930s and 40s, the country's football authorities called in two Spanish referees – Donato Pes Perez and Manuel Fandos – in an attempt to bring some kind of order to the escalating chaos. Presumably the Spaniards, themselves a nation of some repute in terms of match-fixing ability, were regarded as the lesser of two evils. However, they received little thanks from the Colombians for their missionary endeavours. Both referees were forced into hiding to avoid the swarm of match-fixers, many of whom threatened to have them killed if they didn't wake up and smell the bent bank notes. In fairness, they never stood a chance against the wilfully corrupt Colombians. Around the same time it was not unheard of for referees to take to the pitch armed, such was the likelihood of games being terrorised by the gun-toting crowd. From a bit-part role in a gentleman's leisure pursuit to this; the South American referee was used to violence and surrealism, but to be asked to officiate in Dante's backyard was pushing it a bit. The best a referee could hope for was an injury or a fall from favour. One or two were even suspected of feigning illness to ensure deselection. It had gotten that bad. The odd moment still existed to provide comic relief, however: Colombian fans had a tendency to throw two or three balls onto the pitch to confuse the referee whenever they felt their team's goal was under threat. Not much fun for the officials, perhaps, but being threatened by a bag of footballs was a damn sight less frightening that facing three days locked up in a dark cellar with a gun pressed against your head.

In Paraguay, officials are so used to teams throwing games that many accept it as an integral part of the national sport. The 1989/90 season saw Sol De America and Olimpia conspiring to rig a game in order that both teams could qualify ahead of Chilean club Colo Colo for the latter stages of the Libertadores Cup. To do so, America had to win and both teams had to score at least three goals each. The plan went swimmingly, with America winning a ludicrously open match 5-4. Colo Colo's enraged president complained bitterly about the result, but with no concrete proof of match-fixing his team's appeal didn't stand a chance. Nor were the referees exactly sympathetic to Colo Colo's plight: when questioned, most agreed that clubs had the 'right' to fix the result.

The Argentine referee is, as we have seen already, an odd species. The country's football fans, however, can be refreshingly unpredictable when they choose to be. In 1975 the Argentine whistler Jorge Alvarez was arrested on a charge of 'sports fraud' after a match between Newell's Old Boys and FC Oeste. Perhaps the only instance ever of a supporter bringing charges against an official. Visitors Oeste gained a 2-2 draw, scoring both goals in the last eight minutes. The first was a hotly disputed penalty, the second in the final minute, after Senor Alvarez had stopped what seemed like a perfectly valid home attack at the other end. Newell's fans rioted after the match, with Senor Alvarez sustaining a very serious eye injury. He was arrested by one of Newell's fans, accompanied by five witnesses and charged under a spurious and little known Sante Fe Province law. The immediate result of the action was a referees' strike in Argentina. When Alvarez was cleared of all charges, the men in black went back to work.

Such tales of South American skulduggery does not mean that Europe is not immune to such problems either. Bribery investigations were launched in Yugoslavia after a series of highly suspicious results, including two League matches in the 1979-80 season which boasted the improbable scorelines of 22-0 and 19-0. It took only a year for the head of the inquiry, tipped off by two former referees, to discover that the Second Division side Maribor had paid around £15,000 from a private account to more than 30 League referees over a period of five years. The difference here was the response. All of them were banned, *sine die*. Match-fixing was a problem in Yugoslavia as early as 1965. It was in this year that the country's FA took the unprecedented step of refusing to publish referee appointments, simply stating that in the future, clubs would only find out which officials had been selected for their match when they arrived for the game. The move was prompted by several top class referees claiming they had been pestered by mystery phone calls threatening beatings if they failed to comply with the terms of the 'fix'.

The 1960s were indeed a golden period for match-fixing. In Greece, 'honest' referees were considered a rare breed indeed, so much so, that in 1962, an impartial German official had to be flown in to referee a League match between AEK Athens and Panathinaikos. In 1973, Leeds felt they were the victim of a scurrilous Greek official during their 1-0 defeat at the hands of AC Milan in the ECWC Final. The referee – Mr Michas – refused three or four Leeds penalty claims, sent off Norman Hunter and acted throughout as if he was part of the Italian line-up. After a UEFA investigation, Michas was suspended and later struck off their refereeing list. Scant consolation for Leeds. Twelve years on, in 1985, the Greeks were still at it. In February of that year, referee Constantine Pellidis was sentenced to four months in jail for accepting a bribe of £1,130 to help the Second Division side Panetolikos win a League match.

Italian football built its initial reputation on two things: winning consecutive World Cups in 1934 and 1938; and match-fixing. Referees take little credit for the trophies, but should be applauded for their unflinching dedication to the bribe. In a series of articles published in Britain, *Times* journalist Brian Glanville uncovered the corruption rife in Italian football, making it clear to a blinkered nation that the involvment of referees in such practices was similarly common practice. "Do UEFA not know", he said, "that it was an open secret that for a decade, that the big Italian clubs and probably (no, more than probably) the international team were wheeling and dealing in referees, bribing them rotten wherever they could, frequently manipulating matters so that they had the referee of their choice appointed for the important games." Liverpool believe they witnessed first hand the apparent hold Italian club teams had over the referee when they played Inter Milan in the 1965 European Cup Semi-final. Liverpool won the first leg convincingly – 3-1 – at Anfield before losing 3-0 away to go out. Bill Shankly raged that the referee Ortiz de Mendibl had fixed the game, a claim born out, for him, by the highly dubious nature of two of Inter's goals. Ian St John summed up the futility of the situation for Liverpool when he said "we knew something was up when we couldn't even get a throw-in". Nothing was proved.

Three years later, in 1968, a similar thing happened again. Malmo were disallowed a vital goal by a French referee during their European Cup tie with, yes, Inter Milan, on the grounds that one of the Swedish players had impeded the goalkeeper. Pictures show that there was not a man within four or five yards of the goalkeeper. Had the goal stood, Malmo would have had a fairly unassailable 4-1 lead. As it transpired, they lost (5-3), in the end – somewhat inevitable considering what they, and thousands watching, regarded as a blatant display of bias by the referee. Their feelings of injustice were compounded when the team's captain, Kristensson, was sent off for asking, in English, how many minutes of the game were left. Again nothing was proved

In the 1960s a major scandal rocked both Italian and Yugoslavian officialdom. It followed the 1964 European Cup Semi-final between Borussia Dortmund and Inter Milan – again – which was refereed by the Yugoslav official Tesanic, a man who might have well worn the Italian team's famous blue and black jersey for all the impartiality he showed during the match. The German side eventually lost 2-0, following a string of spectacularly biased decisions by Tesanic. An anonymous letter, 'inspired' by the game, but mainly just sickened by its refereeing, appeared in Zagreb's *Sportske Novosti*, soon afterwards: "While I was on holiday in Italy I found, to my consternation and embarrassment, that one of our referees had allowed himself to be bought for a handful of notes and has lowered himself to be the position of a beggar. I learned, in fact, that two referees were staying here in Milan at Inter's expense, and that the Italian club were also giving them daily pocket money. What I want to know is, who permitted our referees to accept an invitation like this? And, how can these referees control a match in an impartial manner?" Naive, perhaps, but it got straight to the crux of the matter. One of the referees in question was, of course, Tesanic, the other turned out to be his Yugoslavian linesman for the game, a Mr Skoric. The other linesman had apparently refused to take part in the fix. Both men were handed indefinite suspensions following an inquiry by the Yugoslavian Referees' Association.

Ever since the 60s Italian players – including, famously, Paulo Rossi, whose ban for his involvement in match-fixing expired just before his wonderful showing in the 1982 World Cup finals – have been dabbling with illegal betting syndicates. As recently as last season, the country's referees were still perceived to be part of the wider problem. As in Spain, Italian referees are constantly accused of showing favouritism to the super-Clubs – Juventus in particular. In March 1998, the vital Serie A clash between the famous Turin club and title challengers Inter Milan became surrounded in controversy when the referee Piero Ceccarini ruled that a blatant foul on Ronaldo in the penalty area was not reasonable grounds for a spot-kick. Inter's coach Gigi Simoni stormed the field in protest at the decision and had to be forcibly removed. Worse was to follow. Minutes after the incident, Juventus striker Del Piero charged forward only to fall over in the Inter penalty box. This time Ceccarini pointed to the spot. Del Piero missed, but it hardly mattered. Juve, already 1-0 up, held on to win, virtually ending Inter's title hopes. Ronaldo, fined earlier in the season for criticising match officials, launched into another protracted tirade after the match. "Shame on the referee," said the Brazilian striker brazenly, "The whole world saw what happened and it cannot go on like this, that the decisions of the referees are always in favour of Juventus…we know they benefit from favouritism. Enough is enough. They can punish me again [they did, banning him for two games], they can give me another fine, but I will not stay silent. Football is about happiness, but you cannot be happy when it is 11 against 12. I feel like crying." *La Gazzetta dello Sport* openly followed the subterfuge line and suggested that the "Championship had not been the cleanest", pointing to several other games that had gone Juventus's way that year. Moratti, Inter's president, was less diplomatic. "Referees always favour Juventus," he said, "it is the rule, not the exception." The ructions over the controversy even extended to the Italian parliament which had to be suspended after fighting broke out during a debate on the Juve-Inter incident.

The conspiracy theory surrounding referees in Italy is backed up by some irrefutable evidence. Months before the infamous Turin débâcle, Livorno, then leaders of Serie C1 (the equivalent of the English Second Division) faced the threat of relegation after one of the league's referees Duccio Baglioni alerted authorities to the dishonourable intentions of a colleague. The federation president Luciano Nizzola was furious: "That this has happened in one of the lower divisions is no reason for us to feel complacent about the state of the game at the highest level. Corruption is like a cancer. It can spread everywhere." The statement followed Baglioni's revelations that, during a telephone conversation, fellow referee Divino Ferrarini had offered him £10,000 to fix a match between Montevarchi and Livorno. At this point in the proceedings, Baglioni suddenly turned himself into Italy's answer to Perry Mason. He told his colleague that he would think about the deal, and to call back later, by which point he had already alerted the federation and arranged for them to bug the next conversation. As the plot thickened, Baglioni pretended to Ferrarini that he was interested, and told him he would be glad to throw the match. As their conversation came to its apparently scheming conclusion, the federation had already made provisions for a third referee – Felice Strocchia – to travel, in secrecy, to the match. Suffice to say, the officials of both Livorno and Montevarchi were rather surprised, not to say extremely unsettled by the arrival of Strocchia, who, when questioned on the whereabouts of Baglioni, explained that he had been "injured in training" and was therefore not fit to referee the match. The match was won 1-0 by Montevarchi. Strocchia did award a (fair) penalty to Livorno, but they missed it. The following day, corruption investigator Biagio Martino turned up on

Ferrarini's doorstep who, after being played a recording of the incriminating phone-call, owned up to his part in the scandal. Mysteriously, it was never discovered on whose behalf the referee was acting. Ferrarini claimed that he had been approached by a man called 'Franco', acting for a third party, but the enigmatic Franco was never traced. Livorno President Caludio Achilli denied any knowledge of the incident, stating, with some incredulity. "It's nonsense. I learned my lesson a long time ago." Indeed he had. Achilli was banned for bribing players in 1989 and Livorno relegated to C2 as punishment.

In 1993 a equally bizarre bribe took place involving another referee, although the short and sweet story has none of the Godfather-like twist in plot inherent in Baglioni's epic. Perugia president Luciano Gaucci was banned in this year for bribing referee Emauele Sernzacqua with the gift of a horse. That says it all really.

Although it is widely – and correctly – accepted that British referees are more partial to a book full of names than a pocket full of dirty money, the offer of the odd sneaky back-hander is thought to have tempted a few. This is UEFA's Directive for Referees concerning standards of behaviour: "Referees and linesmen must refuse firmly but politely any exaggerated and too-generous form of hospitality. Acceptances of valuables is strictly forbidden." In 1978 Scottish referee John Gordon and linesman David McCartney fell foul of the small print. They were suspended for their part in AC Milan's UEFA Cup second round match with Levsky Spartak of Moscow, though their crime was stupidity more than anything else. Whilst on a shopping trip in Milan prior to the game, Gordon and McCartney popped into a fashionable menswear shop to check out the latest Gucci gear. Unfortunately the tight-fisted duo landed themselves in hot water when the Milan officials accompanying them stepped in to pick up the bill for £800. Very generous. AC Milan were fined £8,000 and offered a rather feeble explanation of the events, alleging that the shop wouldn't accept pounds and that the Scots didn't have any lire with them at the time. The club's sports director Sandro Vitali later added: "We didn't ask for the money back later because we wouldn't dream of behaving that way to any guests of ours." Milan's president, Felice Columbo, was more honest in his interpretation of the incident. "It was a naive gesture of courtesy," he said "UEFA fined us, I think, recognising our good faith but meaning to tell us that we must not have this kind of relationship with officials." John Gordon should have known better. He had been a registered FIFA ref since 1967, but then Italian clothes can do strange things to a man. And so too, in a rather more benign fashion, can Scottish knitwear. The former top Welsh referee Clive Thomas incurred the wrath of Hibernian football club for having the gall to allow Leeds to beat the Edinburgh side in a 1968 Fairs Cup fixture. An official from Hibs had met Thomas at Waverley station and susequently offered to 'present' the referee and his linesmen with a set of tartan blankets that had caught the Welshman's eye during a sojourn around the local knitwear stores. But when Thomas failed to stand between Leeds and their victory (Hibs lost 0-1), the club steadfastly refused to produce the freebies: "In the hotel after the game, the charming young man who had ordered the blankets refused even to acknowledge me," said Thomas, "with the result that I lost my temper...but when we left the following morning there was still no sign of the blankets." Poor old Clive.

If Real and Barca are, as has been vociferously claimed, the favoured teams of Spanish referees, then in Scotland it's undoubtedly Celtic and Rangers who face the charges. If you believe the press, the portals of Ibrox and Parkhead have for years provided shelter for hordes of referees, who repay their generous tenants on the pitch by ensuring that the rest of the Premier League teams get nary a sniff of the action. As if the minnows don't have enough problems without, as their fans see it, refs siding with the Old Firm cabal. Yet in a city of football fanaticism, where sectarian divisions and discriminations have long been a fact of life, rumours and paranoias are to be expected. Any refereeing blunder instantly provokes cries of 'foul play' from the injured party. No rumour has ever been proven, yet it is still a conspiracy theory the locals love.

The latest instalment in the saga came in Rangers final home game of 1997-8 against Kilmarnock with just a couple of points separating the Old Firm teams in the title race – a game known among Celtic fans as the 'Bobby Tait testimonial match'. Tait, accused on the terraces of being more than just a little partial to the occasional strange handshake and rolled trouser leg, had requested to the SFA that he be allowed to take the game at Ibrox as some kind of valedictory appearance as a referee. It was indeed, his last appearance as a Premier League official. It was heavily implied in some sections of the Press, that Tait had attempted to provide the home side with a much needed victory by allowing eight full minutes of injury time at the end of a game Rangers were drawing. However, disaster struck for Rangers when, in the 95th minute, Ally Mitchell scored for the visitors. Killie held on to win 1-0. Rangers lost their title to Celtic the following week.

Celtic's main concern over the last ten years has been an empty trophy cabinet. While Rangers amassed all the silverware, Celtic fans kept themselves busy putting together an extensive dossier on bluenose referees, which, they hoped, would prove once and for all that it hadn't in fact been the signature of a succession of low grade strikers, but rather bent officials who were really responsible for their unceasing misfortune. To the

Parkhead faithful, their side's dismal record against the 'Gers in the early to mid-90s suggested one of two things, either Celtic bottled the big games or Rangers had an extra man on the park.

Jorge Cadete, Celtic's one time Portuguese striker, landed himself in hot water after making highly libellous allegations against an official following two contentious Old Firm penalty incidents. Meanwhile, a group of the club's more industrious fans decided to take matters into their own hands by hiring a private detective to stalk another referee, Jim McCluskey of Stewarton, in their quest to uncover what they saw as his obvious Masonic tendencies. It was often said among the Celtic faithful that McCluskey's twin loves were disallowing Celtic goals and gifting Rangers late match-winning penalties. McCluskey retired last year, but before turning his back on the famous Old Firm drama, he found time for one last cameo role. Celtic and Rangers were due to play at Parkhead on 19 November, 1997 with McCluskey refereeing. But before the game he withdrew himself, citing a mysterious 'injury'. After the game the public houses of Govan were alive with rumours that he had been removed by the SFA in the light of widespread allegations of his bias toward Rangers.

The real drama, however, came in the match. McCluskey was replaced by John Rowbotham, a man most familiar to Celtic fans (and other Premier League teams) for his part in what the conspiracy theorists view as another Rangers 'stitch up', this time against Aberdeen in October 1995. The two games became inextricably linked. It was Rowbotham who failed to send off Paul Gascoigne in the Aberdeen match when England's clown prince capped a thuggish performance by first elbowing Stewart McKimmie in the face and then head-butting John Inglis. Rowbotham was an inexperienced referee, but this fact didn't prevent his inaction being widely interpreted in the media and on the terraces as a blatant case of favouritism towards Rangers.

When TV evidence showed the true extent of Gascoigne's misdemeanours, the player was suspended, and Rowbotham's reputation was irrevocably tarnished. Celtic fans' fears that yet another referee was lost to the Ibrox cause was, much to their surprise, not realised. Rowbotham made amends in their eyes when he stepped into McCluskey's shoes and became the first referee to dismiss Paul Gascoigne on Scottish soil: this time Gazza was largely blameless. Walter Smith, the Rangers manager, was not inclined to comment on McCluskey's mysterious withdrawal from the Celtic game but nevertheless made it easy enough for Celtic fans to read between the lines when he spoke out on the Gazza dismissal. "I don't feel that anything that happened in the game is entirely the referees' fault", Smith began, cutely veiling the condemnation that would follow, "because there is no way he could have refereed that match in an impartial manner. He did what he did to Gascoigne under the pressure of that previous Aberdeen match. I really don't think he should have been appointed to the game." For the record, Celtic equalised in the last 10 minutes of the match. After Gazza had taken an early bath.

One recent addition to the saga has a peculiar literary slant to it. When bestselling cult author Irvine Welsh published his second novel *The Marabou Stork Nightmares* in 1995, it featured a scene in which a group of Hibs fans are airing their views on a referee, a character called David Symes, and particularly regarding his involvement in a disputed penalty claim during a Hibs v Rangers Cup game. The referee was fictional, or so Welsh's editor had been led to believe. That was until he received a phonecall from Mr Symes' lawyer who was rather perturbed at the libellous references to his client's sporting allegiances. The referee, a well-known Scottish Premier Division regular, was portrayed in the novel as being, shall we say, more inclined toward the Glasgow side. The book's description of this inclination was scattered with Welsh's full quota of trademark four-letter words, not to mention suggestions of Masonic machinations at work. The matter was swiftly settled out of court with a tidy sum going to Mr Symes and his lawyer; subsequent paperback editions of the book have the offending paragraph removed. Some would gladly pay for the privilege of a walk-on part in one of the celebrity author's novels. Symes chose to be paid for *not* appearing.

It's not just the Glasgow teams' managers that get drawn into the Old Firm conspiracy theory. Alex Ferguson spent the best part of the late 70s and early 80s winding up the Old Firm opposition with allegations that Scottish referees consistently favoured the 'West coast' teams. He wasn't talking about Stranraer or Ayr United either. Scotland manager Craig Brown, Ferguson's assistant in the 1986 World Cup, insists that it was a deliberate ploy on behalf of the then Aberdeen boss, used solely, and with some great effect, to instil in his players a sense of persecution that he hoped would spur them on against Rangers and Celtic. It worked: Aberdeen won more games in Glasgow during Fergie's reign than at any other time in the club's history. Fergie, born in Govan, and reared at Rangers as a player, was probably only getting into practice for his Man Utd psych-outs.

More serious were the allegations in the season 1997-8 that English referee Paul Robinson had accepted money from the non-league club Solihull Borough after their FA Cup first round tie with Darlington in November. The game finished 1-1, but Darlington won the replay on penalties. Representatives of Darlington claimed they had witnessed Robinson receiving a payment in the bar after the game, but Peter Willis of the Referees' Association spoke out for the official once his name had been cleared. "The only mistake Paul made was to buy drinks for his colleagues and accept the change. As a true Yorkshireman he should have allowed the colleagues to buy him a drink."

More recently, the Belgian club Anderlecht hit the headlines following its appeal against UEFA's decision to ban the club for a year for an incident which occurred 14 years before. Prior to their 1984 UEFA Cup Semi-final match against Nottingham Forest Anderlecht officials were found, and later admitted to, paying a Spanish referee around £12,000 to fix the match. Anderlecht recovered a 2-0 deficit in controversial circumstances, going on to win 3-2 before receiving their comeuppance in the Final, where they lost on penalties to Spurs. Forest were particularly galled by the Court for Arbitration of Sport's decision in 1998 to over-rule UEFA's ban, clearing the way for Anderlecht to compete in the same year's competition.

VIOLENCE

The Russians are not exactly renowned for their sensitivity – just ask the Romanovs – but some of the country's football hierarchy have in recent years taken the whole idea of 'blood-letting' a tad too far. Referees, of course, figure prominently in their 'most wanted' list.

In March 1996, a Russian referee was beaten up and knocked unconscious in the dressing room of Premier League team Dynamo Moscow after awarding a 'controversial' penalty to visitors, Spartak Vladikavkaz. Remarkably, the culprit wasn't a player but Dynamo president Nikolai Tolsykh. Trembling with rage at this perceived injustice (in fact it wasn't a penalty at all, more of a blatant shirt-pull), Tolsykh followed the match referee Yury Chebotaryov into the tunnel at full-time, bundled him into the home dressing room and began "to swear at and threaten" him. He then brutally beat the referee around the head and

A match in progress in 1891 shows the referee to the right of the goal wearing a full suit and carrying a flag.

An illustration of a match between Blackburn Rovers and Notts County at the Kennington Oval in 1890 again shows the referee armed with a flag.

Belgian official Jean Langenus (centre) watches over the exchange of pennants before the 1930 World Cup Final. Something of a maverick, he refereed the game wearing a red stripped tie, dinner jacket and plus fours.

A Pools ad. from 1952 has some fun with the different styles of 'sound judgement' on display with the day's referees. Many of the types on show are still recognisable today.

'Tubby finds a knuckle-duster' – the 'Boy's Own' vision from *The Champion* magazine in 1940 of what a referee needs to look out for. When the referee blows the whistle those other guardians of the peace – the soldier and the policeman – aren't far behind.

In 1972 Jimmy Hill came down from the Press box at Highbury to run the line in front of 45,000 fans and the TV cameras during a match between Arsenal and Liverpool after linesman Dennis Drewitt was stretchered from the field.

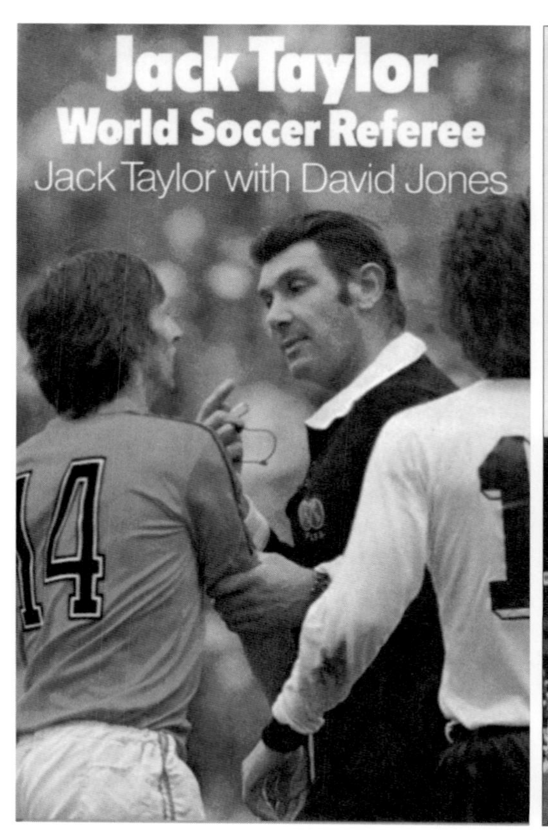

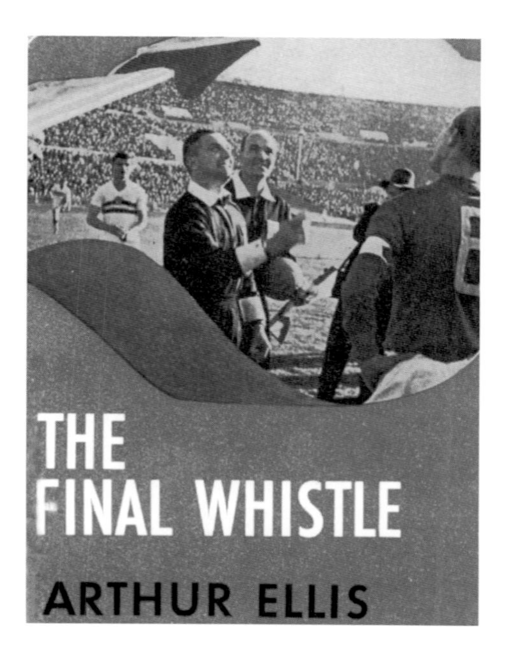

The refereeing autobiography – a classic genre with inspired titles to boot. Arthur Ellis, Jack Taylor and Pat Partridge talk us through their favourite sendings off.

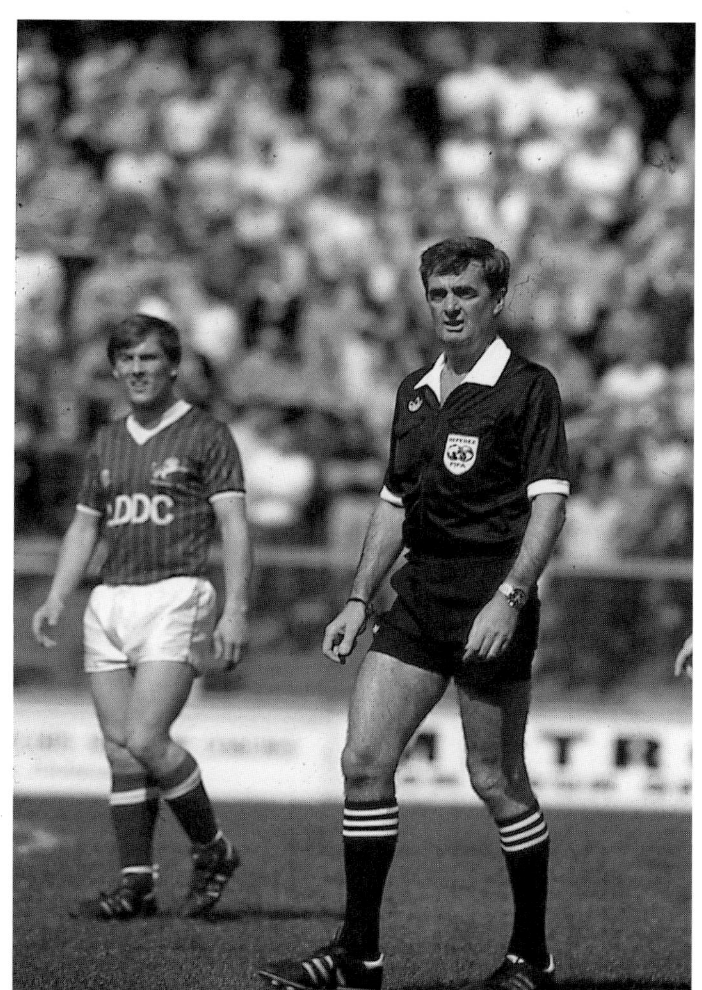

Left.
'Doubting' Clive Thomas, the man who dared to question the FA's methods, referees a Millwall match in May 1984 during his exile from the top flight.

Below
Ike Caswell 1938/39 – the man who pioneered the British refereeing presence in South America is escorted from the field of play by Argentine police – an early example of the referee as public enemy No.1.

Gazza enacts every players dream – showing referee Dougie Smith the yellow card after the official had dropped it during a match at Ibrox in 1995. Smith promptly showed the card straight back to Gascoigne for his trouble.

knocked him to the ground. "I was lying on the floor for some time," said Chebotaryov, who lost consciousness for almost a minute. Not that this prevented the mad-eyed president from continuing with his verbal dressing down, although it obviously prevented the referee from being as receptive as he would have liked regarding the more salient points being offered. Tolsykh was subsequently banned from appearing at the stadium's 'official places': "Until November, he can only watch matches as an ordinary spectator," added the secretary of the Premier League, oblivious to the fact that here, unquestionably, was one of the least 'ordinary' men ever to have taken a seat at a Russian League match.

The Ukraine may have severed its umbilical cord with mother Russia, but temperamentally, its football managers still hold a torch for the old country.

Yuri Pohrebynak is a case in point. Head coach of one of the country's lesser known outfits, Metallurg Mariupol, Yuri was banned for life from football in October 1997 after seriously assaulting a referee and his linesman off the field of play. Not content with just one scalp, Pohrebynak "and some mates", according to one eye-witness, had burst into the match officials, hotel room after losing 5-2 to Vorskla Poltava in a crucial League game and left the referee with a broken nose and his assistant with fractured ribs, the latter no doubt contemplating the variable joys of room-sharing.

Attacks on referees by managers are uncommon. Attacks on referees by religious figures, however, are about as frequent as a Stan Collymore goal: they are that rare. Even in Ecuador, where in November 1997 referee Byron Moreno was physically accosted by the club's 75-year-old priest after sending four players off – it's not known to happen very often.

Sometimes a mere beating doesn't appear to be sufficient punishment for the referee. Having been accosted by both players and fans of the Romanian First Division side Universitatea Craiova for awarding a hotly disputed penalty during their match against Sportul Studentesc in March 1997, it was thought unlikely that referee Daniel Illescu would take up the invitation to attend an official Football Association dinner later that night. This underestimated the mettle of the man. For he did turn up, and was greeted by Craiova's club President Eugeb Arnautu with a firm slap across the face. He received another metaphoric one shortly after, this time from the Romanian FA who handed Illescu a one match suspension for giving the very penalty that had resulted in his bruises in the first place. Presumably, he didn't much appreciate the irony.

But back to the Spanish. As we have seen, they have their own peculiar way of dealing with the man in the middle. Referees there are rarely treated with anything but venomous disdain, although occasionally one or two are singled out for 'special' treatment. In May 1997, Jose Miguel del Rio had to be taken to hospital after a pellet fired from a gun lodged in his arm while he was refereeing a regional match between Santa Cruz and FC Lovio. The accident occurred after he had the temerity to book a player. Spanish police launched an inquiry into the incident, although the proximity of the pitch to a local forest prompted most of the 50 spectators to suspect a hunter's stray bullet as the likely source, a theory angrily dismissed by del Rio. "I don't believe it was an accident," he fumed at reporters, his anger fuelled by paranoia, "I'm six foot tall and look nothing like a rabbit." If only Ronaldo could say the same.

When Spanish fans do stray from their favoured sniper's vantage point, it's normally worth keeping an eye on the rascals. Never ones to miss an opportunity for a good visual gag, Barca's notoriously unhinged extremist fans set to work on up-and-coming referee Brito Arceo. Following the official's disastrous Nou Camp début last season, where he awarded a penalty to the visitors – a capital crime in itself – though it was clear the foul had occurred at least a yard outside the box, the most unforgiving fans in the world were eagerly awaiting Brito's return to the Nou Camp.

Some months later, they got their chance. The referee didn't have long to wait for the fun to begin: almost as soon as the game kicked off a Barca fan released a young pig onto the pitch, dressed in a black referee's jersey with the words 'BRITO ARCEO' emblazoned on its back. A massive television audience and a near full Nou Camp watched as Arceo endured the ignominy of waiting for the animal to be rounded up before he could continue.

Italian football has been plagued with similar disciplinary problems for longer than most care to remember, and when the clubs put their minds to it, they are capable of some brutally burlesque moments. One lower league Italian club was banned from using its own ground for seven months after fans raided the pitch to attack the referee. About 30 supporters of FC Bastardo (sic) were involved in the incident which occurred during the second half of the game with Virtus La Castellana, in January 1997. "They repeatedly slapped and punched me, causing me pain and great dizziness," commented the official, who, despite his bizarre parlance, hailed from Umbria, not the Bronx. The Italian game is littered with such casualties. Only the names change.

The ground-closing punishment is something of a tradition in Italian football. In 1977, Napoli had the right to play at home suspended for the eighth time since the war – a record – after linesman Agustino Binzagi was hit on the head with a Coca-Cola bottle following a disallowed goal. The real thing indeed.

In April of the same year a referee and his two linesmen had to be rescued by police helicopter after the crowd at the Serie B match between Palermo and Ternana poured onto the pitch. This peculiar form of 'ref rescue' had a precedent too: in 1969 referee Antonio Shardella was given a police escort to his aerial escape following the abandonment of the match between Palermo and Napoli.

The supporters of some small-time Italian clubs are not quite so adept as their elder siblings at isolating the frailties of the man in black. And it doesn't get much smaller than a match between two rival bar teams from Rome. In April 1979 Bar Miki were 4-0 up against Bar Acquario when their match was rudely interrupted by the sound of a shotgun being fired from the small crowd. Though the players immediately dived for cover the referee remained upstanding, waiting until the bullets had ceased whizzing overhead before calmly informing the two teams that he thought the target had been Bar Miki's star player. That it might have been him obviously did not cross his mind. However, his blind arrogance didn't pay dividends. A cluster of supporters armed with guns ran on to the field and one approached the official, who indeed had been the intended target, ordering him to bend down and lick his boots. As he was about to comply, the plucky assailant, perhaps hearing the sound of Mama calling him in for dinner, fled. Bizarre.

The Italians are run close in their wilful disregard of authority by the Scots, whose amateur leagues pay scant heed to football's judge and jury. Kenneth John Croft was hauled up in front of the magistrates in 1972 for his actions against an amateur League referee. Croft took exception to a retaken penalty that had levelled the scores, and unable to put the decision behind him and get on with his life, he strode over to the referee and with one punch knocked him unconscious. The game, nicely poised at 1-1, had to be abandoned as no replacement official was available. Croft was fined £40 with £20 costs, and bound over for a year, not to incapacitate any more referees until 1973.

THE VICE SQUAD…& ODD STUFF

It is a rare and grateful profession which doesn't at some point have to deal with sex, drugs and alcohol. Alas football is not one of those lucky few. Late in the season of 1997-8 in Brazil, referee Oscar Roberto de Godoi was persuaded to take a drug and alcohol test after São Paulo defender – and World Cup stopper – Junior Baiano complained that the official had been drunk on the pitch. De Godoi's antics during the São Paulo State Championship derby match between Corinthians and São Paulo angered officials of both teams – he sent off five players and booked eleven, including five in as many minutes. But the hip flask was never found and de Godoi escaped punishment.

The sober, happily married and affable image of the British referee is not always to be believed. There's always one greedy beggar who finds it impossible to resist the good things in life. Like free sex, for example. In 1995, a year after he had retired, the former FIFA and Premiership referee Howard King went to the *News of the World* with the story that for years he had been accepting prostitutes and other free 'gifts' from foreign clubs attempting to bribe him into rigging high profile European matches. Not that King was ever foolish enough to give in to the demands of football's pimps. He just bedded the girls and to hell with the consequence, his reasoning being that the clubs could hardly report him if he failed to show them favouritism on the pitch without incriminating themselves; if they got the hump, as it were, it didn't really matter either: he might be given the cold shoulder should he ever return, but it was a small price to pay.

King's first conquest came while he was in Belgium to referee a UEFA Cup tie – an ex-FIFA official chaperoned him over the border to a Dutch brothel, where he received his first 'gift'. Soon after he was sampling the hospitality of clubs dotted all over the continent: Denmark, Spain, Portugal, Russia, Germany. He became like a dog straining on a leash whenever the chance to get away on European duty arose. On one bizarre occasion King had sex with a Czech girl who had seen him refereeing a Sparta Prague game on TV. Later the same night the two met at an after match party where the girl demanded he make love to her in his official uniform. King loved every minute of it, as he did during his many visits to Portugal – the country, he said, with the best prostitutes in Europe. During his 44 matches on the continent – and they were all major European games – King reckoned to have slept with at least 15 whores. He also insists that he was by no means the only referee involved, stating that he and his colleagues used to while away the dead time before a match comparing notes on the various sexual favours offered by different clubs. But King categorically denied that any British clubs were involved, saying "It went on everywhere else...but it was hard enough to get a cup of tea out of them."

Referees are generally an affable bunch. But, push them too far and they can often surprise their cowardly assailants. After all, turning the other cheek will only get you so far. In Peru, in October 1978, referee Hugo Bustamante knocked out Atletico Chalaco defender Escobar when he tried to prevent a free kick being taken quickly in a match against Nacional Iquitos. This kind of retaliation, however, is polite compared to some of the assaults committed by non-League referees in Britain. Referee

Stuart Iley was arrested at half-time during a friendly match between Newport Pagnell Athletic and Wicken Sport for head-butting midfielder Philip Flannery. Flannery was sent off in the first half for "joking with a friend of mine on the other side", and went to quiz the official at half-time. "I was just being friendly to him, when all of a sudden he got really angry and told me to 'Fuck off'. He then turned round and head-butted me without saying a word."

A curious illustration of the referee's intimidatory powers occurred in the Persian Gulf in April 1962 when referees were allowed to sport a rubber truncheon and had the authority to dish out some heavy on-the-spot discipline. Interestingly, during this experimental period, there were no registered fouls.

MORE BIZARRE TALES

Threatening to sue a referee during the course of a game is not exactly common practice on this fair isle. But it has happened. Referee Andy Young was forced to halt play and check his insurance arrangements with FA officials when a player approached him and said, apropos of nothing, "I'm going to sue you ref, if I get my leg broken." A tad harsh, and certainly unprecedented. The player, a full-back for Portsmouth RN, felt he wasn't being sufficiently 'protected' by the official during his side's Jewson Wessex League match with Thatcham Town. The referee – who took no action against the player – was obviously the sensitive type.

Even more weak-willed was the official who succumbed to his nagging wife's frankly unreasonable demands during an Endsleigh Cheltenham League Division One match in April 1997. Referee Phil Pawsey was ordered to leave the field by his beloved spouse Trish who walked onto the pitch and told her husband she had locked herself out of their home and needed him to fetch his keys from the dressing room. Immediately. The black-shirted but yellow-bellied Pawsey skulked off the field to derisive laughter, and returned only to find the pitch in darkness and the players gone. "It was embarrassing," he said. Just a bit.

Some officials find true love in their vocation. To the point where it becomes totally absurd. Teeside referee Mick Johnston's dying request was not for 'The American Trilogy' to be played at his funeral, but that he be 'sent off' resplendent in his full man in black garb. Johnston's family, recognising what refereeing had meant to their loved one, duly obliged, sending him off in full kit complete with notebook, cards and whistle. Johnston obviously had some unfinished business to attend to in the big football park in the sky.

Sending off players is an occupational hazard for referees, but often they do get it wrong. Very wrong. In a match between the Southampton Arms and Hurstbourne British Legion in May 1998, referee Melvin Sylvester turned his jurisdiction on himself. After throwing a punch at a player, Sylvester, so sickened by his actions – despite claiming they were in self-defence – sent himself off and took an early bath. A spectator picked up his whistle, which Sylvester was subsequently banned from using for six weeks.

Women referees can encounter all sorts of problems on the pitch – but off it, it seems, they have all the fun. Janet Fewings was fined £15 and subsequently relieved of her duties as an official when it was discovered she had been taking after-match showers with the boys. The Devon FA wriggled out of a potentially tricky situation by citing Fewing's overzealousness in dishing out cards as the reason for their actions. Irate wives and girlfriends began threatening Fewings to stay away from their men, but she insists she didn't have to force herself onto them. "The first time I showered with them," said the brazen official, "It was because there were no facilities available for women. They were very open-minded and just said, "You look exhausted, you look like you could do with a shower." Despite Fewing having a natural's feel for the soft porn pick-up line, she insists no funny business took place. "They treated me with so much respect. I grew up very open-minded…"

THE REF ON THE COUCH

the motives of the men in black

BEARING in mind some of the horror stories already documented, it might be concluded that only a bug-brained half wit with a masochistic streak wider than the Mississippi would even consider becoming a referee. Even in a sport with a proud canon of prosaic observations which would shame even Max Bygraves, "Who'd be a ref" is hardly philosophical contemplation of the century. However, what the inquiry lacks in sophistication it makes up for in mystique: in footballing terms it's the equivalent of the riddle of the sphinx. Generation after generation have tried and failed to come up with a solution to the vexed question, but then the referee is not exactly renowned for his straight answers.

"The majority of us do it because we love the game, or haven't been good enough players," says former League referee, and Spokesman for the Association of Premier and Football League match officials, Keith Cooper. "I was no different. I played local football, up to county level, but got an injury to my knee when I was 16. I had my knee-cap taken out. I could still run, but I couldn't kick a ball. I just wanted to put a bit back into the game." Cooper refereed in the old First Division, at FA Cup Semi-finals, ran out in the San Siro for high profile European matches. He has pennants and mementoes from Juventus, Milan, Benfica. In terms of club football, he's seen it all, and he was legitimately paid for his troubles. So while it may be clear why Cooper persevered at being a referee, the case of Dave Braddish, 39, takes a little more explaining. Once on Chelsea's books, he too was forced to give up playing through injury, but there the similarities end. He took up refereeing in the Sunday Sportsman's League in London in 1982, supplementing his income as general manager of a window cradle company with the £15 a game plus travelling expenses he was paid. Why on earth did he decide to become a Sunday League official?

"I do it to keep involved. You're putting something back into the game, which is very satisfying," he insists, echoing Cooper's sentiments. Then there's Tony Leake, a Football League referee from Lancashire. What's his excuse? "I picked up an injury when I was relatively young and still wanted to be involved. Refereeing seemed the best option." Hardly a revelation. From the top of officialdom to the bottom a pattern is nevertheless discernible. Nobody claims to enjoy it, and presumably they don't set out with the ambition to be a referee above all else. It's just something people do when they can't play football anymore. But the intriguing part of the answers they give concerns what exactly they 'took' from the game in the first place and their subsequent overwhelming urge to 'put' it back in. After all, it's not as if football ever gave them all that much. Jim McMaster, a 66-year-old schoolteacher from Edinburgh, who was once a Scottish League referee and still officiates Old Boys matches in Midlothian, tries to explain. "I was a player, and I would have kept on being a player if I knew I had been good enough to make it. But I wasn't, so I became a referee. It's certainly not something I ever dreamed of doing. I don't think anyone chooses to be a referee. But if you are passionate about football then you want to stay involved. Being a referee is as close as you can get to being a footballer, without actually being one. You are part of the game, part of the atmosphere – if you are lucky enough to reach League status – and I feel a certain pride that I have been able to help the game in some way, been involved in its development."

The idea that the referee merely wishes to remain involved in the game and savour the sense of occasion is one thing. But to claim that referees are acting on an obligation, the footballing equivalent of the matriarchal bond that decrees we will return to look after the ones who cared for us when we were young (a not entirely inappropriate analogy given that one recently retired Premiership referee still lives with his mother) is quite another. Such largesse and a shared sense of responsibility to football seem excessively noble reasons for picking up the whistle, especially given that most of these men were mere amateurs. Where does all this gratitude come from and what is it hiding? McMaster's comments are certainly more revealing. He admits to feeling proud of his work as a referee, even hinting that he regards himself as an integral part of the game and its future. So, perhaps it's the ego that secretly motivates them, the pursuit of power that drives them to endure the job.

Premiership referee David Elleray concedes this point. "I realised I wasn't a very good player...and I suppose I must of had a power complex from an early age," says the man who inspired Ian Wright to accuse all referees of being "little Hitlers". For some Elleray forms the classic negative stereotype: an inflexible, aloof disciplinarian. A "frustrated player, unlikely to play for the first eleven", he has refereed since his early teens. As a youngster he felt somewhat removed from the other boys: "they probably thought I was a bit weird, but they were also probably glad I wasn't on their team". Like the most evangelical of traffic wardens, Elleray seems to almost revel in his continuing lack of popularity among Premiership players. A housemaster at Harrow, the waiting area outside his study is bedecked with visual reminders of his authority – "One of me sending off Dunga, the Brazilian captain, and another sending off Abou, of West Ham." He is entirely dedicated to his pupils and the whistle. If he hadn't become a disciplinarian of the classroom and football field, he claims he would have liked to have been a barrister. "My sister and brother-in-law are in the police, and my father was a customs officer…we have quite a lot of law enforcement in the family." He also seems to take a perverse pleasure in the 'public enemy' celebrity status that is bestowed on today's referee: "The [Harrow] boys like it if there is controversy…I did a game at Anfield last year, not particularly well, and there was a headline in the *Daily Mail* – 'Elleray You Blew It' – and 40 or 50 boys held this up to me at assembly. I know who they were."

Elleray's honesty about his motives is shared by Pat Partridge, who brazenly makes a case for his ilk: "All referees are egotistical, it's part of our make-up, and if we love praise then we must accept crticism too." Keith Cooper is partly convinced, but stops well short of naming names. "I'd be a little naive to say that there isn't some of them [egotists] about," says Cooper. "There has to be. But the majority do it because they love the game…" Surely years of abuse on the pitch would diminish anyone's 'love' of the game. There must be more to it than this. The money isn't great, even for top officials. The job involves traversing the length of the country, and the most obvious perks would appear to be being sworn at and threatened in public. But then there's the authority; and the knowledge that whatever you decide on the pitch cannot in any way be legitimately questioned. As early as 1935, it was recognised that the referee wasn't wearing black solely because his dream of becoming the next Dixie Deans hadn't been realised. "His reward is the psychological feeling of being in control," wrote one anonymous author. Still, if the 'frustrated footballer' tag sheds some light on their motivation, referees can't quite hide their streak of self-importance. When asked to describe himself recently in a newspaper interview, Premiership referee Steve Lodge could only think of the reply: "A failed local footballer who took the hard option of keeping involved in football by becoming a referee." The rather forced insinuation is that a referee should be thanked, not castigated, for his unselfish dedication to football. The general tone suggests a favour born of great individual sacrifice, and yet nowhere in the laws of the game does it mention that you must pick up a whistle when you've hung up your boots.

One current Football League referee who at least had the decency to get his boots dirty before he slung them away for the last time is Steve Baines. For 14 years Baines was a professional footballer – a "steady, honest, centre-half" – who played for Nottingham Forest for two years in the early 70s, then Huddersfield, Bradford City and a clutch of other lower league clubs before retiring, aged 31. During his career he clocked up 438 League appearances, three sendings-off and "I wouldn't know how many bookings – a lot", so was presumably not inclined to walk away from the game for a career in refereeing. It would have been a bit like John McEnroe packing it all in to become a Wimbledon umpire. "I wanted to go into management," says Baines. The opportunity never came his way. When he read a newspaper article in which former hardmen Tommy Smith and Ron 'Chopper' Harris advocated players becoming referees: 'I thought, 'what a good idea'." Whether the 'boys' had been on the wind-up or not, Baines was hooked, and has now safely negotiated his second season as a Football League referee.

"Steve is excellent," says Ray McHale, former manager of Huddersfield Town. "Playing hundreds of games like he has must stand you in good stead. He knows the score." Baines, who looks a bit like Tom Selleck would have done if he'd grown up in Mansfield, runs his own insurance company when he's not on the pitch, but even that hasn't prevented his rapid rise to the refereeing summit. On average it takes 12 years for most officials to graduate from sorting out Sunday League fights to moving a wall back at Notts County. Baines did it in seven. And McHale reckons most ex-players could make the Football League grade in five years given the time and, obviously, the interest. So far the exodus from the playing ranks hasn't materialised, something Arthur Smith, general secretary of the Referees' Association, doesn't find particularly surprising. "It's a totally different trade. A lot of them [ex-players] won't even cross the road to see a game once they've retired." Smith admires Baines's determination to stick to the trade, and dismisses the idea that it was nepotism that got him to the top so quickly. "In any profession there are always people who will say that so-and-so has got where he is because of who he knows," retorts Smith, in the knowledge that Baines has had to put up with a fair bit of sniping in the last two years, sadly even from linesmen, reluctant to work with him because of what they saw as preferential treatment. "But there is no question Steve Baines has progressed entirely on his own merit. If he wasn't up to it he wouldn't be there".

Philip Don isn't so keen on former professional players becoming officials; he fears that they would inevitably get to the top quicker than the rest, thus discouraging others from taking the long route to the top. "I can't see how there can be shortcuts," he says. "If you bring in a three-year scheme for ex-players for example – which is something that has been talked about recently – then you're going to lose a hell of a lot of other referees who have started at the bottom."

Out of the 18 Premiership and 54 Football League referees currently operating in the game in England, Baines remains the only one who can look back on a career as a professional footballer. In cricket, it's much more common for players to become officials. Of the 26 umpires taking first class cricket in the summer of 1995, 25 had played to that level.

Footballers in general don't want their playing days to end. The real world frightens them. But when the curtain does finally descend you can be certain most without a managerial or media career mapped out for them want to get as far away from the game as possible. It hurts too much apparently. The options for the retired player are still limited, however, especially now the heyday of the player's pub (once a national institution) is over. The majority of the generation that spawned Baines and many other good, solid professionals, can't afford the luxury of a life of leisure. But having witnessed first hand the levels of abuse aimed at referees – most will admit to being part of the problem – players were and still are a lot less likely to yearn for the black shirt and shorts once they finish playing. The fact is this: former professionals, even those who retire without a penny, would never dream of becoming a referee. It would be almost like a betrayal. Once a poacher, never a gamekeeper.

Still the reasons that motivate the referee remain vague and varied. Thus far, one former League footballer has suggested he became a referee solely on the advice of two bruisers from the 60s. The rest either claim to be fulfilling an obligation that wasn't there in the first place or else taking the only route left open to them in football after disastrous careers in the amateur game. It is possible to comprehend the struggle having been worthwhile for the likes of Lodge or Cooper, although there's a rather obvious downside to life at the top for a referee. But what of the thousands that never get further than Hackney Marshes? Even worse, what of the thousands that never get further than Hackney Marshes, but had their heart truly set on becoming the next David Elleray? Does such a species exist, and if so, do they get out much?

There are approximately 33,000 qualified referees in England, and although around 6,000 new recruits join the system every year the total stays remarkably static. There is only room for 72 referees on the national list – comprising 'refs from the top four professional leagues – so roughly 32, 928 of these men, women, and teenagers will spend every Saturday of their refereeing careers giving free kicks against the cream of the Bass NW Counties League, booking pub players and dodging punches from their partner's 'ex' who runs the video shop down the road.

In truth, it doesn't take too much to make it onto the lowliest rung on the refereeing ladder. A Grade 3 certificate is barely worth the price of a referee's pencil. It's purely a classroom qualification, but even the Clive Thomas's of this world have to start here. Candidates have to pass a 12-hour course on the Laws of the Game, which normally entails attending an evening class for 12 weeks, one hour a week, before taking a short oral and written exam. A colour blindness test sifts out those who can't tell the difference between a Liverpool home kit and a Chelsea away. After which the aspiring ref is broken in with a (supposedly) friendly mixture of low level parks football and boys' games for a minimum of one year. There are usually around 15,000 referees in this grade at any one time. To reach Grade 2 status – which allows officials to take control of a slightly better standard of local parks football – a referee has to apply to his county FA which, having assessed the marks awarded by the junior 'Grade 3' sides, then decide whether or not to promote him. Again, all referees must officiate at this level for at least a year. These are the not so hard facts. What about the reality. To what extent does the Sunday League referee conform to the stereotype of the balding ex-amateur in his mid-30s with a paunch you could balance a small dugout on? And can these arbiters really enjoy their hobby? The answers, apparently, are 'Not a lot', and 'yes'. David Higgs, (72, hair, small paunch, still going strong) loves being a ref. "I still like refereeing now and always have done," says the Grade 2 man and former inside-forward for Woodlands Albion who is now in his 40th year as a referee. Higgs officiates mainly in the Old Boys and Southern Olympian Leagues in London, and doesn't have much truck with officials who fail to see the obvious benefits to be derived from the much pilloried pastime. "You get well treated and you have a nice meal and a drink after the game...I still do it mostly because of the people I meet." Fair enough, but as most of us know, hot dinners, a fine draught ale and pleasant company can all be fairly easily located on a Sunday afternoon without ever straying too near a football pitch. Maybe someone should tell Mr Higgs about the pub lunch.

Colin Braithwate and his mother Lisa took up refereeing two years ago, because they were "both players and big football fans who wanted to find out what refereeing was really like". Colin is 17 and has just started refereeing adult matches – "I get a lot more stick" – whereas Lisa, right back for Sutton United, fits her whistleblowing in around regular Saturday morning playing duties. Although she officiates mainly at adult level, it's the youth games that cause her the most problems. "You get parents giving you so much grief when you give decisions against their kids," she says.

She's not kidding. During a cub scout game in January 1997 Michael May lost the plot when he thought his son had been punched by an opposing player. He ran onto the pitch and viciously head-butted the referee Martin Rolfe, leaving him bleeding heavily from a deep cut to the nose. However, May wasn't merely an aggrieved dad. He was also the linesman. Rolfe's parting shot said it all: "I am finished with football now. Refereeing is the most difficult job in the world." Especially, he might have added, if your so-called colleague is prone to moments of madness. The oft-quoted desire to give something 'back' to football sometimes finds the game to be a reluctant recipient, seemingly more intent on giving the referee a little present instead. Like a broken nose.

Nevertheless enjoyment still seems to be a motivating factor for most referees at this level, even if it is tempered by the occasional contretemps. Perhaps it stems from the psychological feeling of being in control of 22 loose canons that drives these men and women. Journalist Bill Borrows, Man City fan, and intemperate referee – "only the once" – seems to know a lot about the misplaced ego of referees: "The amateur footballer knows that anybody prepared to sit through and memorise the 52 pages of rules in the Laws of Association Football is the kind of person who will derive an almost sexual thrill from being able to exercise authority." It becomes clear Borrows harbours a vicious and deeply felt grudge against the whole of officialdom as he continues, "Teachers are a natural constituency for referee recruitment...by virtue of the fact that most of them are small-minded dictators obsessed with maintaining discipline and protecting their own authority with zealous determination." So speaks a man obviously at one time well acquainted with the joys of the after-school detention. So, what does the referee have to say about all this? One South London non-League official tries hard to trot out the "I-like-it-and-it-keeps-me-involved" party line but his ego easily gets the better of him. "Once you get the experience you then have the authority to impose yourself. You learn how to let them know who's boss, send them off." He grins like a hanging judge at the very thought of it. Another London referee, 28-year-old Georgina Christoforu, also prefers to rule with an iron rod, and it's not just to stop all the childish tittering at her name. "I'm in the police force," she says, "so I'm used to dealing with difficult people. If you lay down the law early on you don't get much abuse."

'Laying down the law' is not just a necessity of the job to these people, it's the main attraction. And although most won't admit it, the craving for control is quite often the instinctive result of run-ins with autocratic officials during earlier playing 'careers'. While the majority of ex-professional players may find even the idea of becoming a referee thoroughly objectionable, for the less gifted footballer the chance to exact revenge is a temptation too good to resist. These are not just the primitive motivations of Sunday League referees either. Many Premiership referees (like policemen) become officials because they were lippy buggers even as powerless lower league players. If someone can't help questioning authority then it's normally because they want it all to themselves. And it's usually these types that take the most pleasure out of pushing people around on the pitch. England World Cup referee Paul Durkin who, as a player, was once suspended for 14 days and fined £6 for persistently haranguing opponents and officials, is a case in point. "I used to play for Portland but wasn't ever going to make it to the top…I used to try and referee and play football at the same time."

If lower league officials share anything with their Premiership colleagues it is this love of authority. They both have it, it's just a matter of relativity: one gets to send off Dennis Bergkamp at Old Trafford; the other, Dennis Jones at Purley Way, Croydon. Do lower league officials actively seek to emulate and copy the big boys of refereeing in the same way that young children mimic their footballing heroes? I'm not sure. A more sinister form of hero worship is barely imaginable. But there's a certain logic to the question nevertheless. Top referees are scrutinised so closely now that an individual's 'style' of refereeing is fairly discernible. In theory, a lowly Beazer Homes League referee might ponder the fact that if Durkin got to where he is today by showing himself to be a merciless task-master on the pitch, then there's no reason why he shouldn't behave in a similar manner and get away with it too. But whilst Durkin can send off Arsenal's Emmanuel Petit for having the gall to accidentally bump into him, without fear of a pitch invasion, a Sunday League official faces much more than just a ticking off from the referee's assessor if he lets his perceived authority get the better of his judgement.

Most non-league referees experience the darker side of the game at some point during their careers anyway: you don't have to be inflated with self-importance – and many are not – to get yourself into serious trouble. At this level, the referee's very presence on the pitch can be like a red rag to an extremely agitated bull.

In 1994, 29-year-old referee Wayne Kirkham experienced a particularly nasty attack from an aggrieved player while refereeing at a Notts County Combination League match between Old Rose and Hucknall Chequers. Kirkham sent off two Old Rose players, and was forced to reach for the red again early in the second half to dismiss another member of the same team. This player took his sending-off as a personal affront, and as a result the match quickly descended into burlesque. Having tired of his vicious verbal remonstrations with the referee, the dismissed player stormed off the pitch, clambered into his van and drove it full pelt straight at the petrified Kirkham, who was only saved by a late dive to his left. The shaken official was shielded from the rest of the lynch mob by the Chequers players, while the driver of the van was taken away to be charged with attempted grievous bodily harm.

The physical dangers of being a Sunday League referee are well documented. But sometimes the verbal assaults can hit just as hard. One incident in 1996, however, put a whole new slant on the term 'abusive language'. When Nick Loughlin of the White Hart pub side in Hartlepool swore at the referee during a local derby match he received his marching orders, and, taking into account previous misdemeanours, faced a three-week suspension from the authorities. Instead the Durham FA appeal court cut the penalty to two weeks after the resourceful Loughlin used a dictionary to prove his argument that 'bollocks' was not in fact a swear word but an expression of disbelief.

Referees too are sometimes capable of semantic ingenuity when faced with a volley of expletives. "A bloke called me a 'fucking cunt' once", recalls 32-year-old Yorkshire referee Harry Inglis, "and technically I could have sent him off, but instead I just said to him quietly, 'You've just missed an open goal mate – who's the fucking cunt?' The player and the captain both heard it and he calmed down and turned to me and said 'I get your point'." If only all man management was like this, there would be no need for the likes of Will Carling.

The rise of 'industrial language', as football's diplomats like to call swearing, became a Premiership issue in 1996, following the dismissal of Everton's Duncan Ferguson by David Elleray for foul and abusive language. "Top refs are quite happy to ignore swearing, but will not tolerate direct abuse," said Elleray in his defence. "If a player says to a ref, 'hey, that was a ****ing corner,' they are unlikely to show a card. But if a player confronts an official and says 'you're a blankety blank', he is likely to be sent off. The public perception that we are shrinking violets not used to industrial language just isn't the case. We are pretty tolerant but not of personal abuse." Those with Tourette syndrome take note.

The lowliest placed officials in the world can only endure so much flack, however. Everyone has a breaking point. For some, it comes after one too many hotly contested red cards; for others, the first physical assault marks the end of the games' appeal. Sometimes getting off the field in one piece is enough to claim a victory – however pyrrhic it may be. For the power-hungry referee, however, the abuse becomes tolerable – even manageable – once the art of supremacy has been mastered. No doubt some even thrive on all the hassle, measuring it as directly proportional to their importance, or get some sort of masochistic buzz out of being punched in the face by 15 stone plasterers. Not many, certainly, but maybe some. And although clinging to the bottom rung of football's ladder can prove more painful than spending a week locked up with an insurance salesman, for the ones who dream of walking out beneath the cantilevered majesty of Ibrox, or the twin towers of Wembley, it's just the trickiest foothold on the climb to the top.

For all this, the idea of entrenched Sunday League violence is a bit of a myth. The tabloids make it out to be an epidemic, when really the disease strikes only a handful of unfortunate individuals every year. Peter Willis of the Referees' Association agrees. "You have to remember that there are something like 90,000 games or more every weekend. There are about 350 assaults a season and you can count the number of serious assaults on one hand." David Ager, the author of *The Soccer Referee's Manual* and a licensed instructor of referees, can give the trembling official a more cast iron assurance: "I did a little statistical exercise and I calculated with the number of referees and assaults that you'd be assaulted once in 40 years. That isn't too bad." Unless you've just started your 40th trouble-free season as a referee, of course.

The biggest problem currently facing refereeing in Britain, however, is not violence but mutiny, with the perceived perils of the profession clearly a contributory factor. Although approximately 6,000 new recruits become qualified referees every year, the same number of men and women also decide to call it a day. The latter statistic is worrying. What was once just a trickle away from the profession is now a haemorrhage waiting to happen; and with new blood increasingly put off by the exaggerated stories of violence, the authorities are justifiably concerned for the future of football officialdom. Keith Cooper acknowledges the problem, but can't see a quick and ready solution: "We have more refs packing it in than coming into the game," he says. "And that's partly because of the problems of park football. We had an incident recently in Wiltshire when a Sunday morning player – who'd obviously had too much to drink – hit the referee, and that was it. He packed it in, right there. Now nobody becomes a referee because of the money – there's not that much about – but at the same time nobody quits being a referee because of lack of money…it's down to other things too. Kids don't want to play as much as they used to. They've got other things to do on a Saturday, like earning some pocket money. It's the same with refereeing, it's all linked to a lack of interest."

Phil Waters, secretary of the Association of Football League Referees and Linesmen, hung up his whistle two years ago after a move back down the career ladder. "When I packed in League refereeing I decided I still wanted to referee. But I found it intensely difficult to move back down to parks football. I'd enjoyed it on my way up but now there was the deterioration of standards – in terms of respect for the authority of the match official. I refereed a local match in Blackpool and while I was up with the action one player 60 yards away actually head-butted an opponent. My back had been turned but when I saw this guy stretched out it was obvious what had happened and who'd done it. I thought, 'I don't need this any more'." Waters, although 45, takes Cooper's theory that children are no longer held enthralled by the promise of a weekend's football and applies it to adults. "Refs who give up can't take the level of abuse that's being levelled at them. They have better things to do on a Saturday afternoon. I decided that if I was not getting the same enjoyment as when I started out it was time to pack up."

Cooper also maintains that there is a serious lack of ambition amongst local park referees which is preventing many from attempting the leap up to national level. Courses, he says, which might have attracted dozens of people in the past now tempt only a few and of those a fair proportion are school teachers or scout masters whose 'career ambitions' are more likely to stretch no further than their local Comprehensive. The knowledge that it could take up to 12 years to get anywhere near Wembley way presumably deters even those decidedly more keen to ditch their 'L' plates.

Of course, with the requisite appetite and dedication, there are always going to be some good referees who will make it to the top. The characteristics needed to become a good referee have long since become the subject of debate.

"You need the patience of a saint, the wisdom of Solomon and eyes everywhere," says Andy Legg, an Icis Premier League referee. "And there is not a referee anywhere who has got all that." Half Dalai Lama, half Marty Feldman, this ideal official does indeed seem to lack any obvious disciples in the game at present. David Ager, clearly a fan of the over-elaborate analogy, likens the referee's task to that of a learner driver. "It's a bit like understanding the highway code. You can know all the traffic laws, understand the breaking distances, but it doesn't mean you can drive." What does it mean then? "During the referees' courses we do role-playing on how to handle things like booking a player. During a game there's lots of adrenaline flowing and it's extremely easy to inflame the situation".

The basic rule is to remain firm and in control, but to show the player respect. Don't bawl him out, wave your arms around, order him about, touch him or lecture him. You have to do things formally, and say: 'I'm cautioning you for ungentlemanly conduct; if you repeat the offence, you may be sent off.' A moral lecture can be disastrous."

Pat Partridge – or 'Penalty Partridge' as he was more commonly known, was famous enough during the 70s to be asked to sign autographs by fans before a Cup Final at Wembley, but is still strongly against egotistical referees adopting screaming tactics. "Some referees go out to take a game thinking that they can't possibly make a mistake and will jump down the throat of the first player who so much as speaks to them. That's ridiculous. I always liked to get along with the players, not antagonise them. I remember once I booked Nobby Stiles for clipping the heels of a winger, and he tried to plead with me that it was an accident. 'It's the floodlights ref. They shine in my contact lenses and I can't see a thing.' Anyway I still booked him, but as I was writing his name down Nobby leaned over and said: 'You spell it with an 'I' not a 'Y' ". So much for the bad eyes. But that was the sort of repartee between player and referee that I enjoyed. It was fun, but full of mutual respect at the same time."

Dave Braddish agrees that personality is the key to good officiating, but recommends a more unorthodox approach than Ager or Partridge. "It's the secret of being a good referee," he says, "You don't bend the laws, but you use them to your advantage. Sometimes you have players doing things off the ball but you can't see it. So you get them on technicalities later and make sure they're out of the game and don't get away with it." Not exactly the kind of method that FIFA might encourage, and not a style particularly suited to top flight football, but effective enough in the park, according to Braddish. Peter Willis advocates good eyesight. "You have to be able to recognise that glint in the eye. A quick card from ten yards can stop an incident, but sometimes it's better to take players aside and have a word."

In the upper tier of the game most observers agree that to be able to control 22 grown men on a muddy pitch, you need first class communication skills.

"Man management is the key," says Keith Cooper, "well, it used to be, but since FIFA brought in all these mandatory laws – for example, if a player kicks the ball away you must caution him – well, it's hardly helped. In my day you used to able to invite players to talk to you on the pitch. You could say 'I might have robbed you there', and they would often turn around and reply 'you're only human'. That kind of rapport doesn't exist anymore." Cooper, however, is not so naive to suggest that he always got on well with players during his time as a match official. "Admittedly, players tend to give you better respect once you've finished refereeing. I've had many players who I didn't think were particularly keen on my style come up to me in the last few years and say 'It was all right when you were around, Coop'."

One current player who is old enough to remember 'old school' referees like Cooper in action is Wimbledon's Robbie Earle. He agrees that the mark of a quality official is his ability to fit in with a game and its participants. "Keith [Cooper] knew how to take the heat out of a situation…I remember on several occasions him advising me to calm down a certain Mr Jones before he was forced to take action. This is the art of good refereeing: interaction with the players."

David Elleray's highly impressive demonstration of the art of "preventative" handling (his words) during Middlesborough's opening League game of the 98/99 season against Leeds would suggest that some of today's top referees have not entirely forgotten how to 'interact' with even the most unruly of players. The

Harrow official showed remarkable poise – not to say admirable patience – with Boro's loose canon Paul Gascoigne, encouraging with one hand, firmly rebuking with the other, and, most importantly, communicating with the player throughout. Earle still believes, however, that in general, referees today lack these vital communication skills. "To talk now of the 'relationship' between players and referees is slightly misleading when on the whole there is none," he says. "One of the problems, I think, is the lowering of the retirement age for Premiership referees to 48. It takes at least a year or two to create some kind of familiarity between player and official. But some may have as little as three years at this level before having to bow out. Just as you are becoming accustomed to each other the relationship is over." Neale Barber and Uriah Rennie, the Premiership new boys last season, might beg to differ: both referees were widely praised for their efforts on the pitch last year, and received markedly less criticism from players and managers than many of their more experienced colleagues.

The veteran BBC commenator Barry Davies has changed his views on the essence of sound refereeing over the years, albeit somewhat reluctantly. "When I first started commentating I would have agreed that man management was the most important quality. People would always counter that by saying 'Well, what about the laws of the game?' Frankly if a referee doesn't know the laws of the game then he shouldn't be there in the first place. Now, because of all the edicts that have been laid down [by FIFA] the primary function of any referee is to make sure that you apply the letter of the law. That needs to be done in order to produce a consistency of performance. [But] with a modicum of exceptions, I think the letter of the law has forced away the spirit of the game for referees. Gary Pallister got booked during a game against Leeds last season for what appeared to be an innocuous challenge. Utd were 3-0 up at the time, and it was almost the end of the game. Whereas a referee from twenty years ago might have let it go with a word of warning, Gary Willard could not afford to because of the FIFA laws."

The phrase that crops up most often from the older generation of officials is common sense". "The best law is the 18th, which is 'common sense", says Joe Worrall. "Referees have always used it, and would not have got to Premiership level if they hadn't. I think they will continue to use it, no matter what the law changes are."

Some detractors, however, argue that many 'old school' referees stretched the boundaries of 'common sense' a little too far, and were often more concerned with keeping on good terms with the players than applying the laws sensibly.

"I don't want to see us going back to the bad old days of referees being over familiar with players," says Philip Don, "the pat-on-the-bottom and get-on-with-it ones who did, and some still do, control the game without really applying the laws. They were out there to please the managers and turn a blind eye to the laws and that's wrong."

Clive Thomas is in total agreement. "The eighteenth law should be used sparingly or the ultra-professional will take advantage," he says. One referee who epitomised the 'old school' approach was schoolteacher Gordon Hill. In the late 60s and early 70s, Hill was undoubtedly the 'players' referee'. On the pitch his tendency to adopt the players' colourful vernacular was symptomatic of his overwhelming desire to be liked and accepted by the two teams. Off the pitch he likened himself to Richard Burton. "Some years ago," he said in 1975, the year he retired, "referees were taken for granted, like the goal posts and the corner flags, but I could have never lived with the 'faceless ref' situation...I could never buy it when people said 'referees should arrive by the back door and leave by the back door'. I felt I was a very important part of the game. I felt an equality with players. I was never jealous of them, in fact I took enormous pride just from being on the same pitch with men like Norman Hunter and Emlyn Hughes. I was popular too. When I arrived at places like Liverpool or Leeds my car was immediately submerged with kids wanting autographs...like Roger Kirkpatrick [another showy 70s referee who was alleged to have conducted a telephone interview with the editor of *Goal* magazine, Dave Cottrell, from his bath] I believed in enjoying 'the theatre of football'. Richard Burton says he enjoys the power he has as an actor and I think you can equate showbiz with refereeing. It is similar because as a referee you have the power to help thousands of people enjoy themselves on a Saturday afternoon."

Pat Partridge, for one, was disinclined to ape the theatrical methods of Hill. "I don't believe it is the referee's function to be the star of the show. A good referee is seen when he has to be – yes – but Gordon always acted like the ultimate achievement was to be popular with the players. I mean I was a 'talker' too, but there the similarity ends. Gordon liked to eff and blind in the belief that he was talking to the players in their own language and therefore gaining their respect. I never swore on the pitch – it wasn't being puritanical, but I never saw the need. It's a shame because the way he went out to attain respect greatly restricted his career. He never made it onto the FIFA list..."

Hill was the most prominent exponent of the glory-seeking method of refereeing, although many others shared his philosophy. But the era when officials commanded the pitch like they were conducting an X-rated version of the last night of the proms is highly unlikely to be repeated. The late 80s ushered in the epoch of strict law enforcement which purged officialdom of its characters. Even the less extroverted, yet capable referees, found it hard to acclimatise. "The change ruined someone like George Courtney," (1982 World Cup referee) says Barry Davies. "I really believe George could not cope with suddenly having to do everything by a rule book. It was a great shame but the game was bound to change. It's a cliché that football mirrors society more than any other sport, but it's also true. The more competitive attitude, the more aggressive nature of players has changed refereeing totally, and hence altered opinions on what is 'good' and 'bad' about an official. I think you are only going to see that old kind of interaction from a referee whose time is coming to an end."

The fitness of top referees is frequently questioned by players, managers and fans. And with no regulated programme of exercise available to the top flight official it is becoming harder for the referee to keep up with the fast-moving modern game. Football League and FIFA tests have shown that, on average, a referee might cover eight or nine miles during the course of 90 minutes, almost as much as a professional player. Most footballers, of course, train daily. Despite the predilections of some wayward souls, most of this work is done in the gym or on the pitch. It's inconceivable that a middle-aged man in black could endure this kind of rigorous and regular exercise. Or is it?

"Most referees do keep themselves in shape," says Premiership whistleblower Steve Dunn, who looks after his waistline by running a newsagent's and writing a referees' column for a Bristol newspaper. "We have to prove our fitness every summer [at Lilleshall] while FIFA give their own tests in October. Nothing to trouble Linford Christie, of course, but enough to make us sweat. There's no official FA training sessions, but I know a lot of referees meet up of an evening and organise work-outs themselves. Road running and sprints – that kind of thing." It seems likely, however, that top referees lacking athletic fitness (no one could ever call Paul Durkin or Martin Bodenham 'well toned', however many laps a week they claim to do) may soon be brutally exposed by the pace of the modern game. The health warning is simple: being out of shape seriously hinders your judgement. As it is with players, referees are most likely to make mistakes of judgement when they are physically low on resources toward the end of a match. Stamina is essential for mental as well as physical sharpness. "You only need to watch a video of a game today and compare it with one from just five years ago," says Ipswich manager George Burley. "The change in pace is incredible, decisions have to be made so much quicker. Consequently, refereeing is much more difficult." The veterans on the Premiership list who face the unenviable prospect of trying to keep up with the whippet-like Michael Owen this season will presumably already be all too aware of this fact.

As Steve Dunn points out, all League referees and assistant referees are tested on their fitness during the summer by officials from the Lilleshall Human Performance centre. It's the one and only day of the year referees are obliged to train. Unless of course, they fail the test. During the course of the day referees' body fat, cholesterol and blood pressure are measured. They also have to take the dreaded 'bleep test', a series of 20-metre shuttle runs controlled by an audio signal, and are timed during a set of 60 metre sprints, each involving a series of turns and separated by only 30 seconds of recovery time. At the end of it all, says the head sport scientist at Lilleshall John Brewer, any official who has not met the required standard (which is not disclosed to the public) cannot continue in either the Premier or Football Leagues. There is a second chance, however. Referees who fail can retake the test, but only after four weeks of intensive training, knowing that if they have not reached the accepted level of fitness by then, they will be struck off the list.

Before the late 70s the Football League did not impose any form of physical test on its referees. Horror stories of rotund schoolmasters, and smoke-filled dressing rooms abounded in the early years of post-war refereeing. FIFA's fitness examination, introduced in 1974 and known as the Cooper test, is a fairly rudimentary examination focusing on correct height/weight ratio and the referee's ability to complete a series of runs within designated times. UEFA did not introduce compulsory testing of their officials until the late 80s. Although all British and world football organisations now set mandatory examinations in health and fitness for match officials, many feel levels are still not as high as they could be. FIFA, in particular, have often been accused of selecting less than fit referees for World Cups. France '98 was the first tournament in which rigorous tests were enforced. In fact, the attention to detail bordered on the ridiculous. "Little things you don't even think about can cause problems," says Michel Vautrot, former World Cup referee and now a member of the FIFA World Cup committee. "For example, even toothache can bring on muscular problems and end up interfering with the referee's ability. So their teeth were checked."

Eight years ago, following the completion of Italia '90, Sepp Blatter, then FIFA Secretary, was prepared to admit to poor levels of fitness amongst the world's top officials, though he rather predictably stopped short of openly criticising their performances. "Many weren't in the best physical condition," he confirmed. "In fact more than 50 per cent failed our fitness test...we discovered our fears were well founded. I'm not going to say we had bad refereeing but we certainly had inconsistent refereeing because certain individuals were unable to keep up with the game. We know that referees run as much as players on the pitch – and with a different rhythm – forwards, backwards, sideways – so he has to be in peak physical condition."

FIFA lowered the maximum age for their officials from 50 to 45 in 1994. The move has been welcomed in some quarters as a positive move toward fitter referees. Players like Robbie Earle, however, might argue that experience – not youth – is, and always has been, the most potent weapon in any referee's armoury.

DOUBTING THOMAS

the life and times of a maverick referee

THE ego of Welsh referee Clive Thomas assumed legendary proportions during the 70s and early 80s, which the intervening years have done little to diminish. In a world where euphemism invariably passes as diplomacy, Thomas was a strict 'disciplinarian' – in much the same way that Graeme Souness was a 'tough player': not by being over cautious and player-friendly did he earn the nickname 'the Book'. In a career spanning 20 years, Thomas attracted more controversy than any other British official in the history of refereeing. And, unlike say, Arthur Ellis, he didn't just happen upon disputes or incidents, he actively courted infamy like it was a friendship waiting to blossom: "I never did aim simply to be a headline maker," he once claimed, not ever convincing himself, well hardly ever. Understanding exactly why Thomas spent half his career on the pitch, and the other half on the back pages and in disciplinary hearings at Lancaster Gate, is easy when the man's philosophy of refereeing – clearly influenced by a combination of Nietzsche and Hobbes – is uncovered. "I am an entertainer," states Thomas, unequivocally, in his autobiography. "I am a performer, who refuses to accept that there are on the field only 22 players. You only have to look at the number of my fellow countrymen in politics and pulpit, in show business and in the classroom," he continues, rather unfairly dragging Neil Kinnock and Tom Jones into the sermon, "to realise that we love the centre of the stage. On the soccer pitch there are 22 players, yes, but there is also me...[and] when I arrive at a ground to find all the paraphernalia associated with television coverage festooned around the stadium...I am unashamedly delighted. I have to accept the criticism levelled at me...that I am a showman, an extrovert. The fact is that I believe some of my best performances – and I use the word here in a professional rather than dramatic sense, though there is a hint of that too – have been in front of the cameras." Thomas retired before he ever got the chance to play 'the Dane', but it seems unlikely he would have ever uttered such brazen words on the subject of television's relationship with the referee had he been speaking during the 'Sky age': for whichever words may spring into the mind of the modern referee facing a barrage of cameras revealing every action on the pitch from a variety of angles, 'delighted' is almost certainly not one of the first.

Although Thomas's narcissistic approach to refereeing was confined to another, altogether less scrutinised era of football, it did not exempt the Welsh whistler from widespread criticism. Neither did it prevent him from becoming one of Britain's most admired and respected officials. In many ways, his hard-headed principles and self-belief forced the country's footballing authorities to wake up and look at the obvious flaws inherent in the game and, crucially, its system of refereeing. Thomas was clearly driven by self-aggrandisement but he also had a surprisingly persistent streak of altruism which pushed him to publicly question the FA and its affiliated organisations in a way in which no match official had ever done previously (or indeed done since).

The fact that little changed as a result of his promptings was not really a poor reflection of Thomas's powers of persuasion; rather it merely highlighted the FA's strident opposition to anything that might endanger the status quo. If Thomas spent the 70s storming around with his head up in the clouds, then it was often through a naive, but genuine belief that he could really do something to improve the lot of the referee. But then the football world's so-called movers and shakers were guilty of a more serious conceit: their heads were stuck firmly in the sand. Change was a dirty word at Lancaster Gate in the 70s, deemed about as obscene as any criticism that might be hurled at the referee from the terraces on a Saturday afternoon.

Thomas earned a reputation as a potential troublemaker early on in his career. After only his first game as a referee, aged 16, Thomas recalls travelling back to his home town of Treorchy on the train, accompanied by the visiting team, who showed their disapproval of some of his harsher decisions by refusing to talk to him. It only made him more determined: "From that moment on," he says, "the general assessment was that I was too strict. But from that moment, too, I certainly made up my mind I was going to be a top referee." Thomas, a high-flyer if ever there was one, didn't waste much time. He became a Class B referee and League of Wales linesman at the age of 18 1/2, earning praise from none other than Mervyn Griffiths, the legendary Welsh World Cup referee, and was a Football League official at 27, one of the youngest ever. Thomas had been no slouch as a player either. Norwich took him on as an apprentice in his teens, and he played regularly in the reserves until a recurring ankle injury forced him to reconsider his aspirations.

However, it is as a formidable League and controversial World Cup referee that Thomas is better remembered as well as the figure who brought new levels of eccentricity and grandiosity to the game. Thomas would sing Frank Sinatra's lachrymose opus 'My Way' in the dressing room before games, and then thunder his way through a selection of Welsh hymns, culminating in the Welsh anthem 'Land of My Fathers', "and never a word of protest from the linesmen sitting with me". It's difficult to imagine today's more straight-laced officials warming their vocal chords by roaring out death-bed show-stoppers and fanatically partisan religious tunes. Thomas's other superstitions included drinking a cup of tea – "always with honey" – before a match and the famous Thomas 'kick start' – a highly peculiar trait employed just after kick-off, which actually gave the impression that the referee was about to ride off into the sunset on an imaginary dirt-track motorbike.

Of course, it was all just show. Thomas was simply living out his fantasies of being an entertainer on the football pitch. He liked to name-drop too. After the 1976 FA Cup Final, won by Lawrie McNenemy's Southampton, Thomas embarked on an evening out in London. Eschewing the invitation to a post-match banquet hosted by the defeated Manchester United team Thomas headed for the West End, more frequently the favoured locale of the city's big spending and big drinking footballers, but ideal for this referee's tastes. Thomas recalls how he ended up at the Talk of The Town nightclub, after refusing to adhere to the traditional FA Cup Final day itinerary for match officials. "I told Ted Crocker [FA secretary] that I would referee the Final but no one was going to tell me what to do after the match. I told them I would be at the talk if they needed to find me in case any controversy had arisen from the game that they needed to discuss...One telephone call to my old friend Frankie Vaughan and within an hour the booking for a table was confirmed." After the match, Thomas jumped into a limousine, picked up his wife and headed for the bright lights, while the unfortunate linesmen were forced to endure the losers' unhappy feast. The rest of the evening saw Thomas receiving guests and their glowing plaudits like Frank Sinatra holding court in some Vegas hotel bar. "We were met by the manager of the Talk of The Town, taken swiftly to our excellent table and found an ice-box with a bottle of champagne in it and a card saying 'Sorry I couldn't be with you this afternoon. I am sure you had a fantastic match, Frank and Stella (Vaughan)'...I scarcely had time to raise my glass when a huge paw landed on my shoulder and nearly knocked me to the ground. It was Lawrie [McNenemy]...who had taken over the place for his 'family'...virtually the whole of Southampton Football club were there. At 1a.m. with the morning still young, we went off to join the linesmen and their wives at the Astor. I told them to forget their evening with the losers and enjoy themselves: and we did. At about 3.30a.m., there was me, this boy from Rhondda, a gold medal in his pocket, eating eggs and bacon in a plush London nightclub. Strange, I thought. I mean, I never eat breakfast." Thomas lapped up the attention like a young boy accepted into his elder brother's peer group. Moreover, he loved the trappings of stardom not normally afforded to the humble League referee. Thomas later missed the opening day of the League season because he had a dinner date with Englebert Humperdink. Allegedly.

Thomas's colleagues were generally opposed to his style of refereeing, arguing that the way he threw cards around like confetti could only be detrimental to the already fragile player/referee relationship. Their disapproval, however, or anyone's else's for that matter, never prevented the whistle-happy Welshman from indulging his more authoritarian instincts. Sometimes his strong-armed approach surprised even players well-versed in the ways of 'Clive the Book'. In March 1974 Thomas refereed the Manchester derby at Maine Road and sent off City's Mike Doyle and United's Lou Macari for fighting. Both refused to leave the field. Having watched the two assailants walk away from him, Thomas picked up the ball, blew his whistle and motioned both teams off the pitch. It was the first time in Football League history that a referee had taken all 22 players from the field of play because a player – or in this case, two players – had refused to obey an order. Thomas, a man keen on setting unorthodox precedents, would no doubt have taken great pleasure from this fact. The game finally resumed without the two red-carded players, who were later fined by the FA for misconduct, but were rather generously spared suspensions. Thomas complained bitterly that the FA had shirked from their responsibilities by failing to publicly back his actions.

Then again he was becoming used to receiving the cold shoulder from the authorities, mainly, it seems, because they had long regarded him as insolent and opinionated. Thomas's fractious relationships with the FA and the Football League became the centrepoint of his controversial career. Thomas was the first referee to openly criticise the venerable organisation's outdated methods. "Once upon a time there was the Football Association," he wrote in 1985, "that, even without a name attached to it was known throughout the world. When the FA said 'We do it this way', the world did it this way. The FA maintained its credibility and charisma in the world game until 1974, when Sir Stanley Rous had to relinquish his hold on FIFA. By then, the standard of English football was accelerating rapidly downhill. Today", he continued, "we have an out-of-date administrative structure that leads only to mediocrity, reflecting a lack of leadership from the top. The people in Lancaster Gate are reneging on their duty to modernise the game by changing the laws; they renege by accepting edicts from FIFA apparently unquestioningly…and the FA does not appear in any way to be interested in the discipline of players or followers…or in supporting its referees." Pretty harsh words. But Thomas stood by his outburst. He had, he said, been singled out and made an example of by the FA during the 1982-3 season.

During this year, even as one of the most experienced officials on the League list, Thomas was not allocated a single FA Cup match – the first time this had happened to him in 17 years. This would be comparable to David Elleray or Paul Durkin being snubbed by the FA today. Thomas was convinced he was being persecuted for previous 'misdemeanours', including an incident during the 1981 League Cup Final between Liverpool and West Ham which he believed to have been especially prevalent in the minds of the committee responsible for selecting the FA Cup officials. After the match, West Ham's manager John Lyall approached Thomas and allegedly called him a 'cheat' – repeatedly – for over-ruling his linesman on a disputed offside decision, which had led directly to a Liverpool goal. Thomas reported Lyall to the FA. Bert Millichip headed the FA Disciplinary Committee which handled the hearing into Lyall's alleged comments, and which subsequently cleared him of a charge of 'insulting and improper behaviour'. The message was clear, at least to the conspiracy-fixated Thomas: the referee should expect and indeed withstand such criticism. The FA seem to have been acting on a desire not to expose managers or players to public criticism on the whim of an apparently jumped-up, power hungry official.

Thomas felt the FA had also used his comments on the subject of the professional foul to justify his exclusion from the Cup list. Speaking to the annual conference of the Association of Football League Referees and Linesmen during the summer of 1982, Thomas strongly urged his colleagues to ignore any directives from the FA, the Football League, UEFA or FIFA with regard to the required punishment of this infringement. It was hardly going to make him a popular figure. Still Thomas received no written explanation from the FA for his exclusion from the Cup fixture list, until, that is, he deigned to approach the board himself for an answer. The letters he received appeared to reveal the FA as a rather clandestine and shadowy organisation, unwilling and in no way required to disclose the rationale behind their selection procedure for referees. Ted Crocker wrote to Thomas to explain: "With only 123 matches to allocate [from first round to final] and almost 90 referees available [i.e. the entire Football League list] it is inevitable that every season several referees do not receive an appointment from the committee." Crocker's mathematical shenanigans aside, Thomas was not convinced. After all, he knew himself to be one of the best officials in the country. But seemingly, merit wasn't sufficient criteria for selection. Three months of correspondence followed, and while Thomas received rare support in the press for what had become a wider issue of FA accountability, Crocker continued to evade the direct question put to him, fobbing off his nemesis with a series of vague assurances that the matter would be dealt with by the Referees' Committee. By this time it was May 1983, the Cup Final had come and gone, and Thomas was cursing the FA's hex like a man possessed. It was a matter of principle. "I now charge the Challenge Cup Committee and/or the Referees' Committee of the Football Association Ltd," Thomas wrote, with typical phlegm on May 26, "with using improper methods in my exclusion of an appointment in the FA Challenge Cup competition in the season 1982-83. In view of the seriousness of the charge, I would make myself available at any time to meet the FA Council to substantiate any charge with necessary evidence." The FA never picked up the gauntlet; they just filed the letter, in the presumed hope that the little Welsh troublemaker would just go away and stop putting the frighteners on them. Thomas suspected that the FA had shied away from a confrontation precisely because they had no evidence whatsoever to back up their decision to exclude him. If they had had reasonable grounds to expect a victory in a hearing with Thomas, then they would surely have taken up the challenge: after all, a countercharge of bringing the game into disrepute would have seen Thomas severely punished, and presumably less inclined to play up again in the future.

The whole furore nevertheless cast a very revealing light on the complex and vaguely Orwellian network of referees' committees and sub-committees working under the auspices of the FA. Thomas knew that the Football League's Referees' Committee appointed officials to League-games (before the Premiership, League-listed referees could be asked to officiate in any of the four leagues); yet he seemed unsure who was responsible for omitting his name from the FA Cup list that season. The FA Handbook states that that the Challenge Cup Committee's duties include appointing officials to matches. The Referees' Committee, on the other hand, deals with matters concerning the regulation of referees. Yet Crocker had initially referred Thomas's grievance to the latter body. It didn't make sense. A member of the Referees' Committee, Dick Speake, has suggested in an interview that Thomas's League marks might in some way have been responsible for his exclusion. Thomas also knew that the FA's appointments secretary – Reg Payne at the time – was in some way involved in the selection process, and was unquestionably an influential figure within the FA. Putting two and two together, he sensed a cover-up. His assessor's marks had been good, and, more puzzingly, Payne had been one of Thomas's more admiring critics. "May I say that your performance from first to last whistle", wrote Payne of Thomas's display during a

League match in April 1983, "showed how a referee should command the players and control the match on the field." It was all rather odd.

The FA wasn't the only governing body to incur the wrath of Clive Thomas. Alan Hardaker, the equally strong-willed secretary of the Football League during the late 60s and 70s had many a run-in with the fiery Welshman. Again, it was generally the 'system', and Thomas's flagrant distrust of the way it treated match officials, that caused the ructions, although even the League's tentative experiments with new methods of selection failed to please a man so keen on change. During his first few years on the League list, Thomas was constantly in trouble with Hardaker, who warned him about his cavalier style of refereeing and bemoaned the young official's unceasing appeals and questioning. One incident brought matters to a head. At half-time in a heated League match between Coventry City and Sheffield Wednesday in March 1970 Thomas stormed into the team dressing rooms to make it clear that he was beginning to tire of all the brutal tackling. The plea for sensible challenges fell on deaf ears. In the second half, Thomas, perhaps more than just a little riled that his authority had been undermined, booked four players, including the Coventry centre half Roy Barry, who had the ignominy of receiving his yellow card as he was being stretchered off with a broken leg. The players appealed, and an FA commission over-ruled all but one of the cautions. Thomas was livid. Although it was the players who had been summoned to substantiate their claims of 'unfair dismissal', Thomas felt it was the referee who was really being put on trial by the authorities. Having vocally aired these sentiments he was duly reprimanded by Hardaker, who told him in no uncertain terms that his job was to referee matches, and not to try to change the way the FA and the Football League operated in one fell swoop.

Thomas was left out in the cold by Hardaker, as well as by the FA Challenge Cup Committee. Between 1974, on his return from refereeing in the World Cup Finals in Germany, and January 1977, Thomas was repeatedly excluded from officiating at First and Second Division league matches. The referees' assessor's marks had been good; Thomas was convinced he was being deliberately ostracised for his outspoken behaviour – this time mainly on the subject of referees' expenses. The press picked up on Thomas's gripe, which was concerned with the fact that the League had started to employ a system of allocating referees to their own geographical areas to cut expenditure. This ploy, however, also had the effect of reducing the number of top matches appointed to officials, including Thomas, many of whom ended up out of pocket.

The League was furious when the press began to champion Thomas's cause: "No room at the top for ref Thomas"; "Baffling as ref Thomas stays in the wilderness". On 17 October 1976, Hugh Johns, in an article published in the *Sunday People*, expressed dismay that one of the country's leading officials was 'going out shopping' on a Saturday because he wasn't being selected to officiate even the lowliest Football League matches. On 19 October, under the headline "Why has Mr Hardaker stuck Referee Thomas up a Mountain?", journalist Peter Batt noted that Thomas had spent three consecutive Saturdays training in the valleys instead of refereeing. The League's policy had, of course, affected many other referees – some of whom complained in the press that there were now too many officials on the list, while others just accepted it. Not Thomas. His outbursts on the subject infuriated the League, and in particular Hardaker. "It does seem a pity that every time there is correspondence between this office and yourself the press seem to get hold of it," he wrote to Thomas, still struggling to get a game outside the Fourth

Division. Although Thomas had in no way leaked information to the press regarding his grievance, he hardly discouraged the headline-makers, and they in turn loved it. Suddenly, there was talk of Thomas leading a revolt against the authorities; players and managers who had previously criticised the referee – with Emlyn Hughes and Brain Clough to the fore – were now falling over themselves to praise him. One paper even published a poll in which League players voted Thomas the best referee in the country.

During the controversy the Football League refused to comment publicly on Thomas's situation, simply brushing enquirers aside with old arguments: "there is no system which guarantees any referee matches"; "the appointment of games has nothing to do with Clive Thomas". In truth, it was not really the raising of the issues of match allocation and expenses itself that so incensed the authorities, but rather the methods employed by Clive Thomas in doing so. This was made blatantly clear during the hearing that – somewhat inevitably – followed the furore. Thomas was told that he was to stop all direct correspondence with the League Headquarters in Lytham forthwith. Any complaints a referee had were to be made through the Association of Football League Referees and Linesmen, said the board. "You thought you would be able to do things yourself," added Bob Lord, Chairman of Burnley, master butcher and member of the referees' sub-committee appointed to 'hear' Thomas's case, "Well you can't."

Thomas was incredulous. "I am astounded to hear you say that one cannot communicate with the establishment. You know my association will not fight for things because they are afraid of all of you. The feeling of referees today is not very good. And the standard has gone back but no one is doing anything about it. The referees have not got the guts to put their names to articles.

I have...but I have never given a story to the press." Thomas's punishment in the end was to be banished to silence. "There were no doubts in my mind", he later said, "that the committee had tried to take me on and, if I was not prepared to toe the line, they intended to strike me off the list." It didn't take long for Thomas to revert back to his old ways. A few years later, as we have seen, he was back to his cantankerous and outspoken best.

Perhaps the most telling comment of all concerning Thomas's troubles with the authorities came from another League official, who was asked by Thomas why he thought he had really been cast off by the Football League into the refereeing wilderness of the lower divisions. The anonymous official dodged the question, but his reply still spoke volumes. "You know it's never been about your refereeing ability," he said. It summed up his whole career really.

In comparison, today's referee is almost cosseted by the game's authorities. Still, there is a lack of an independent and sufficiently empowered body to provide protection and encouragement for the embattled official. Local referees' associations are still disinclined to approach the feared powerbrokers at Lancaster Gate on behalf of their members. And although the FA generally back the country's leading officials during a crisis, no efforts have been made to introduce suitable deterrents for lippy players and managers. A fine doesn't prevent anything. It still leaves the referee exposed, a fact one prominent referee recognises with a resigned tone. "To an extent, we are out on a limb," he says. "The FA back us, tell us we have no need to justify our decisions, but we still have no real channel for our grievances."

In Thomas's era, managers and players who publicly criticised the referee were often exempted from suspensions and fines. Often, it must be said, on the promptings of referees who rather than report individuals for inflammatory comments, would take them aside and try and talk the matter through. After a League match at the Dell in 1982 Manchester City manager John Bond called Thomas and his refereeing 'a disgrace'. The referee followed Bond into the dressing room and offered him the opportunity to explain what he meant. Bond, struggling at City and clutching at straws to find consolation in defeat, couldn't articulate the words to elaborate on his accusation. Thomas didn't report him. Fifteen years later, in November 1997, the name-calling hadn't stopped, but the refereeing niceties had. When West Ham's John Hartson called referee Mike Reed "a shithouse", "a homer", "a disgrace" and "an absolute joke" after his team's defeat at Leicester, he was swiftly hauled up in front of an FA disciplinary committee and charged with misconduct. Hartson escaped suspension but was fined £1000.

Thomas never tired of his one-man assault on the footballing world. Whether it was niggling over the nuances of stud checks on players' boots, querying the FA's archaic expenses system, or even designing his own referee's kit in a bid to enliven the official's appearance, Thomas was always in the midst of a controversy. One Football League Referees' Committee plan that he did approve of, however, was the introduction in season 1972-73 of teams of officials, selected on a geographical basis, but this time for the apparent benefit of officials. Where previously – and subsequently – the referee would expect to be handed different linesmen for each game, the Committee now invited five referees to have the same linesmen throughout the entire season. Thomas was selected for the trial and given Colin Wade and Joe Wright for his games in the north of England, and Jim Sims and Gerry Faulkner for southern matches. The object of the exercise was to build 'teams' of officials, who, on the basis of working together for long periods, would strike up an instinctive understanding and therefore operate more effectively as a unit. Thomas was sold on the merits of the idea. "It worked very well," he says, "I was able to introduce many innovations, like introducing the linesmen to the captains before the toss-up, which are still in use today, and we reached the stage of having almost telepathic communication..." Thomas also claims that during the trial period he persuaded linesmen to stand at the corner-flag for corner kicks for the first time and also gave his assistants the sole authority to make offside calls. Both developments remain in place today, though the experiment was dumped by the FA "for administrative reasons" after less than a year's trial.

Thomas's ability and ego were best suited for the world stage. He was selected by FIFA for both the '74 tournament in West Germany (where he complained that he was put in an embarrassing situation when presented with pendants, badges and other gifts from his World Cup colleagues: the Welsh Football Association had given him nothing with which to return the favour) and, four years later, for the '78 event in Argentina. It is for his actions during the latter tournament, in the first round game between Brazil and Sweden, that the Welsh whistleblower is perhaps best remembered.

In injury-time, with the game nicely poised at 1-1, 'Olive' Thomas, as he was listed in the FIFA program of officials, awarded a corner to the Brazilians. "I had time to look at my watch while standing near the Swedish goalkeeper, Ronnie Hellstrom, who asked me in broken English how much longer there was to go," recalls the referee. "'Not long,' I replied. With just seconds to go, the corner was eventually taken. I blew the whistle after the ball had travelled about ten yards, turned and pointed to the tunnel to show that the match was over. Behind me there was uproar. There was a roar from the crowd, I saw the Brazilian players jumping for joy and I turned to see the ball in the back of the net, apparently headed in by Zico." Although the Brazilians protested to Thomas, he received none of the apocalyptic assaults that Ellis had suffered 20 years earlier. Still, he realised it was the probably the last game he would ever referee in the World Cup.

Although backed by certain sections of the press (mainly British it has to be said), Thomas was heavily criticised by members of FIFA's Referees' Committee. His detractors felt he should either have awaited the outcome of the corner before terminating the game, or blown for full-time before the set-piece was taken. Nobody, however, was able to point to a football law to back up their arguments. It didn't matter. Thomas was deemed to have dropped a clanger, and paid the price. Bristol referee Steve Dunn replicated Thomas's 'mistake' in January 1998 – albeit not in the World Cup but during an FA third round match between Wimbledon and Wrexham. Dunn cut it even finer than Thomas. He blew for full-time as the ball was on the way into Wrexham's net after Marcus Gayle's powerful header. He, too, was condemned, mainly by Dons boss Joe Kinnear who felt strongly that the referee had committed a serious error of law. Again, he hadn't. Thomas jumped to his defence in the press. "I have been waiting 20 years for someone else to do that", he said. "Twenty years I have been praying, every cup tie. I would like the FA to say 'Well done, Steve Dunn, you made the right decision'. But I'd bet £1.50 that they won't." His money was safe. Although the referee has the law on his side, Keith Cooper believes common sense must prevail in these circumstances. "My view is that there is always a nice place to call the end of a game. We all know that if the ball's in the centre of the pitch then there's no hassle. Life is never about the dead second. I can't quote Steve, but I'm sure he wishes he'd stopped the game earlier or later." Thomas, for one, was delighted he hadn't.

When the time finally came for Thomas to retire in 1984, he reflected on his time as a referee with characteristic brio: "...and one man in his time plays many parts. I do not know that I played all of Shakespeare's seven ages of man during my escapades, but many of the roles cast upon me were eminently suitable for comedy, tragedy or high drama." Curtain.

AMONG THE VULTURES

the referee under attack

ALMOST since his inception, and long into the latter half of this century, the man in black had been football's *persona non grata*, the party pooper. Despite the persistent hints – veiled or otherwise – from fans, players and managers that the party would go with more of a swing should he choose to stay at home, the referee always insisted on turning up. Metaphorically turning the music down; figuratively lighting shadowy corners, he was only really happy when assured that nobody else was. That was his role, and everybody knew it.

Lately, however, he seems to have become more bothersome, and the value of his contribution has been subject to overwhelming debate. Performing under greater pressure than ever before, facing irate inquisition from all quarters, the referee increasingly resembles one of those Guy Fawkes effigies sitting on top of a bonfire. And nowadays, everybody has a box of matches.

In the past the referee's presence may have been unwelcome, but few of those privileged enough to watch their football without having to pay for the pleasure took that much notice of him.

Admittedly, he was given a rough ride by the players and the managers – and sometimes by the newspapers – but the animosity rarely festered, as Keith Cooper recalls: "I've lost count of the number of times a player would come into my dressing room at the end of a game and say, 'Look, I know we probably saw too much of you today, but thanks for the game'. I'd go for a couple of pints in the players' room, then go home." This doesn't happen anymore, at least not at the top of the game, where even the players rarely venture into the players' bar anymore. But then a referee of Cooper's vintage – he started officiating in 1966 – would be hard pushed to recognise today's game, let alone referee one 'according to the laws laid down by FIFA'.

Old-style officiating was all about controlling the game according to the laws the referee decided to implement, and those he chose not to. This is how Roger Milford, probably Britain's best known modern official until his retirement four years ago, describes the way in which he once dealt with a defender struggling to contain a centre-forward, following the introduction of restrictions on the tackle from behind: "This guy said to me – 'Look, Rog, I'm not as quick as he is. I can't tackle him from behind now, but I've got to stop him somehow.' And I said, 'Well, let me put it this way. If you kick him from behind, you're going to hurt him, and you're going to get a yellow. But grab his shirt and you may not get cautioned, and you've got the same end result – you've stopped him." Not the kind of advice you might expect from one of the game's most respected referees, and hardly words to encourage flowing football – or centre-forwards – but it was nonetheless effective in certain contexts. The point Milford was making was that a referee's main task in the past was to try and control a game by whatever means necessary, to apply the rules selectively according to the characteristics of each individual match. If it meant humouring some players, but coming on like Chuck Norris in shorts with others, then so be it. At heart, refereeing used to be about flexibility, or "being human" as Cooper likes to put it. As we know from the arms of the law in the real world – from the High Court judge to the Bobby on the beat – despite the fact that the 'letter' of the law exists, it is always about contigency and interpretation. However, now that FIFA have removed the human element from the job description, referees can no longer afford to operate in this way. By imposing a strict ban on flexibility, Zurich's meddling administrators have finally taken away the one thing that allowed players to tell referees apart: personality. If, as FIFA decrees, the laws are rigidly applied to every situation in every game, then the referee risks becoming a robot in charge of 22 life-size Subbuteo models.

There is a more direct disadvantage to the man in black himself. Without the right to exercise a little leniency or diplomacy, the referee is left brutally exposed to accusations that he is unsympathetic and rigidly didactic. Players committing an infringement of the laws can no longer be quietly taken aside and told to cool down – instead, they must be booked. It's hardly likely to make the referee more popular.

This is merely on the pitch. Off it, a whole new host of detractors have assembled in newspaper and magazine offices to take aim at the referee, not to mention those perched in TV studios behind banks of video screens and computer gadgetry specifically designed, it must seem to the embattled referee, to help expose his shortcomings and frailties. Any problems, once resolved on the pitch between the referee and the players – with the fans in the ground taking an active but short-lived interest – are now open to the scrutiny of the public as a whole. With the eyes of the entire fooballing fraternity firmly focused on him, the referee has become like a specimen sample trapped under a powerful magnifying glass that rarely flatters. Cooper agrees that it's not so much the problems faced on the pitch by the referee today that make him increasingly vulnerable to criticism, but the external interference which inflicts the real damage to his battered confidence. "It's not necessarily any harder refereeing matches, it's just that everything comes under so much more scrutiny now," he says. In footballing terms, that's the understatement of the decade.

Satellite TV's Sky Sports has perfected the art of trial by television. Where once acquittals were common on the grounds of insufficient evidence – a kind of sporting version of murder not proven – now condemnation is the likely outcome for most referees. Men and women everywhere are all too ready to don the black cap, and there appears to be little referees can do about it. Ken Ridden, the FA's Director of Refereeing, is adamant that it's not falling standards in officiating that are to blame for this trend. "Television has a lot to do with it," he insisted in a recent interview with *Four Four Two* magazine. "It's a tremendous influence on the criticism of referees. At live matches there are now anything up to 16 different camera positions [Sky had 31 for the FA Cup Final]. Obviously they pick up lots of things three sets of eyes can't see. Going back ten or fifteen years there were just one or two cameras and no replays. Now you would get to see everything." Ridden, of course, is bound to back the officials. It's his job. But by the same reckoning, it's Sky's job to provide their paying subscribers with the most comprehensive football coverage possible, and if that means seeing what a goal really looks like from inside the top right-hand corner of the net, or savouring that programmed 'whoosh' every time the director cuts to another angle, then so be it. Even if it means a half-crazed Andy Gray twitching excitedly amidst a bewildering array of technology which probably cost more than the entire Wimbledon first team.

In a hugely competitive industry, Sky exists to excite. And that's not a word normally associated with the referee.

If supporters want mumbled solidarity for the plight of the official and replays seemingly inspired by some of Ingmar Bergman's more reflective films, then they can always watch ITV's regional football coverage instead. Ridden is not sufficiently blinkered to realise that his cause is probably a lost one, but he nevertheless sticks to his utopian dream like mud to Paul Gascoigne. "I know it sounds like moralising," he admits, "but I don't think it's helpful for the game to be super-critical of referees. It dents their confidence and makes their decisions less credible in the eyes of the public." It's a little disingenuous, however, to presume that Sky's overriding concern when broadcasting football is to criticise referees. The channel's multi-angled replays are there because the channel can afford the cameras which provide the technology the viewers want. It's as simple as that. And if the ref is implicated as a result, it is surely more by association than design.

Sky is catering for a different kind of football fan – a less fortunate one most would say – who cannot obtain, or perhaps, afford tickets for their team's matches. Whatever their reasons for watching at home or in the pub, they want to be entertained. Whereas a warming pie and Bovril or a flick through the match programme – traditionally soundtracked by music apparently being played on a wind-up record player – is enough to occupy most fans during half-time in League grounds around the country, Sky takes the opportunity of the break to show – and comment upon – detailed highlights of the first half. This routine is duly repeated after the game. Indeed, within 10 minutes of the final whistle, it's not unusual to have the views of both managers and the inevitable studio panel regarding all aspects of the game. This is the case whether the referee has made a mistake or not.

It's all part of the entertainment. Andy Gray, overlord of Sky's virtual replay says, "Sky are no more guilty than the BBC or ITV. We have a duty to show a decision for what it is. You can't alter the fact that those pictures are there. In a sense, it's educational because everyone has a chance to learn from them." Referees who are punished by the press and media for decisions made in good faith during a fast-moving Premiership game are presumably less inclined to agree with Gray's upbeat theory of the learning curve.

On paper, indeed on TV, his argument is a sound one. But in reality Gray would struggle to find a single referee who claims to have learnt anything from his hyper-sensitive virtual replays. Multi-angled slo-motion replays of a game's flashpoints are certainly fun to watch, but when the spotlight falls on the referee, it invariably highlights him making a mistake. Conversely a referee's correct decisions are by nature less visible than his mistakes – they are ascribed a neutral value rather than a positive one, they are simply expected rather than applauded. Philip Don, who is vehemently opposed to the use of TV evidence, suggests that referees are in a no win situation: "At the end of the day, [a referee's] judgements are based on [his] angle of vision and what he sees. If you haven't got a camera looking from exactly the same angle as the referee, you can never show exactly what he is seeing. I would only ever have taken notice of a video if the camera angle was identical to my own. It never was." Sky's cameras are unforgiving, and as Andy Legg said, no referee has "eyes everywhere". Paul Durkin agrees that the technology available to Sky makes life extremely difficult for any referee trying to do his job, but admits that officials have always made errors during matches, the only difference now is the merciless way in which Sky exposes them: "At the moment...we're there to be shot at," he says. "The live coverage of games, the slow-motion replays...all these things highlight a lot of errors of judgement, the kind that have always been there...people make errors in every walk of life, unfortunately ours are played out on the TV." There is one group who remain overlooked in these rueful tales from the televisual frontline: the players. Try explaining the troubled lot of the referee to the striker whose ill-timed scoop in front of an open goal is being re-examined for the 28th time on a wet Sunday evening. Then try explaining why any of us should feel sorry for men earning a comfortable annual wage in seven days. That – and the fact that no referee has affiliated 'fans' fighting his corner – is the difference.

If it is generally felt that referees get a raw deal at the hands of Gray and his colleagues, then one man, unsurprisingly, disagrees. Jimmy Hill claims, with characteristic conviction, that TV has been a blessing for referees. "Replays actually get referees off the hook more times than they incriminate them," he says. "The one thing TV doesn't do is accuse a referee of making a mistake when he hasn't made one." Philip Don and others might refute this by saying that TV is incapable of telling apart a genuine error of judgement from an obvious cock-up. Hill, however, believes that as well as aiding officials, TV coverage has also led to improved accuracy in the press. He argues that before the presence of cameras and replay facilities, journalists, forced to come to conclusions with their own eyes, would frequently criticise referees unjustifiably in the following day's papers. True or not, access to modern technology has in no way reduced the criticism of Britain's top referees. In many ways, it can be said to have had the opposite effect; safe in the knowledge that their opinions can be corroborated by TV evidence, journalists can now lay into referees with absolute impunity.

During Chelsea's controversial match with Leicester in the 1996 FA Cup, the activity in the press box vividly bore out this line of reasoning. The match was nicely poised at 0-0 in extra-time when referee Mike Reed awarded a penalty to Chelsea for a foul on Erland Johnsen. As chaos ensued on the pitch, the journalists in the press-box shared their opinions on the decision: nobody was sure whether it had been a penalty or not. A quick call to their offices, however, and they were immediately assured by colleagues watching Sky's coverage of the match that Reed had messed up. Badly. Immediately they had their back-page lead – Reed's clanger – and with the added ingredient of Danny Baker's rabble rousing on his radio show that night, a witch-hunt ensued. Reed was harangued by angry Leicester fans for weeks, received threatening phone-calls and letters, and his daughter was harassed by the press on her way to school. That is what TV evidence can do for a referee.

Ironically, all this hue and cry is as yet essentially meaningless in terms of the referee's role. While the criticism undoubtedly hurts, it amounts to little more than letting off steam on a national scale. For what TV evidence can't do as yet is the one and only thing that matters in a practical context: it can't change the decision made on the pitch.

When the recent outcry over an incident between Alan Shearer and Neil Lennon erupted, the FA refused to be swayed by TV evidence. No matter that the rest of the country could view– thanks to the video replay – an act overlooked by the referee that night. The original decision stood. The referee, for all the braying punditry and tricksy technology swaggering around on the touchlines, remains top dog on the field. The question hanging on everyone's lips is, 'For how much longer?'

Fans are perhaps the referee's most unforgiving and brutal critics. It's no longer just referees at the bottom of the pecking order that are being forced to endure physical abuse. Last season, a number of Britain's League officials were subjected to attacks from football fans, acting, it would seem, like they had been reared on the blood-soaked pitches of Buenos Aires. In August 1997, referee Phil Richards was assaulted by a Notts County fan after he was alleged to have committed a double sin against the Meadow Lane side. Richards dismissed County striker Devon White mid-way through the second half and then allowed Lincoln's Phil Stant to score a winner, which the home crowd strongly felt should have been disallowed for offside. As the home players remonstrated with the official, a supporter broke onto the pitch and pushed Richards to the ground.

In January 1998, an altogether more serious incident took place at Portsmouth's Fratton Park when linesman Edward Martin was knocked unconscious by a Sheffield United fan, John Crocker, following the dismissal of the visiting team's goalkeeper Simon Tracy. Martin, who was well positioned to see Tracy impede Steve Claridge and then handle the ball outside the penalty area, informed referee Mark Hasley that the keeper had to go, and was then assaulted. "I actually saw what happened," recalls Hasley. "This man came running along the sideline and threw a punch. I was just numb really. I have never seen anything like it in all my years of football." Martin, a chirpy grocer from Somerset was admitted to hospital with concussion, but, incredibly, vowed to keep running the line. "I am quite sore, a bit battered and bruised, but I will survive," he said after coming to. "I have never felt in any danger before. Running the line is the highlight of my week, and I'm certainly not going to let one idiot stop me doing what I love. I'm having one week off and then I'll be back on the touchline." Resilience and bravery indeed.

The sickening and cowardly acts of intimidation continued during the rest of the season. Two months later in March, Premiership referee Gary Willard was on the receiving end at

Oakwell, during and after Barsnely's 3-2 defeat at the hands of Liverpool. Having sent two Barnsley players off – the second, Chris Morgan for elbowing Michael Owen in the face, albeit, with little obvious intent – Willard was attacked by several spectators. Fortunately a rugby tackle from Jan Aage Fjortoft dealt with one offender, and before Willard could be assaulted by the others a quick-acting steward had escorted both the referee and his linesmen off the pitch. They stayed off for four minutes until tempers had seemingly cooled. On re-emerging, however, and with minutes to go, Willard sent off a third Barsnley player, Darren Sheridan, prompting another minor pitch invasion. This time Liverpool captain Paul Ince stepped in to wrestle the assailant to the ground. Any residue of goodwill left in the home end had long been used up by this stage. At full-time Willard was pelted with coins and forced to take shelter amidst a huddle of Oakwell stewards as he ran off the field. It was not until 6.30p.m. that a rather nervous-looking Willard, flanked by two police officers, came out from the sanctuary of his dressing room and was shepherded to his getaway car. "The one or two who tried to get to the referee deserve to be banned for life," said the Barsnley boss, Danny Wilson, before adding that he thought Willard had only antagonised the situation by leaving the field without warning. Liverpool manager Roy Evans, was more inclined to succinctness. "Strange game, strange day," he sighed. In a less publicised incident on the same day, an Everton fan made for the referee Neale Barry after he awarded Aston Villa a penalty at Goodison Park. Three weeks later, on April 21, linesman Russell Tiffin was assaulted by a spectator as he ran the line during a Second Division match between Carlisle and Grimsby Town. "Things are getting out of order and opening the door for a potential fatality," commented the spokesman for Premiership referees, Keith Hackett.

These incidents inevitably sparked a new debate over the need for enhanced stewarding at grounds, and greater protection for referees. Unlike in Italy, where ground-closing became a regular punishment in the 80s for clubs whose supporters invaded the pitch to attack officials, no deterrent has ever been made available in Britain. The individuals are banned, most are charged, but little changes. The initial furore elicits promises of inquiries and investigations from the authorities; but they tend to renege on these with time, until the violence starts happening again. "We study carefully all requests for tighter security but at the moment we are not planning to do anything about it," said FA spokesman Steve Double after the Carlisle incident. It's little wonder England's referees feel isolated.

In many ways, however, the root of the problem lies not with ineffective stewarding, but in FIFA's constant meddling with the laws of the game. The more pronounced suffering of officials today is often caused by fans struggling to comprehend why a player has to be sent off for an infringement that previously might only have merited a caution. On the basis that prevention is the best cure of all, it would surely help matters if FIFA re-introduced the intent clause in Law 12, relating to fouls and misconduct. Since 1995 the question of intent has been removed from all offences except handball and now demands a red card for a player who "denies an obvious goalscoring opportunity to an opponent...by an offence punishable by a free kick or penalty kick". Previously, the ruling stated that a player had to be found guilty of "intentionally committing" such offences before a dismissal could be justified. A subtle change, but one with wide-ranging implications for the referee. No longer would he be permitted to make allowances for accidental infringements occurring during a goalmouth incident. *Guardian* journalist David Lacey believes that Willard could have avoided at least one of the red cards in the Barnsley match had he been allowed to make allowances for intent. "If Willard felt that Chris Morgan's arm had caught Owen in the face, then under the laws he was justified in dismissing the player," he says. "Common sense might argue that Owen's pace had taken Morgan by surprise...but referees are no longer supposed to exercise their discretion in such matters." It might be further added that Willard could have avoided amassing many of his eight red cards (the second highest total among Premiership referees last season) had the laws on intent not been modified.

Then again, the FA made it quite clear last season that any referee failing to send off a player for an infringement of Law 12 would be forcibly dealt with. Dermot Gallagher was suspended for one Premiership match in February 1998 following criticism of his handling of a Chelsea-Arsenal game. Again, the rule book, and Law 12, in particular, conspired against him. Gallagher booked seven players during what was admittedly a highly physical match, but came under fire for failing to send off Arsenal's Steve Bould after the defender had committed a 'professional foul' on Chelsea's Gianluca Vialli.

The man responsible for Gallagher's suspension, FA's Director of Refereeing Ken Ridden, stressed that the referee's ban was not implemented as a knee-jerk reaction to recent criticisms of officials, and that this form of disciplinary procedure had been written into the statutes when the Premier League was formed in 1992. "This is not new," he said, "It is rare, but it is not a precedent; it has happened before but perhaps not received so much attention. When Premiership referees sign their one-year contracts at the start of the season, part of the deal is that they have to produce satisfactory performances. If they are not fulfilling these responsibilities then action can and will be taken. Though [Gallagher's] other games were taken into consideration, we looked at the match observer's report of the Chelsea-Arsenal match and were disappointed by the overall standard. The area we are talking about is if a referee acknowledges he's seen an incident but doesn't take the action as required by law." In Gallagher's case this made him guilty as hell. Vialli was clean through on goal and was therefore "denied an obvious goalscoring opportunity". Even Steve Bould admitted he was lucky to have stayed on the park. Adding insult to injury, however, was the match observer. In his report, he also criticised Gallagher for failing to caution a player for kicking the ball away after the award of a free kick, thus contravening the terms of another new, and most would say, wholly unnecessary law.

The public nature of Gallagher's humiliation was condemned by both Referees' Association members and, more surprisingly, by several leading Premiership managers. Such action would only put more pressure on the already severely burdened whistle-blower, it was argued. "I am not at all in favour of this suspension," said Secretary of the Referees' Association, Arthur Smith. "People will now be demanding that referees are suspended every time they make a bad decision. If they were going to suspend him they should not have made it public." Arsenal manager Arsene Wenger and Blackburn boss Roy Hodgson also made remarks supporting the Banbury official. Incredibly, in the wake of the furore, the terraces did not erupt with cries of 'suspension' on every occasion the referee raised his hand or blew his whistle. At least, not seriously. But it showed little consistency on the part of Ridden that others didn't follow Gallagher into the dunce's corner: there were certainly worse refereeing performances during the season. The only banishment comparable to Gallagher's occurred during the summer prior to the commencement of the 1997-98 season when the Leicestershire referee Paul Danson was struck off the Premiership list for persistently failing to rigidly enforce the laws of the game. However, he was never suspended for an individual performance.

David Elleray was clearly dismayed at Gallagher's suspension, but hoped that it might stop critics from accusing officials of having it all too easy at the top. "Everybody is saying that referees aren't accountable for their performances", he said, "and this is one way in which they are shown to be. Players get dropped if they don't perform to the correct level and so do referees." Elleray's argument was fatally flawed however: only one referee was publicly suspended – unless, of course, Ridden is hiding something – and that was Gallagher. Gerald Ashby, another of the Premiership's 18-strong coterie, certainly isn't aware of a precedent. "I've never heard of this happening before," he says, "But now I suppose that, deep down we know what the ultimate consequence might be if we don't do the job." Barry Davies is opposed to the pubic persecution of referees. "There has to be a better way to discipline them," he says. "I believe that it is wrong to condemn them for one bad performance. If a referee is not performing to the required level then it might be useful to have a panel of experienced ex-Premiership referees watch him for, say, six games…rather than rely on the findings of just one match observer."

Fears that reprimanding referees in this public manner might increase the pressure on officials and undermine their confidence were in some way realised when Gallagher returned to the fray. In 1980 Colin Seal returned to referee an FA Cup Semi-final replay after being widely criticised for his handling of the first game and likened himself to "a pilot who has been in an air crash and has had to climb back into the cockpit". Gallagher presumably experienced similar feelings of trepidation. Only a few games after he had served his suspension, Gallagher received a verbal battering from Wimbledon manager Joe Kinnear for allowing Manchester United two controversial, and in the end, vital goals, during the second half of a League match at Old Trafford. Once again Gallagher appeared to be found wanting in his knowledge and application of new edicts. TV evidence showed both goals to be clearly offside. According to the law, Gallagher should have pulled up Paul Scholes, who had run back from an offside position to score United's second goal: he was certainly "involved in active play". That the referee allowed the strike to stand cast serious doubts on his ability once again, and further emphasised the problems referees are currently experiencing in interpreting the laws of the game.

Despite these hairy moments, Gallagher had a relatively successful season, and during the course of it, received high praise from many Premiership managers, Joe Kinnaer excepted. He finished fourth in one newspaper's Premiership referees table, where points were awarded on levels of fitness, tendency to book and dismiss players, and clarity of judgement. But, if the criticism of referees continues unabated this season, it would be foolish to think that the suspension of Dermot Gallagher was an isolated and never-to-be-repeated experiment. As Ken Ridden makes clear – the FA have the power, and they alone call the shots.

The stringent application of modified and mandatory rulings may seem like the sensible solution to inconsistent refereeing. But in reality, it causes the referee no end of heartache. A series of incidents in Scotland during the 1995-96 season highlighted the fact that without room for interpretation referees can be made to look decidedly humourless and petty. Paul Gascoigne, somewhat predictably, was involved in two of the controversies. The *enfant terrible* of British football became the most noted victim of the Scottish Football Association's clamp-down on goal celebrations when he was booked by referee Jim McGilvray for jumping a set of hoardings to celebrate a goal against Partick

Thistle; the referee interpreting the act as one of "incitement".

Earlier in the same match McGilvray had cautioned Partick striker Rod McDonald for crossing himself as he ran onto the pitch after half-time. Again the charge was 'incitement' – presumably on the basis that it wasn't exactly the Rangers fans' idea of an acceptable expression of religious devotion. The decision was hotly debated, the referee's critics pointing out that although in certain areas of Scotland the act may have been interpreted as inflammatory, it was certainly not regarded as such in Catholic countries like Italy and Brazil, where players would frequently cross themselves without fear of punishment. In this instance, FIFA's plans for a uniformed interpretation of the rule book, were shown to be short-sighted and ill-conceived. McGilvray recognised the ludicrousness of the situation himself. One of Scotland's top officials, he stood down as a League referee not long after this match, citing new, "unacceptably harsh" FIFA rulings as the one development that had caused him to question his position as an official. Reading between the lines, McGilvray felt he was unable to continue as a referee so long as the influence of spurious rulings continued to prevent the man in the middle from doing his primary job as an arbitrator of two football teams. In short, the laws were destroying the game and making a mockery of the referee.

Gascoigne too was on the receiving end of another referee driven to new levels of harshness by FIFA's thoughtless tinkerings. During a league match against Hibs in December 1995, the former Rangers midfielder was booked by referee Dougie Smith for playfully 'showing' the official the yellow card he had dropped on the pitch. Even the chortling Hibs players conceded that, for once, Gazza's spontaneity had produced, not an act of wanton self-destruction, but a moment of subtle humour. It didn't matter. Rules were rules and his name went into the book.

* * *

No other sport in the world treats the referee the way football does – with disgust, disdain and scant regard for his capacity as a human being. Having said that, as the pressure to win becomes greater and greater in other sports too, so the referee is likely to be held up to ever more intense scrutiny and accountability. In tennis, we are all familiar with the fashion John McEnroe set for abusive player-umpire relations. While even cricket, once solely the domain of the gentleman and thought beyond refereeing controversy, has seen increasing flare-ups in recent years. The most famous case of a cricketing player-umpire *contretemps* was an incident involving England's Mike Gatting and Pakistani umpire Shakoor Rana during an England tour of Pakistan in 1987. The two came near to blows on the square over a series of contentious decisions. At the time it was not necessary to secure an umpire from a neutral country to referee an international cricket match. Shortly after this débâcle it was ruled that one of the umpires must always be neutral. Even now at county level, the officials need not be from neutral counties to umpire a game.

Cricket umpires are no longer beyond the wrath of the crowd either. It is not unknown for first class umpires to be pelted with oranges and even bottles in some parts of the world for their dubious decisions. Even one decision made by the great Dickie Bird (to suspend a game for longer than necessary because of bad light) saw members of the MCC throwing their chairs onto the pitch in disgust during the early 80s. More recently, the England-South Africa summer Test series in 1998 was marred by a spate of verbal assaults on umpires. South Africa's Allan Donald was fined £550 for criticising umpire Mervyn Kitchen in a radio interview, and the experienced official talked about retiring as a direct result. Another umpire drafted in at the last minute was widely condemned for being woefully incompetent. It should be noted too that the use of video replay technology in cricket has if anything undermined the traditional authority of the umpire. Of course, cricket umpires are still only rarely subjected to these kind of atrocities, while their footballing colleagues are forced to endure them on a weekly basis.

In the United States, however, it is a different story. The referee is an honourable and well-thought-of individual, as much a part of the fabric of sporting life as the Super Bowl and the World Series. Well, almost. "In our major sports – baseball, grid iron football, basketball and ice hockey – the referee is a respected figure", says *New York Times* sports correspondent, Jack Bell. "Most fans accept that referees are human and therefore are going to make mistakes. They certainly don't swear at him or threaten him. At least not in general or for no apparent reason. There is no tolerance whatsoever for fans who blame referees for their team's defeat." Admirable all-American sporting sentiments indeed. But not necessarily a reflection of the superior ability of baseball or hockey officials. "Standards are good, but not so good that some decisions are not disputed," insists Bell. "But supporters really do feel that criticising referees is a futile act; nothing can alter the outcome of a game, so it doesn't make sense to harbour grudges. Also, errors have an uncanny habit of evening themselves out over the course of a season. No team is ever seen to prosper or suffer at the hands of one, or a number of referees. Officials don't throw games, or fix them: the issue of bribery and favouritism doesn't ever come up."

Players and managers too, it would seem, are unlikely to become embroiled in verbal confrontations with referees. Common sense tends to prevail. "In baseball especially," says Bell, "strict punishments are enforced on coaches and players who make unfavourable comments about officials after a game. Most are sensible enough to realise that any outburst is going to cost them a lot of money and perhaps a suspension, so they tend to keep quiet. Coaches are particularly guarded. And the press certainly don't go digging for juicy quotes – they're much more interested in the games." A strange and novel attitude indeed from the 'soccer' world's perspective.

THE FUTURE IS BLACK

bringing the referee into the 21st century

THE referee has come a long way since 1891. Yet the experimental steps toward professionalism and technological innovation announced by the English Premier League in September 1998 (to be implemented by autumn 1999) are by far the most momentous in the referee's history. The Premiership proposes to employ at least 10 full-time professional referees. Their salaries will be in the region of £40-50,000 per annum. The Premier League also plans to lobby FIFA to allow these referees to wear sponsors' names on their shirts to help finance the wage bill (a *Guardian* cartoon cheekily suggested the RNIB might be an appropriate donor). The 'choosen ones' will be given full media training (if it can work on Gary Lineker then why not a ref?) and encouraged to discuss their decisions in the press. Altogether the changes will turn the life of a Premiership ref on its head. It's a transformation that will, for better or worse, bring him further into the limelight ultimately changing his role from that of a civil servant bureaucrat into an fully accountable minister.

If all this wasn't remarkable enough, the FA have also unveiled plans to utilise video replays to rule on goals when it is unclear whether the ball crossed the line. Such technology, however, will not be employed for penalties, free-kicks or bookings and therefore will not unduly interrupt the flow of the game.

Throughout much of this century, the referee has increasingly resembled an unpopular child being dragged uphill by his self-appointed elders and betters; bullied by players; picked on by fans; undermined by the press and scrutinised by the TV cameras. But will these changes finally convince the embattled referee to ride the wave of criticism? In the past, peace-seeking tactics have ranged from constructive debate (such as managers meeting referees more frequently) to more radically modern schemes (tagging, virtual replays, professionalism). Technological innovations and the introduction of full-time officials may seem the way forward, but can they really change the fundamentals of the relationship between official and the rest of football, an uneasy union built on a bedrock of mistrust?

With professional referees, employed on a full-time basis and paid accordingly, levels of consistency among match officials would improve and consequently, the game would benefit too. So the argument goes. To some it's an enduring and convincing theory, to others, it's simplistic and misleading. Most advocates of this plan are, it has to be said, managers and players. When you are a full-time professional, it is perhaps too easy to see an inherent weakness and fallibility in amateurism, whatever the realities.

That a plan for full-time refereeing has been so slow coming to the table in Britain is largely down to ignorance of what the reality might entail. The theory sounds almost utopian – increased and more intensive training of referees, improved communication between officials and managers, consistency and understanding – but nobody knows what shape it will assume in practice. Before drawing up their blueprint the Premier League and Football Association studied the Italian model. The Italian match official is not full-time as yet, but he is close to becoming so. This is how it works: Serie A and B referees have to work three days a week under the supervision of an Italian FA physical trainer, and a further day on their own following a prepared programme. Once a month the referee has to report for a two-day session at the Italian FA technical centre in Coverciano, where their physical condition is closely monitored. Typical Italian methods of retribution are enforced if the referee fails to reach the required standard: he is swiftly removed from the National List. The physical demands of the job, however, are by no means compensated by bountiful financial rewards. Serie A officials receive a retainer of £1,300 a season plus £200 a match, fairly poor by European standards. Currently Premiership referees enjoy a £2,000 retainer and £375 a match, plus expenses of 35p a mile and £18 meal allowance. It's little wonder that some Italian referees have had to resort to other means of supplementing their income over the years.

At the moment, the FA in England is relying on FIFA lifting their ban on referee sponsorship to free them from the financial ties of professionalism. Regardless, the training regimes implemented by Italian football's governing body impressed Referees' Association observers in Britain. "I preach to referees that they must ensure they are capable of coping with the pace and demands of the modern game," says secretary Arthur Smith, "any referee worth his salt will do everything necessary to remain on the list and that includes regular training...In view of the way the game is going, the Italian method of monthly checks may be something for the FA to consider."

Away from Lancaster Gate and the manager's office, the concept of the professional referee has few advocates. Barry Davies is one such opponent of the idea. "Referees are professional enough in my opinion. Making them full-time would only result in them becoming more robotic. Moreover, think of what it might do to the referee's life. If an official makes a mistake now he might incur the wrath of the authorities, but he can still afford to pay the mortgage. Make him full-time and professional and he could arguably be out of a job if he makes an error.

Nobody's really thought the whole thing through properly. What the hell would they do after they retired?"

Paul Durkin, for one, isn't at all certain. "There isn't the structure at the moment for professional referees. Before we do anything, we have to try and encourage more young people into what is becoming a fading profession. If we started at the bottom instead of the top and introduced young professionals at grass-roots level then, maybe. But, remember all of us on the Premiership list have full-time jobs already – some better paid than others – and we would have to consider our pensions. What would happen to us when we reached 48? Where would we go from there? There are a lot of things to consider. You can't just start paying Premiership referees." Would Durkin consider turning professional himself if it were an option? "I would certainly consider it," he says. "I know quite a few of the others in the Premiership would too." Is he jealous of players' pay packets? "No, you get what you can out of life. If you earn £20,000 a week then good luck to you." (Durkin, speaking last April must be rather pleased with the way things have turned out. With professionalism now no longer fantasy, Durkin and Co. presumably have every reason to bless their luck and look forward to next season's windfall.)

Some would say, of course, that Britain's top referees are already semi-professional. During the 97/98 season the 19 Premiership referees averaged about 20 games each, not including Cup ties and (for the eight qualified) European Cup fixtures.

At approximately £450 a match including expenses, the figure earned annually by most of the elite would be at least £11,000. Not bad, for a job that entails one or two days' work a week and no compulsory training.

Keith Cooper believes that the fitness of referees is more important than ever, but, "I cannot see any vast improvement to levels of refereeing that could be made by going full-time. It may assist a bit in fitness levels, because a referee would obviously have more time to get fit, but I'm sure the clubs would still find fault." The last point is a particularly salient one. The advocates believe professionalism will produce better referees. And although a fitter official may be better equipped to keep up with the pace of the modern game, he would still make mistakes and, as a media figure, be subjected to even closer scrutiny by a whole host of critics waiting for him to trip up. As one top referee says, echoing Barry Davies, "Paying officials more money and making them train three times a week wouldn't make that much difference. In some ways, it would put referees under more pressure, and that cannot be a good thing. Also, what you have to remember is that referees will always make mistakes – nothing will change that – and fans and some players will always enjoy hassling officials. One of the reasons people go to football is to give the ref a hard time. It's not nice, but it's a fact."

John Hartson, who during the 97/98 season had a few choice words to say about the performance and personal attributes of Premiership referee Mike Reed, is not, as one might expect, a strong supporter of the campaign for professional match officials. "I don't know whether they should go professional or not," he says. "I don't think it would make a lot of difference to be honest. I still play some games and come off the pitch thinking 'the ref was brilliant, he really let the game flow'. I realise that it's a hard job and all the TV cameras don't help, but if you make it their livelihoods then it could be even worse, as they could be under even more pressure." The managers don't see it quite the same way, of course. "Now is the time for full-time referees, like players and managers," said Gordon Strachan after Coventry were beaten by Derby during the 97/98 season, "They should have to earn the right to be a referee. For some of them it's just like a hobby and the vehicle to be a celebrity. I wouldn't mind being a part-time manager and, say, an accountant during the week." In the heat of the moment it's an easy solution, but the figures don't add up. Professionalism won't succeed without the support of players and managers like Strachan, and as long as they are as unwilling to meet and talk with referees many of the problems will remain unsolved. At one Forum last year, organised by the FA to allow managers to air their grievances in the company of referees, just two of the Premiership's top bosses turned up. Sniping in front of the cameras is one thing; actually speaking constructively to a referee, it seems, is an altogether more disagreeable option.

Failed attempts to make the referee a professional have a long history. In the late 70s, FA secretary Ted Crocker strongly backed such a move, stating that he would like to introduce six – or at the most 12 – full-timers, who would officiate at 50 to 60 games a year. The implication being, incredibly, that better-paid referees wouldn't tire of this regime. Pat Partridge, at this point nearing the end of his career as a referee, strongly opposed Crocker, fearing his plan might lead to referees accepting bribes: "Imagine a referee with only a few months to go to enforced retirement ...with no recognised trade to fall back on, being approached by some unscrupulous character offering him £10,000 [this was 20 years ago] in ready cash." Partridge's slightly paranoid conspiracy theory, however, was accompanied by the most sensible words uttered on the subject. Doubting the benefits of full-time training for professional referees, Partridge says: "No amount of training could improve two of the referees' greatest assets – his eyesight and his courage."

The high esteem in which American sports referees are held could be seen to be a result of their well-honed professional structure. Baseball has employed fully professional referees for almost 30 years; the National Basketball Association and National Hockey League both function to a similar level, but the NFL are yet to follow suit – "their referees still parachute in for games after a day's work". Professional referees are well-paid – "almost as much as some players" and supported by a durable infrastructure. "Officials don't have to worry about money," says Jack Bell of the *New York Times*, "They are organised in unions and are well catered for in terms of benefits and pensions. It's not the case that they will have to look around for work once they've finished refereeing. Plus, there are no strict mandatory ages imposed for retirement – many go on well into their fifties. Most are fit enough to do so." Apart from the wily black and white striped baseball refs, that is. "Well, yes, they do tend to be these porky kind of guys. There was a bit of a problem a few years ago when several of them went down with strokes or had heart attacks while on the field. And they don't even have to do that much running about."

Still, if not exactly in the prime of health, baseball officials are at least well organised as a result of their full-time status. "They travel from game to game in a crew," says Bell. "The same four officials stick together for a season, rotating positions [on the field] as they go. It's a very efficient system and it certainly ensures consistency. Each man gets to know exactly how the other three work – and as such the team becomes almost telepathic. It's a popular system with the players." And one employed in the NBA too, where teams of three become roommates for the course of a season.

Improved communication between the football referee and his adversaries is certainly to be encouraged. But it's not just managers who are reluctant to attend discussions. The modern day referee is regarded by many as aloof, untouchable even. Few make the effort to speak to managers or players before games, and virtually no referees seem prepared to make the required effort in the aftermath of a match. Joe Kinnear responded to Dermot Gallagher's dubious performance during the 97/98 season's Wimbledon-Manchester Utd match by attempting to locate the official in his dressing room, allegedly for a 'chat'. "I couldn't get near him after the game for an explanation because he locked himself in his room," said the clearly livid Kinnaer. Simply 'disappearing' after games is a common, although somewhat understandable precautionary act. It hardly helps though. "Professional managers and players get very upset when referees slam doors in their faces and refuse to talk," says Barry Davies, who would like to see referees under some kind of obligation to justify their decisions. Davies suggests sports shows like *Match of the Day* might provide a suitable forum and atmosphere for referees to discuss controversial decisions. If the FA does not renege on its recent promise to make professional referees available to the media this may soon be commonplace. Several Premiership referees appeared on sports panel shows during the 97/98 season (Graham Poll and Dermot Gallagher being two such participants) but, frankly, with many lacking humour and personality, and without the relevant probing questioning of ex-managers and other experienced football personalities (Eamon Holmes just won't do) it's not a real solution to the problem.

Keith Cooper supports moves aimed at bringing referees and clubs closer together, and believes regular meetings would help managers in particular to understand the ramifications of new laws when they are introduced. "We [at the Association of

Premier and Football League Referees] want to arrange meetings with clubs, officially organised by the League, so that there are no surprises when a new season starts. We could talk through with managers and players the interpretation of new law amendments and how we intend to implement them. But the clubs have to want this too. Certainly, some referees seem reluctant to meet club officials – I presume some don't have the confidence in their communication skills, which never used to be a problem, I could talk the hind legs off a donkey, still can – but some kind of arrangement has got to be made for discussion. Straight after a game, when passions are rising, is not the right time however."

It is the right time according to John Barnwell, chief executive of the Managers' Association, who, toward the end of season 97/98, launched a campaign he hopes will eventually bring some semblance of harmony to this tempestuous relationship.

The former Arsenal and Wolves star met referees, managers and members of the Premiership executive to discuss his proposal that England's flagship league adopt after match 'talk-ins'. The idea is for the two managers, the referee and the Premiership match observer to meet for discussion after every League match. In theory, it sounds like a winning idea. Managers get to air their grievances in appropriate surroundings, and the official is given the opportunity to explain any controversial decisions made during the game. The observer would be expected to keep the peace. Of course, in reality, it could easily turn into a slagging match, with confidences later betrayed to the press and public. Meetings can address problems. But, in football, they rarely solve them. One problem would be a manager coming face to face with an official he already holds a grudge against. Feuding bosses would only further add to the quarrelsome atmosphere. On the other hand, the plan is a positive one, that at least shows that some kind of collective desire to improve the situation exists. Barnwell for one is hopeful the idea will come to fruition. "There have been meetings over the years with little or no success," he said, "but this time it proved very constructive. I am not saying we have cracked it, but we have certainly made considerable progress towards establishing a structure of communication." And that can only be a good thing.

Arsenal manager, Arsene Wenger, although as critical of the referee as the next manager, has also offered suggestions for change. During the 97/98 season he vaunted the idea of using two professional referees – one in each half – which, admittedly, hardly sent shock waves of anticipation around the world. But his call for the publication of a Premiership Referees League Table elicited strong support from within the footballing community. Wenger wants the lifting of the secrecy presently shrouding the marks awarded to referees by match observers (or assessors as they are known in the Football League). His belief is that if fans, managers and players knew a referee's rating, the official would be 'kept on his toes', and thus improve his performance. Others might argue that it would make matters considerably worse, by loading even more pressure onto the top officials, or, conversely, giving the referee an excuse to revert back to his showman's tendencies. At any rate, Premiership spokesman Steve Double insists that introducing a competitive nature to officialdom is not in any way an option. "We ask referees to meet an acceptable standard in observing the laws of the game," he says. "We are not interested in seeing who is top of the pecking order and can't see that there would be any benefit in the general public knowing who is top." Benefit – maybe not. But interest? Undoubtedly.

At present Ken Ridden's Premiership referees' office compiles an end-of-season table based on reports from observers who award grades (and add remarks) in each match. E is exceptional;

I impressive; G, good; B, below expectations (whose precisely is unclear); and D, disappointing. At the end of the season these are converted into marks and a table compiled. Referees receive bonuses ranging from £1,000 to £100 each according to their position in the table, but even the luckless ref does not find out his final 'League' placement. He is merely informed of which bonus segment he stands in – top six, middle six, or bottom seven. In theory, referees can be relegated for finishing near the bottom of this table. A couple of seasons ago, for example, Paul Danson was demoted back to the First Division after a string of poor performances left him (we can only presume) propping up the spot all footballer's (and patently referee's) fear.

Arthur Smith, from the Association of Premiership and Football League Referees, was happy to see Wenger's plea rejected. "I don't see what purpose the publication of a merit list would serve, although perhaps referees at the top might be happy to see it," he says. "Referees are already closely monitored and marked, but I think it is better for the details to be kept in house...every referee goes out to do his best, but I don't think it comes across in a competitive way. I don't think they are going out to do better than their colleagues."

Amendments to and tinkerings with the laws of the game have been a prominent feature of the last 10 years. The offside rule, the goalkeeper's handling rights, misconduct laws and indirect free kicks have been meddled with, some say, with little positive effect. "I'm firmly opposed to any further tinkerings with the laws," says Barry Davies, before adding, "but I'm a great advocate of the rugby law regarding free kicks. There are few things more unsightly in football than the refusal of a wall to stand 10 yards from the ball. Moving the offenders back a further 10 yards until, if the ball has to be placed in the box, it's a penalty, would almost certainly deter players from continuing this practice. I don't agree with awarding penalty goals however." Paul Durkin is particularly keen to see FIFA introduce the '10-yard rule'. "It's a bit of a hobby horse of mine," he says. "The 10-yard scheme would, I'm certain, wipe out dissent in the game. There's actually a pilot scheme going to be tested in Jersey. The last thing we want to be doing is be cautioning players for not going back the required distances, but we've got to try and sort out the problem once and for all."

In general the consensus is that the laws have been messed with too much in recent years. Most referees appear happy with the rule book (although many would argue that some look more comfortable implementing it than others), but the popularity of the '10-yard' rule for dissent and time-wasting amongst British officials, and the FA's introduction of a trial run of the proposed amendment, suggests that it will become part of the game very soon.

In the light of the France 98, a crackdown on diving and play-acting was inevitable. Keith Cooper says that with more money resting on the outcome of matches, players are increasingly resorting to foul play as a means to outwit referees and steal an advantage on their opponents. "Although I have to say that I'd never call any player a cheat," he says, "I think they stretch the laws to the nth degree now. When a new rule comes out a certain amount of players take time to circumvent it." During France 98, Croatia's Slaven Bilic – though he was by no means the tournament's only perpetrator – did a sterling job of tricking the referee into sending off the French captain Laurent Blanc, ensuring his suspension for the Final. Preventative measures to be inforced in the Premiership starting with the 98/99 season should see players like Bilic forced to rely on more traditional methods to win games. Like defending or trying to score goals. "Our officials are determined to prevent such unsporting behaviour developing," insists Philip Don, who claims referees will take a tougher line on players feigning injury, holding and pulling, and – in line with FIFA's infamous World Cup 'tackle from behind' edict – "strong action" against dangerous challenges.

Women officials are still a rarity in football, although the tide is slowly turning. Wendy Toms, who during the 97/98 season became the first ever woman to officiate a Premier League fixture, remains the only League-listed female official in Britain. Toms has yet to be given the opportunity to referee a game in the top flight, but the signs are promising – she is only 35 and her startling rise through the ranks have impressed her peers. "She was extremely capable, much better in fact than the other two [male] officials if I recall," said Chelsea's Frank LeBouef after his first encounter with Toms last season. "She was a very quick learner," says Toms agent Lawrence Jones, a fellow referee. Toms is still a hungry student, attending games with Jones solely for the after-match discussion of decisions (like the majority of her colleagues, she claims never to have supported a particular team). However, if Toms is to succeed as a female referee in the men's game she will have to develop an immunity to the more entrenched chauvinistic tendencies of some players. In one game during the 97/98 season an Everton player was clearly caught on camera calling Toms what looked like a "fucking stupid woman". Then again, it's the fate of any touch judge to be sworn at and cursed regardless of gender, and it's not as if Toms doesn't know what to expect from footballers. Having refereed in the Vauxhall Conference for two years she has plenty experience to draw on.

The paucity of female officials currently operating in football leagues around the world – and in other sports – suggest Toms may not have too much female company in the dressing room for some time yet. However, in the 1998-9 season in Spain, Carolina Domenech became the first referee to take charge of a Spanish (third division) professional match. And, Sonya Denoncourt, a Canadian woman referee, reached the highest levels in South America in the early 90s, refereeing several Brazilian National Championship games and high-profile friendlies involving the likes of Maradona and Romario. In theory, there is nothing standing in the way of woman referees. The raised profile of the game in recent years has attracted many women to sit the referees' exam; and FIFA has its own women's list, which at least shows that the desire exists amongst the authorities. Sepp Blatter has – rather condescendingly – commented that women are well-equipped to referee, because they are more level-headed and often naturally fitter than men. Blatter, it's alleged was president of the all-male World Society of Friends of Suspenders in the early 70s. This gives you some idea of his views on women's lib.

The most mooted innovation in recent years is the embracing of technology. Electronic eyes, tagging devices, and video replays for the benefit of a fourth official sitting in the stand, have all been vaunted as accessories that might give assistance to referees and cut out some of the criticism they receive for making contestable decisions.

Experiments with technology in other sports have seen varying degrees of success. Cricket has recently taken some bold steps towards embracing the electronic age. A third umpire sits in a booth overlooking the field and can be called upon to pronounce on run-outs, or whether the ball has crossed the boundary line or carried for a catch. By using a simple signal box with red and green lights he can deliver his verdict to the umpire at the crease within seconds. It hasn't proved remarkably successful, with the third eye often criticised for failing to get the call right. Recent controversies over disputed lbw decisions have also seen plans tabled for the introduction of mini-cameras, situated both behind the stumps and at right-angles to the batter on the boundary, and linked digitally to the third official. Tennis has been successfully using electronic eyes to judge disputed line-calls for years.

Video technology was tried out in American football's NFL, but scrapped recently because it failed to give the referees adequate support. "Basically, it didn't work," says Jack Bell. "It got to the stage where referees were becoming afraid to call any decisions without consulting the video replay. It made them far too tentative. It was being used to back up almost all their decisions and the constant breaks were becoming unbearable. [This is even in a game in which breaks are frequent and natural.] Sometimes, it took five minutes for a decision to be reached. That was OK if you happened to be watching on TV, because you got to see their replays, but for the crowd, it was really tedious – they didn't know what the hell was going on. A whole panel of officials would be watching the TV feeds in the stands, and they would take an age to reach a decision. Plus, every game was different. For smaller games, maybe only six cameras could be consulted, but for the big matches, up to 15 or 20 might be available. It was all down to the whim of the TV stations."

Bells says one positive idea has come out of this experiment: to bring back the video replay, but to introduce a deterrent for managers tempted to call for its utilisation. "In (American) football, each team is allowed three time-outs in each half. But there is talk of penalising coaches by deducting one time-out from their allocation each time they call for video evidence and it proves his appeal to have been wrong. It might stop so many stoppages...anyway, we're back to the old system now – with no technology – and it seems to be working fine." If there is a lesson to be learnt, then it is that where technology is concerned sparing moderation is the key.

Ice hockey has fared much better with the third eye. "The replay is only used for goal-calls," says Bell, "and it's been very successful. It's very hard for a referee to see a puck moving toward goal with the naked eye. So, the way it works is the goal judge (positioned behind the goal) flashes a red light if he has been unable to verify a good goal, and then the replay will be looked at. Sometimes a puck can travel into the net and come back out before the referee's eyes have had time to register its movement – it's that fast. So, it's useful in this sense. In the NFL I think it was more a case of the authorities having too much money available. They could afford the technology, they brought it in. But the game didn't need it. Basketball doesn't use replays because there are very few disputed calls, and baseball...well, it's very much the traditional game in America – much like cricket in Britain. Disputes are rare, and I don't think the introduction of technology would go down too well with anyone involved in the game."

Sky TV have started providing giant replay screens at top Rugby League grounds for the benefit of officials. And they, of course, already use Virtual Reality Replay (VRR) equipment, which employs technology pioneered by the Israelis to track missiles during the Gulf War. On a more profound level, the three-dimensional recreations have recently shown, for example, that Alan Shearer's goal for Newcastle against Stevenage in season 97/98's FA Cup should not have been awarded. Their simulation proved the ball had not crossed the line. The VRR equipment also cleared up one of the longest running controversies in British footballing history. Geoff Hurst's goal never crossed the line in 1966; the only hat-trick ever scored in a World Cup Final has thus been written off by a computer. Not that this indelible evidence moved English opinion one jot. The power of the crowd, and even a nation, to believe what they want to believe should never be underestimated when pondering the impact of video footage. Sometimes, no matter how much you bounce those players up and down with fast forward and rewind, opinions will still differ.

Regardless, VRR is the kind of equipment that could be used to adjudge similar incidents during League and Cup games, ridding football of mistakes caused by the frailties of the human eye. This is the argument, in any case. The reasons for introducing the TV replays and VRR to the wider game are clear enough. Today's referees receive more criticism for disputed offside and penalty decisions than for any other offence. Yet, although TV is able to expose refereeing frailties, match officials cannot be held accountable, or punished, in any way by the authorities. TV often shows referees to have been wrong, but as yet the irrefutable evidence it provides is being ignored, save for the odd reversal of a red card decision. It is argued that by providing a fourth official – seated in the stand – with a TV monitor and a Sky subscription, many unsightly post-match confrontations and back page exposés could be avoided. In principle the video replay might work like this: a referee sees a player fouled around the box, but is unseen, and so does not feel sufficiently confident to award either a penalty or a foul. He therefore gives a signal to the fourth official indicating that he wishes the incident to be looked at again. The third official watches a replay of the incident on TV and gives his verdict. Simple – according to the nemesis of the British referee, Danny Baker. "Everyone is up to speed with videotape and its findings," he insists. "If the referee gives a decision that a ball has crossed the line and 20,000 voices scream that they are going to tear the ground apart based on that decision, he only has to halt play, and, via a radio mike, ask for the help. Then after 10 seconds if it is announced that the ball really didn't cross the line, people will buy that. They may swear and groan but they know that, when they themselves see it on TV later, it will be real."

There are two problems here. Firstly, the referee cannot be allowed to be intimidated into calling for help merely because the supporters or players don't like his decision, otherwise the game would descend into farce; and secondly, it must be assumed that the referee believes in good faith that he is making the right decision in the first place. Why, therefore, should he call for the fourth official? And what would happen if players were allowed to influence the appeal system? Surely it would only result in an even greater torrent of protest from the team against whom the appeal had been made.

The FA's decision to use a limited replay facility in 1999 to adjudge whether the ball has crossed the goalline or not seems a sensibly cautious dip of the toe in what could be turbulent waters. As FA spokesman Steve Double asks, where do you draw the line? "TV could help to determine whether a ball has crossed the line or not. But we wouldn't want it for anything else. Replays would slow the game down too much. Where would it stop? Would we want replays for offside decisions, handballs, throw-ins, fouls?" The constant breaks in play that would result from regular use of TV replays cause the former FIFA referee John Lloyd particular concern. "How long would you leave the crowd waiting? It's all right in cricket and Rugby League where there are natural breaks but football is a continuous game."

The traditionalists argue that TV technology is against the spirit of the game. "Part of football's attraction is that it is a simple game, played to the same rules throughout the world," says FA chief executive Graham Kelly, somewhat naively. FIFA has rejected giving referees TV replays twice in the last three years. According to Sepp Blatter, "We are anxious television does not take over the game by controlling the referee." His anxiety is shared by referees, many of whom have misgivings regarding electronic devices because they fear change will eventually result in their extinction. "I didn't become a referee to be replaced by a machine," said the Premiership's arch pessimist Mike Reed.

It seems highly unlikely, however, that Reed, or any other referee, will ever be replaced by machines. But mistrust of the unknown – a perennial fear amongst football's bureaucrats – risks standing in the way of progress if indeed that is what technology represents. TV replays would help the referee – not hinder him, some argue. And there seems to be few alternative remedies to the unceasing criticism of referees.

FIFA's Director of Communications Keith Cooper believes that if players stopped trying to cheat referees there would be little need for such technology. While this may apply in regard to actions like diving and shirt-pulling it doesn't take into account the full diversity and variety of the game. It would be a resourceful FIFA official indeed that could find a player who has been guilty of deliberately 'cheating' the offside ruling. Contentious offside decisions could arguably become a thing of the past with the TV replay. It has already been proven – by research conducted in Spain – that linesmen's eyes are scientifically incapable of keeping up with the split second movements of attacking players.

The traditionalists also argue that errors of judgement, however badly they might effect the game and its officials' confidence, generally don't serve to benefit one team over another. "Every side in the world has a hard luck story involving a referee," says one FA official. "But these decisions level out in the end. That's the game. If we change to suit TV we might ruin it forever." To deny referees the opportunity of an eagle-eyed and impartial electronic companion is, some say, to deny football the opportunity to rid itself of unsightly confrontation. However, the argument for preserving football in its 'natural' form remains strong.

How many of the referees' harshest critics – the fans – would really be happy to ditch the 'Bastard in the Black' chants for a system of unequivocal, fair-minded equality all round. To many it would deprive them of an integral and fundamental aspect of their afternoon's entertainment. The idea that fans would merely shrug 'fair enough' after video evidence was used to award a disputed goal against their team is somewhat improbable. And anyway, it's not much fun hurling obscenities at a camera.

Bristol City supporter Michael Baker is surely in the minority when he says, "Personally I would love to see replays in use. And I'm sure most referees would welcome some back up on the pitch. It would benefit fans and officials, and probably take a lot of the animosity out of the game. That has to be a good thing."

The TV replay until recently seemed on football's distant horizon yet is now soon to become reality. But what about the highly advanced 'virtual pitch'? A prototype for the football field of the future has already been drawn up by pioneers who believe the financial demands of the game will soon be such that there will be no room for any human error. The system utilises an under-pitch grid which is able to track players exact locations by a chip located in their boots, and hence confirm offside infringements. A series of electronic fields would enable linesmen and referees to tell immediately if the ball had gone out of play or crossed the line. The referee would wear a mini 'head-up' display (a little like a scientific monocle) to view replays, and carry an electronic notepad and a buzzer. His watch would be linked to an electronic stadium clock. It's football Jim, but not as we know it.

Experiments are already taking place with buzzers on linesmen's flags, and Crystal Palace are even experimenting with a form of tagging. Presumably they could do with keeping a better eye on their players. Sci-fi football, however, is a long way from becoming reality.

That the introduction of even TV replays will drastically alter the game is debatable. The question of just how unsure an official has to be before he calls in the electronic arbiters is significant. Cricket has certainly witnessed its fair share of important decisions which have later been exposed as mistakes through video evidence. However, the umpire clearly felt sufficiently secure in his call at the time to make no use of the video back-up facilities afforded to him. The point is that referees – being human – would be unlikely to call for replays on a regular basis. Firstly, they mostly believe they are right anyway. Secondly, it would represent an admission of error or inability, and referees, on the whole, are rarely seen to admit their mistakes – on the pitch at least. And thirdly, it would seriously undermine the referee's authority in the beady eyes of the match observer, and therefore place him in a compromising situation with the authorities. The alternative would be for *players* to appeal for a third opinion; but down that path lies certain chaos. Even in cricket, tennis and rugby technology is used only sparingly. And in football it will be used sparingly too. Why? Because ultimately, football is a human game, with human interaction. Control is essential in the game, and although he has seen some ups and downs over the last hundred years, the referee is the one person humanly capable of exerting it. In the end, someone has to make the decisions. Someone has to be there to talk, cajole and protect. Someone has to take a deep breath, lower his eyes and point to the spot in the last minute of a blood and guts local derby. And if – or when – every inch of the pitch is being scutinised by digital tracking and hyper-sensitive micro cameras, someone, ultimately, has to decide whether or not to call on all that technology. And really, who else would – could – do that but the referee?

The managers don't trust him, the players don't like him, many fans claim to 'hate' him. Yet most would shed a tear if the man in black threw down his whistle, packed up his cards and disappeared down the tunnel never to emerge again.

'AN ABSOLUTE DISGRACE'

a refereeing diary 1997/98

AUGUST 13 1997
"I'm a referee that's black, not a black referee but I'm always aware of my culture and identity." So says Uriah Rennie, a leisure centre manager from Sheffield, who became the first black referee to officiate in the Premiership. Rennie's top flight baptism doesn't go too smoothly. He is forced to abandon the Derby-Wimbledon match because of floodlight failure at the Rams new ground, Pride Park.

AUGUST 23 1997
Referee Phil Richards is attacked by a supporter during the Third Division match between Notts County and Lincoln at Meadow Lane. Meanwhile, at Selhurst Park Joe Kinnear gets straight to the point. "The linesman was a waste of space. We were too quick and too smart for him," he fumes after a dubious offside call lets Sheffield Wednesday's Paulo Di Canio in for an equaliser.

AUGUST 27 1997
Ian Wright and the Leicester Captain Steve Walsh are reported to the FA by referee Graham Barber for "adopting an aggressive attitude towards each other," during a post-match fracas at Filbert Street. Martin O'Neill, for one, is perplexed by the ruling. "What does 'aggressive behaviour' mean anyway?" he pipes, "When there has been no physical contact. I've never heard of that before

and I've been in the game 25 years. Will we now have to ban the Aussies for sledging?" he adds, cryptically. Wright, who had been substituted in the 3-3 draw, ran 40 yards to join in a posse of players protesting at the six minutes added on by Barber, which allowed Leicester enough time to equalise.

SEPTEMBER 5 1997

Only a month gone but Arsene Wenger is already calling for professional referees. "They need more time to prepare for matches without having to think about work or business commitments ...the sooner they get properly paid for the tough job they do, the better for them and the game in general." Not satisfied with one fully paid ref, Wenger also suggests the game have a ref for each half of the pitch. Clearly, he's a glutton for punishment.

SEPTEMBER 19 1997

Ian Wright is cleared of misconduct for the Leicester incident, but Arsenal's assistant manager Pat Rice is fined £500 after admitting to making unseemly comments to referee Graham Barber after the same game.

SEPTEMBER 20 1997

Manchester United's Gary Pallister receives the first red card of a distinguished career and Bolton's Nathan Blake walks too following a fairly minor altercation at The Reebok Stadium. Bolton players are quick to rush to the defence of Pallister, the less culpable of the red-carded pair. "It was a derby and maybe the ref [Paul Durkin] was trying to stamp out trouble before it got out of hand," says John McGinlay, "But it was just a bit of pushing and shoving really. To get a three match ban for that is crazy." The red faced Durkin sneaks out of the ground under a police escort without taking the opportunity to comment on the incident.

Elsewhere Everton's third goal – a disputed penalty – in a 4-2 home win against Barnsley, gets Danny Wilson hot under the collar. "Never in a million years was that a penalty," he seethes. "I told [the referee] that the player dived and he just said that my players had been doing that all afternoon."

SEPTEMBER 27 1997
Dion Dublin is sent off for 'elbowing' Colin Hendry during Coventry's 0-0 draw at Blackburn. TV evidence later shows that no contact was made – Dublin's outstretched arm missing the bridge of Hendry's nose by a good few inches. "It was a joke decision," moans Dublin as he is led away. "I never touched him." His manager Gordon Strachan calls for the FA and the referee Peter Jones to study video footage in the hope that the red will be expunged.

SEPTEMBER 30 1997
Leicester manager Martin O'Neill may be forced to face a UEFA enquiry after comments made about French referee Remi Harrel. O'Neill is incensed by the performance of the official during his team's UEFA Cup defeat at home to Atletico Madrid. The referee sends off Gary Parker for taking a free-kick before the whistle, for a second bookable offence, and turns down three Leicester penalty appeals. "I felt we couldn't win," says O'Neill. "There are shades of 1984 and Anderlecht and all that type of stuff [the Belgian team recently admitted to bribing the referee during the UEFA Cup defeat of Nottingham Forest]. You do feel, 'What's the point [of appealing]?' But then you think there is a point: to prevent it happening again. What happened was absolutely disgusting."

OCTOBER 7 1997
The German FA order a match to be replayed, ruling that the goal scored by Sean Dundee to give Karlsruhen a 2-2 draw against Munich 1860, crossed the line after the ref had blown for full-time.

OCTOBER 18 1997
Elland Road. David Elleray is forced to change into a borrowed blue Leeds United t-shirt when players complain that his traditional black kit clashed with Newcastle's navy blue away strip.

OCTOBER 26 1997
Wenger is at it again. This time he complains that referees are booking Arsenal's star player Dennis Bergkamp because they want his name as a trophy. Paul Durkin is the day's target, following a 0-0 draw with Aston Villa, in which high drama was the order of the day. The French midfielder Emmanuel Petit is sent off for allegedly shoving Durkin in the chest with both hands, and four other Arsenal players are booked for various acts of indiscipline. The Petit incident causes a furore which lasts for weeks, sparked by Wenger's insistence of his player's innocence. "Petit did not run to the referee to push him," he insists, "It was my impression that he was just holding out his hands to stop them colliding. We will appeal about the decision."

OCTOBER 28 1997
Hartson's tirade against Mike Reed is lapped up by the tabloids. Hartson, who had previously called the referee "a shithouse", is fined for his comments after defeat at Leicester. The Welsh striker labels Reed a "homer" and a "disgrace"; Reed, in turn, threatens to sue, before relenting. "I looked at the video later and felt I had a good game," he remarked somewhat phlegmatically.

Hartson's team-mates aren't so enamoured. "We felt the referee was awful," says Hammers' defender David Unsworth.

Leeds go down 1-0 away to Wimbledon, and George Graham finds fault with the referee – Graham Barber on this occasion – for giving a penalty after David Hopkin's penalty box challenge on Michael Hughes. "I think the player dived and the referee fell for it," he growls. Joe Kinnear – for once – applauds the ref's decision. "I thought he was in a perfect position to see the penalty." Well he would, wouldn't he?

NOVEMBER 8 1997

The referee's traditional winter of discontent has well and truly arrived. Several curious decisions, not least the six bookings and one sending-off, mar Crystal Palace's 1-1 draw with Aston Villa and make Jeff Winter a wholly unpopular man. Palace boss Steve Coppell openly criticises the official's handling of the game. "When a referee becomes a bigger personality than the players on the pitch...then questions have to be asked...He was a bit too uptight about everything. He should chill out." Talk about the pot and the kettle. The *Guardian*'s Neil Robinson agrees, but his question is a broader one. "Imagine what a sterile game football would be if referees really were backed up by the all-seeing eye of new technology. No ridiculous decisions, no angry managers spitting venom from the touchline and, worst of all, nothing for the supporters to get steamed up about on the long walk home," he says. "There is no doubt Winter's inadequacies added splendidly to an otherwise ordinary game...a campaign could be launched: stand up for frequently erratic referees. Suffer, in short."

NOVEMBER 19 1997

Paul Gascoigne is sent off for the first time on Scottish soil by referee John Rowbotham, and is subsequently banned for five games. The Celtic-Rangers encounter at Parkhead, in which eight players are booked, also sees Rangers manager Walter Smith, his assistant Archie Knox and striker Gordon Durie land themselves in hot water for remarks made to the referee after the game. Durie is given the equivalent of a sending off by Rowbotham for bad mouthing him in the players' tunnel. Walter Smith makes a formal complaint to the Scottish Football League about the official. "The club will be making their feelings known," he says, "We believe that the referee should not have been allowed to take the match." The match also saw missiles thrown at Gascoigne and Stuart McCall, and fueled the debate on whether video footage should be admissable as evidence.

NOVEMBER 25 1997
Emmanuel Petit receives a one match ban and a fine of £1000 for pushing ref Paul Durkin.

DECEMBER 2 1997
Second Division mayhem. Referee Ken Lynch equals a record set only 10 months ago, when he sends off five players in the Wigan v Bristol Rovers match. Rovers, down to seven men by the 71st minute, lose 3-0. On the same night, in the dying seconds of the match between Luton and Gillingham at Kenilworth Road, the referee has to contend with an 18-man brawl in which three players are booked and one sent off. Meanwhile, across the channel, Marseilles striker Fabrizio Ravanelli complains of a campaign by referees to drive him out of French football. The whinging Italian says after a game at Nantes, in which he hotly disputes almost every decision, "the referee's behaviour was not professional. Everyone saw there was a penalty, except him. Ever since I've come here the refereeing on me has been catastrophic."

DECEMBER 3 1998
The world's top-rated referee Sandor Paul is banned from officiating at European matches and the World Cup following his failure to punish Feyenoord's Paul Bosvelt for an horrific foul on Manchester United's Denis Irwin during a Champions League match in Rotterdam on 5th of the previous month. Paul failed even to book the Dutchman after he brutally stamped on Irwin's leg, leaving the defender with badly damaged knee ligaments.

DECEMBER 6 1997
Mike Reed, otherwise known as The-man-who-got-Danny-Baker-the-sack (from Six-o-Six), has obviously not heard the last from his frankly childish nemesis. "As if anyone gives a monkey's why this puffed up and easily fooled official got into football in the first place! It's isn't about you, slick! You are old-fashioned, dangerous, arrogant and in the way." Some might say the same about Baker.

DECEMBER 13 1997
The Battle of Stamford Bridge. A replay of the 1970 FA Cup final is deemed appropriate for the Billy Bremner Memorial. And the fiery, flame-haired midfielder would surely have enjoyed this one. Referee Graham Poll sends off two Leeds players and books ten other men. Leeds manager George Graham isn't impressed by Graham Poll's handling of the proceedings. "The ref was far too quick to brandish yellow cards," he says. Indeed, it's unlikely that Bremner would have taken too kindly to some of Poll's quick-draw tactics. Booking Leeds Gary Kelly in the first minute for standing too close to a corner kick hardly sent out signals of leniency. "He was not so quick in the second – because he was running out of players..." Poll though, thought he had a rather good game in the circumstances. "It could have got very nasty

...but because of my decisions, there were no serious injuries. Yellow cards should have an effect on players but this time they didn't. I have never refereed a game like it." "The referee had to do something", says Ruud Gullit.

DECEMBER 20 1997

A selection of choice cuts follow another weekend of controversy. "It was the most obvious penalty you could wish to see," fumed West Ham's Harry Redknapp about his team's failure to be awarded a spot-kick by Gerald Ashby at Blackburn. "If that's not a penalty I'll pack this job in." He doesn't of course. Swindon boss Steve McMahon is thoroughly peeved at a red card incident involving one of his players during Saturday's game with Birmingham. "I'll get into trouble for saying this [a phrase rapidly becoming every manager's favourite]...but the referee should be relegated. We played ten men against 12." Dalglish doesn't mince his words either. "You've got to look at the referee. He was the worst man on the pitch." None of these three bosses register a win on Saturday. Not that you could tell from their comments.

DECEMBER 28 1997

The festive season brings little joy for one Scottish referee. Martin Clark suffers cuts to his lips, forehead and shoulder – the result of coin-throwing – during the Scottish Third Division match between Montrose and Arbroath at Links Park. Before the game, which Montrose won 1-0, a man wearing only socks and shoes streaked across the pitch. "It was an eventful day all round," said the Montrose Chairman Mike Craig.

JANUARY 3 1998

Martin O'Neill is charged with misconduct by the FA for confronting referee Jeff Winter in the players' tunnel at the end of

Leicester' s 1-0 defeat by Everton in December. West Ham's Steve Lomas faces a similar charge after allegedly grabbing the referee Gerald Ashby in his side's defeat at Blackburn.

JANUARY 4 1998

It's Steve Dunn's turn for a critical hammering. Dunn blows for full-time in the FA Cup third-round match between Wrexham and Wimbledon just as the ball is travelling into the net following a Marcus Gayle header in the final second of the game. Joe Kinnear hands out the by now inevitable panning.

JANUARY 5 1998

The *Observer* peeks its head over the parapet to fire off a round or two at the referees at the centre of the latest controversies. "Too many top referees combine school-ma'am fussiness, scattering cards like confetti, with an inability to root out real misbehaviour... An objective report on refereeing standards and monitoring is long overdue and should be commissioned forthwith." Mike Reed is presumably one referee the newspaper would like to see given the once over. The man who loves to brandish the red does it again, sending off Leeds keeper Nigel Martyn in the last minute of a Cup match at Elland Road for a highly innocuous and accidental challenge on Oxford City's Jamie Cook. "Dangerous conduct" according to Reed. "If that was dangerous conduct," writes the *Guardian*'s David Hopps, "it will be no surprise if Paddington Bear is revealed today as a serial killer."

JANUARY 6 1998

Middlesborough's 1-0 win over Reading in the quarter final of the Coca-Cola Cup is surrounded in controversy. Boro's winner arrives four minutes into injury-time, courtesy of a disputed free-kick, given first to one team, then to the other and then as a drop ball and finally back to Boro by the clearly confused referee George Cain. When Neil Maddison eventually takes it, the Reading players – still remonstrating with the official – are caught unawares, and Criag Hignett scores. "The game was too much for the referee," says Reading boss Terry Bullivant afterwards. "The players knew full well what I'd given," counters Cain somewhat unconvincingly.

JANUARY 16 1998
The criticism of referees is quickly becoming an epidemic. Arsenal and Coventry share a physical but entertaining draw at Highfield Road, but Gordon Strachan is apoplectic at referee Stephen Lodge for a series of decisions – culminating in the dubious sending off of Paul Williams for an alleged trip on Dennis Bergkamp. Since November, when Strachan exchanged full and frank views with David Elleray at half time behind the locked door of the referee's room at Pride Park, the Coventry boss claims his team "has had nothing, nothing, absolutely nothing from referees." Today, he turns on Lodge, whom he calls "an absolute joke," or alternatively, "an absolute disgrace." After a fleeting appearance at the press conference – to condemn Lodge – Strachan leaves muttering about the possible consequences of his outburst: "The FA can come after me if they like"...They do.

JANUARY 22 1998
A Carling survey discovers that a staggering 92 per cent of football supporters think the men in the middle should be professional. Nearly 9,000 fans took part in the Internet survey which followed Coventry manager Gordon Strachan's blistering attack on Lodge.

JANUARY 29 1998
Strachan is charged by the FA after his outburst. Strachan apologises to Lodge saying "I shouldn't have said he was an absolute disgrace, but that he made some disgraceful decisions". Lodge was presumably overjoyed at Strachan's repentance.

JANUARY 30 1998
West Ham's Steve Lomas receives a one match suspension for his "misconduct" during the previous month's game with Blackburn.

JANUARY 31 1998
Linesman Edward Martin is knocked unconscious by a fan during Portsmouth's 1-1 draw with Sheffield United and taken to hospital. He later vows to continue running the line.

FEBRUARY 1 1998
Barnsley's Danny Wilson launches a venomous attack on Jeff Winter after defeat at Chelsea. "That was the worst refereeing performance I've seen all season," he barks. "I think he was throwing cards at Chelsea players at the end just to pacify us."

FEBRUARY 2 1998
Paul Durkin and Hugh Dallas are chosen to represent England and Scotland respectively in the World Cup.

FEBRUARY 4 1998
Spurs striker Les Ferdinand calls ref Gerald Ashby "an absolute disgrace" during an interview with Sky Sport after his team's defeat at home to Barnsley in the replayed FA Cup tie (3-1).

FEBRUARY 5 1998
Punishments are handed out. The FA fines Leicester City player Garry Parker £750 for foul and abusive language to a referee – but not while playing for Leicester. The incident occurred when Parker was acting as a linesman in a recent Oxfordshire Sunday League match. Leceister City manager, Martin O'Neill, doesn't get off so lightly. O'Neill is fined £2,500 for using "insulting and improper language" towards the referee Jeff Winter after Leicester' s game with Everton in December. To round off a good day's work for the FA's disciplinary committee, they fine Southampton's lippy defender Carlton Palmer £1,000 for verbally abusing referee Gerald Ashby in the FA Cup defeat at Derby. You would have thought anyone with Palmer's record of blunders might be more careful about who they choose to call a "disgrace".

FEBRUARY 8 1998
Dermot Gallagher sets himself up for a fall at Highbury by failing to send off Arsenal's Steve Bould for hauling back Vialli, through on goal. "He has to be sent off," says Ruud Gullit, in the knowledge that he was undeniably correct. "If you commit a foul like that in any country in the world it's a sending-off. But the referee wants to do it his way and this is not on. If he had given that decision in the Nou Camp he would not have been allowed to go out." Gallagher gets out of the ground alright but the FA quickly put him under house arrest. He is suspended for one game. The same day, Coventry's Gordon Strachan tells the *Times'* Oliver Holt how he really feels about the men in black. "I know there is an element of futility about criticising referees. But you either do it or you have a heart attack," Strachan insists. "I do not know what is wrong with somebody saying the standard of refereeing in this country is not very good. It is like saying the buses are bad… or British Airways charge too much. It seems that free-

dom of speech is OK unless it is with referees. Maybe I'm totally wrong, but you cannot fine me for being totally wrong." Well, no, a *Times* journalist can't Gordon.

FEBRUARY 16 1998

More griping from Wenger about the perceived persecution of Dennis Bergkamp. "We will have to buy Dennis an extra shirt", he whined. "The referees in this country are not used to man-marking and when it happens they don't know when to whistle". Referee Martin Bodenham's *laissez-faire* approach to the Arsenal-Crystal Palace FA Cup encounter – he disallowed two stonewall penalties, one for each side – doesn't impress the *Guardian*'s David Lacey either. "This was another day when Bodenham's refereeing smacked of two wise monkeys rolled into one. He heard no evil and saw no evil". Presumably the Cornish official was too busy dreaming of more pleasant ways to spend his Saturdays. He retires from the Premiership list at the end of the season.

FEBRUARY 17 1998

Andy Gray and Alex Ferguson cross swords. The referee gets caught in the middle. Gray claims visitors to Old Trafford never get penalties – "no team has had a penalty there since 1995, that's the proof," and Fergie retorts by calling the Sky presenter "anti-Man U." Gray nearly goes as far as to accuse referees of being frightened to point to the spot, in the wake of Mike Reed's blunder. "It's only natural that a referee is far more likely to react to 50,000 fans screaming for a penalty... referees are becoming more and more wary of making unpopular decisions."

FEBRUARY 23 1998

Finally, something gives. The FA ban FIFA referee Dermot Gallagher for one match following a string of unsatisfactory performances which – though they won't say as much – peaked during the Arsenal-Chelsea game in which the Banbury failed to send-off Steve Bould for a professional foul on Gianluca Vialli.

MARCH 1 1998

The cards keep coming. Rangers captain Richard Gough is red-carded during a home draw with Hearts, but vehemently disputes the decision. Bad move. Gough is later called into the referee's dressing-room and promptly shown another one. Earlier in the season Aberdeen's bad boy Dean Windass received the equivalent of three red cards in one match and was suspended for six games as a consequence.

Abroad, Swedish referee Leif Sundell, is dropped from officiating the following week's European Cup Winners Cup quarter-final between Real Betis and Chelsea after he and his two linesmen for the game were spotted enjoying the hospitality suite at the Spanish club's ground before taking their seats in the Director's box for a league match.

MARCH 9 1998

Alleged racist remarks made six days previously by Liverpool's Steve Harkness about Villa's Stan Collymore failed to be recognised by referee Graham Poll: "Stan told me on the pitch that things had been said to him. I could see he was incensed about something and asked him what was wrong. It is not in my report. If I put everything in my report that players told me was being said on the pitch, I would be writing all week." On the same day, Norwich boss Mike Walker is fuming over a controversial late penalty which hands Bury a home victory over the Canaries. "The referee was their best player. It is hard enough without having refs like that around."

'AN ABSOLUTE DISGRACE'

MARCH 14 1998
A rare moment of light relief for the beleaguered referee. At Highfield Road, a police escort is sent to fetch a set of socks from Coventry's training ground to lend to Sheffield United's players, after an assistant linesman complains of a colour clash. At Birmingham, there's little cause for laughter when a mobile phone is hurled at a linesman during the game with QPR. "You cannot condone incidents like this," says Blues boss Trevor Francis, "Why would anyone want to do it?"

MARCH 28 1998
Three players are sent off and referee Gary Willard is the victim of two attempted attacks by supporters, who also throw coins at him after Liverpool's match at Barnsley. Supporters at Goodison try to get to referee Neale Barry. Two players, one from each side, are sent off at the Bolton-Leicester match. In total, 12 players – 10 in England, 2 in Scotland – are sent off in one day's football.

MARCH 30 1998
Not the best of Monday mornings for Gary Willard, who gets it in the neck for his handling of the Barnsley-Liverpool fiasco. "This man is a menace," scowls the *Sun*'s Michael Morgan, "He must certainly shoulder the lion's share of the blame for all the aggro…he should carry a government health warning." Barnsley's Labour MP Eric Illsley joins in the refereeing witch-hunt. "Some of his decisions were appalling. He bears a large responsibility for what happened here." If these men had their way, Willard would be charged with inciting a riot. Still, it's a neat way to avoid criticising the real miscreants.

On the same day, every referee's favourite manager Joe Kinnear calls for Dermot Gallagher to be banned – again – after two controversial late goals sealed a victory for Manchester

United at Old Trafford. "He was like a muppet for them," seethes Kinnear, "His cowardly decisions did more damage to my team than the United players. Can you imagine what would have happened if he had allowed two dodgy late goals against them? There would have been a riot. He got a one match ban for his last cock-up he should be locked up after this one. I know there's a possibility that I'll get into trouble," continues the man who has already amassed £20,000 in fines for previous outbursts against the men in black, "But I'm sick and tired of these people getting away with it."

APRIL 7 1998

Tottenham striker Les Ferdinand is fined £2500 by the FA for his comments on referee Gerald Ashby's performance in the FA Cup defeat at Barnsley. "If the FA are fining me for what I said, I hope they are fining Ashby for his performance," said an irate Ferdinand.

APRIL 25 1998

End of term blues for the man in black. And a heavy workload for the SFA disciplinary committee. At Parkhead, where Celtic falter with a 0-0 draw with Hibs, the Edinburgh side's manager Alex McCleish and the Parkhead club's assistant manager Murdo McLeod are ushered to the stand by referee George Simpson after a heated verbal collision on the touchline. Elsewhere, at Tynecastle, where Rangers beat Hearts 3-0 to revive their title aspirations, a linesman is the target for an empty whisky bottle.

MAY 18 1998

World Cup ref Paul Durkin starts a week in which he takes part in the England team's training sessions at Bisham Abbey to help them prepare for FIFA's new world cup directives, particularly with the ruling on tackling from behind.

VITAL STATISTICS

the FIFA-listed 'big eight' referees

DAVID ELLERAY

Age: 44
Home: Harrow-On-The-Hill, Middlesex
Occupation: Schoolmaster
League debut: Colchester v Torquay, Div 4, 12/9/86.
Premiership debut: Liverpool v Sheffield Utd, 19/8/92
Total league games: 254
Prem. and old Div 1 games: 143
Career penalties: 52, Career sending-offs: 51
FIFA listed: Since January 1992. Elleray is currently the Premier League's longest serving FIFA referee
Biggest games: 1994 FA Cup Final (Man Utd v Chelsea); Euro 96; 1995 World Club Championship
Remembered for: Too many reasons. Dished out the fastest ever booking in a league match when he showed the yellow to Vinnie Jones after 4 seconds of a match in 1991.
Style: Prudish
Fact: Elleray collects framed pictures of his most notorious matches and hangs them outside his Harrow office.

DERMOT GALLAGHER

Age: 41
Home: Banbury, Oxon.
Occupation: Printer
League debut: Wrexham v Peterborough, Div 4, 25/8/90
Premiership debut: Spurs v Coventry , 19/8/92
Total career games: 169; (99 Prem./ old Div 1)
Career penalties: 22; Career sending-Offs: 20
FIFA listed: Since January 1994
Biggest games: 1996 FA Cup Final (Man Utd v Liverpool) – the dullest final of recent years; Euro 96.
Remembered for: That ban last year.
Style: Unpredictable
Fact: Gallagher is the only Irish referee on England's National List. During Euro 96, Gallagher was 'substituted' during the France–Bulgaria match after he seriously injured his knee. It remains the only instance of an official leaving the pitch during a top class International because of injury. Paul Durkin replaced him.

PAUL DURKIN

Age: 43
Home: Portland, Dorset
Occupation: Housing Association Officer
League debut: Torquay v Wrexham, Div 4, 15/8/87
Premiership debut: Arsenal v Sheffield Wed., 29/8/92
Total league games: 257; 134 (Prem./ old Div 1)
Penalties: 48; Sendings off: 29
FIFA listed: Since January 1994
Biggest games: France 98 – Italy v Austria (his only World Cup game); 1998 FA Cup Final (Arsenal v Newcastle); also refereed two separate European club tournament Semi-Finals 1997-8
Remembered for: Sending off Emmanuel Petit for getting too touchy; failing to spot Eric Cantona stamping on the head of a Norwich player during a 1994 Cup tie.
Style: Convivial (unless you happen to be a pony-tailed French midfielder)
Fact: Durkin's League debut fell on his birthday. Was once a big Manchester City fan – but, unsurprisingly, claims no alliegance now.

GARY WILLARD

Age: 38
Home: Worthing, W Sussex
Occupation: Financial consultant
League Debut: Walsall v Torquay, Div 4, 25/8/90
Premiership debut: Spurs v Everton, 24/8/94
Total League games: 158; 78
Penalties: 37; sendings off: 23
FIFA listed: Since January 1996
Biggest games: 1998 League Cup Semi-Final (Liverpool v Middlesborough). No Finals or top Internationals
Remembered for: The Barsnley v Liverpool fracas last season
Style: Bureacratic
Fact: Sent off eight players last season. Attributes many of his cautions to "dangerous play".

GRAHAM BARBER

Age: 40
Home: Pyrford, Surrey
Occupation: Sales manager
League debut: Colchester v Torquay, Div 4, 13/8/94
Premiership debut: Nottingham Forest v Sunderland, 21/8/96
Total League games: 110; 44
Penalties: 18; sendings off: 21
FIFA listed: Since January 1998
Biggest games: League Cup quarter Final last year; reserve referee for 1998 FA Cup Final
Remembered for: The 3-3 draw between Arsenal and Leicester. Barber added on 6 minutes of injury time and was nearly lynched at the end of the game. First referee to report two players (Ian Wright and Steve Walsh) for 'adopting an aggressive attitude' toward each other. Produced 25 yellow cards in his first four Premiership games.
Style: Zealous
Fact: It took the prodigious Barber only three and a half years and 100 League games to become a FIFA official.

STEVE DUNN

Age: 40
Home: Bristol
Occupation: Newsagent
League debut: Cardiff v Darlington, Div 4 15/8/92
Premiership debut: Spurs v Aston Villa, 23/8/95
Total League games: 147; 59
Penalties: 18; sendings off: 10
FIFA listed: Since January 1997
Biggest games: An FA Cup quarter Final in 1997-8 and Newcastle's famous 5-0 win over Man Utd in October 1996.
Remembered for: Following in the footsteps of Clive Thomas by blowing as Wimbledon were in the process of scoring against Wrexham in last season's Cup.
Style: Mischevious
Fact: Dunn writes a weekly column called Come On Ref in the *Bristol Evening Post*'s results paper, The Green 'Un.

GRAHAM POLL

Age: 35
Home: Tring, Herts.
Occupation: General Sales manager
League debut: Rotherham v Burnley, Div 4, 17/8/91
Prem debut: Southampton v Sheffield Utd, 2/10/93
Total League games: 156; 98
Penalties: 23; sendings off: 32
FIFA listed: Since January 1996
Biggest games: 1998-9 Charity Sheild (Man Utd v Arsenal)
Remembered for: A fondness for cards. Season 97/98 there was the Battle of Stamford Bridge; in 1994 there was the match between Southampton and Wimbledon in which Poll sent off one player and cautioned 10. Led the red card chart (with 10) season 97/98. Being the first referee to send off Michael Owen in a Premiership match – last season at Old Trafford.
Style: Stoical
Oddities: In 1986 he became the youngest ever League linesman at 23; second youngest ever League referee when he was promoted, aged 28, in 1991. Claims his top International game was Aberbajzan v Finland.

PETER JONES

Age: 44
Home: Loughborough
Occupation: Runs his own building firm
League debut: Scunthorpe v Hereford, Div 4 27/8/88
Premiership debut: QPR v Sheffield Wed. 24/8/94
Total League games: 212; 85
Penalties: 19; sendings-off: 18
FIFA listed: since beginning of season 1996/7
Biggest games: 1997-8 League Cup Final (Chelsea v Middlesborough).
Remembered for: Booking 9 players during a League game between Southampton and QPR in April 1995, and getting slaughtered in the press as a result.
Style: A lot less interventionist since 1995

INFORMATION ON THE REST OF THE CURRENT CROP OF PREMIERSHIP REFEREES IS GIVEN IN A TABLE OPPOSITE:

NAME	AGE	HOME	OCCUPATION	LEAGUE DEBUT	PREMIERSHIP DEBUT	CAREER GAMES League/Prem.	PENALTIES/ DISMISSALS
Paul Alcock	44	Halstead	Shopping centre manager	Cambridge v Grimsby Div 4, 28/8/95	Coventry v Man City 23/8/95	199/45	37; 29
Neale Barry	40	Scunthorpe	Planner at British Steel	Bury v Northampton Div 4, 14/8/93	Crystal Palace v Barnsley 12/8/97	148/20	31; 29
Robert Harris	41	Oxford	Car sales	Hereford v Doncaster Div 3, 13/8/94	Charlton v Southampton 22/8/98	126/new97-98	31; 22
Stephan Lodge	45	Barnsley	Local government officer	Wrexham v Hartlepool Div 4, 22/8/87	M'boro v Man City 19/8/92	255/121	29; 24
Keith Burge	47	Tonypandy	Executive officer in civil service	Exeter v Orient Div 4, 23/8/86	Wimbledon v Arsenal 5/9/92	260/121	35; 20
Mike Reed	47	Birmingham	Area supervisor	Wrexham v Colchester Div 4, 24/8/85	Notts Forest v Liverpool 16/8/92	333/170	77; 36
Uriah Rennie	38	Sheffield	Leisure centre manager	Darlington v Preston Div 3, 13/8/94	Leeds v Crystal Palace 23/8/97	117/19	15; 24
Mike Riley	33	Leeds	Accountant	Scarborough v Barnet Div 3, 20/8/94	Leicester v Southampton 21/8/96	93/40	9; 13
Alan Wilkie	47	Chester-Le-Street	British Telecom	Mansfield v Northampton Div 3, 27/8/88	Leeds v Chelsea 24/3/93	205/98	42; 36
Jeff Winter	43	Stockton-on-Tees	Bank manager	Carlisle v Walsall Div 3, 15/8/92	Notts Forest v Chelsea 23/8/95	140/59	21; 21
RETIRED AT THE END OF 1997-8 SEASON							
Gerald Ashby	49	Worcester	Office job	Crewe v Southend Div 4, 17/8/92	Leeds v Wimbledon 15/8/92	318/143	64; 35
Martin Bodenham	48	East Looe	Guest house owner	Bournemouth v Crewe	Manchester City v QPR	400/184	31; 28

MORE STATISTICS

The first table (opposite) is the FA's statistical breakdown of one referee's disciplinary record (Paul Durkin, picked at random) for the 1997/8 season. It has never been published in full before. It is one of 19 such tables (the sheer volume makes it impossible to print them all here) that, together, form a complete record of every Premiership referee's actions during a season. Each table lists every player booked, sent off or reported by the 19 top flight refs, and states the infringement which necessitated each action.

The most revealing aspect of the lists are these 'statements' – the real reason given for each caution or dismissal (that is, the particular clause of Law 12 under which all players are disciplined). Most of these 'statements', which are standardised phrases, are obvious and non-controversial: foul tackle, time wasting, tripping, shirt pulling, striking an opponent, pushing an opponent, deliberate obstruction, encroaching on a free kick, violent conduct, dangerous play, deliberate obstruction, deliberate handball. But a number are more nebulous and potentially open to interpretation: showing dissent by action, showing dissent by word, persistent infringement of the laws of the game, adopting an aggressive attitude and unsporting behaviour. The ambiguous rulings all concern dissent and gamesmanship and potentially offer a window of opportunity to a showman ref to administer justice in less orthodox ways.

Of course, even when penalising a player for a seemingly obvious infringement, the referee can still get it wrong. But this at least is merely a *bona fide* error of judgement. With the more intangible infringements it is harder to account for the precise motive of the referee. This is the where we enter the twilight zone of individual interpretations of the Law issued from the hip for indeterminate reasons. Terms like "persistent infringement…", for example, bring to mind the offences listed by the racist policeman in the *Not the Nine O'Clock News* sketch, who would arrest a black man for just about anything he could, including "walking on the cracks in the pavement" and "wearing a loud tie in built up area".

What is beyond the pale as far as player verbals are concerned? "Dissent by word" is a cautionable offence, while "foul and abusive language" is a sending-off offence. But what about the grey area in between? The minute of the law governing the disciplinary powers of the referee (law 12) hardly makes for a riveting reading. But the information each clause conveys can provide an insight into the personalities and priorities of England's top referees. These caution 'statements' allow us to differentiate between the sticklers – those who rigidly enforce the letter of the law; and the 'performers' – those referees who throw cards like confetti, often for seemingly petty infringements.

Using the statistics, we can separate each referee's total number of cautions into two groups: one, ambiguous (performer) and two, non-ambiguous (stickler) lines to offer up some surprising insights. During season 97/98 Uriah Rennie issued 30 per cent of his Premiership cautions for 'ambiguous' reasons (with Graham Barber and Jeff Winter in close proximity). While the most 'non-ambiguous' Premiership cautioner was, perhaps surprisingly, David Elleray issuing only nine per cent of his cards for these more nebulous offences (with Graham Poll and Martin Bodenham not far behind).

One bizarre anomaly was the caution statements offered by Gary Willard, top of the league table for carding (p 238). Over a third of his total cautions are listed as being issued for "dangerous play". Every other referee issued only a couple for this offence all season. Strange?

The stats could, no doubt, throw up other interesting nuggets when put under the right scrutiny. For instance, last season Paul Alcock refereed three matches involving Coventry; and three involving Crystal Palace. He booked eleven of Strachan's men but only one from Palace. These figures could suggest one or a combination of three things: one, the Coventry games – and players – were substantially more heated than the Palace matches; two, Alcock had a rush of blood during his encounters with Coventry; three – Alcock is Gordon Strachan's old headmaster. Or maybe more simply, like Arsenal last year, Coventry struggled with disciplinary problems.

PAUL DURKIN'S PREMIERSHIP VITAL STATISTICS, SEASON 1997/8

09/Aug	BURROWS, D	Coventry	Chelsea	C	Unsporting tackle	4
09/Aug	HUCKERSBY, D	Coventry	Chelsea	C	A foul tackle	4
09/Aug	HUGHES, M	Chelsea	Coventry	C	Unsporting Behaviour	4
09/Aug	LEBOEUF, F	Chelsea	Coventry	C	Showing dissent by action	4
09/Aug	LIGHTHOUSE, K	Coventry	Chelsea	C	A foul tackle	4
09/Aug	SINCLAIR, F	Chelsea	Coventry	R	Charge under FA rule 26	0
09/Aug	WILLIAMS, P	Coventry	Chelsea	C	Pers:Infr:The Laws of the game	4
09/Aug	WISE, D	Chelsea	Coventry	C	A foul tackle	4
13/Aug	CARBONE, B	Sheff W	Leeds U	C	Unsporting behaviour	4
13/Aug	DI CANIO, P	Sheff W	Leeds U	C	Adopting an aggressive attitude	4
13/Aug	HOPKIN, D	Leeds U	Sheff W	C	Adopting an aggressive attitude	4
13/Aug	KELLY, G	Leeds U	Sheff W	C	Adopting an aggressive attitude	4
13/Aug	MOLENAAR, R	Leeds U	Sheff W	C	A foul tackle	4
13/Aug	STEFANOVIC, D	Sheff W	Leeds U	C	A foul tackle	4
30/Aug	APPLEBY, M	Barnsley	Derby Co	C	A foul tackle	4
30/Aug	DAILLY, C	Derby Co	Barnsley	C	A foul tackle	4
30/Aug	ERANIO, S	Derby Co	Barnsley	C	A foul tackle	4
30/Aug	LAURSEN, J	Derby Co	Barnsley	C	Deliberate obstruction	4
30/Aug	SHERIDAN, D	Barnsley	Derby Co	C	A foul tackle	4
20/Sept	BECKHAM, D	Man U	Bolton W	C	A foul tackle	4
20/Sept	BERGSSON, G	Bolton W	Man U	C	A foul tackle	4
20/Sept	BLAKE, N	Bolton W	Man U	S	Striking an opponent	12
20/Sept	COLE, A	Man U	Bolton W	C	A foul tackle	4
20/Sept	FRANDSEN, P	Bolton W	Man U	C	A foul tackle	4
20/Sept	IRWIN, D	Man U	Bolton W	C	A foul tackle	4
20/Sept	NEVILLE, P	Man U	Bolton W	C	Showing dissent by action	4
20/Sept	PALLISTER, G	Man U	Bolton W	C	Adopting an aggressive attitude	4
27/Sept	GINOLA, D	Tottenham	Wimbledon	C	Adopting an aggresive attitude	4
04/Oct	CARBONE, B	Sheff W	Everton	C	A foul tackle	4
04/Oct	DI CANIO, P	Sheff W	Everton	C	A foul tackle	4
04/Oct	GERRARD, P	Everton	Sheff W	C	Showing dissent by action	4
04/Oct	THOMAS, T	Everton	Sheff W	C	A foul tackle	4
26/Oct	BOULD, S	Arsenal	Aston Villa	C	A foul tackle	4
26/Oct	PETIT, E	Arsenal	Aston Villa	S	Violent conduct	12
26/Oct	SEAMAN, D	Arsenal	Aston Villa	C	Deliberate handball	4
26/Oct	SOUTHGATE, G	Aston Villa	Arsenal	C	Shirt pulling	4
26/Oct	VIEIRA, P	Arsenal	Aston Villa	C	Deliberate handball	4
08/Nov	ALBERT, P	Newcastle	Coventry	C	A foul tackle	4

08/Nov	HALL, M	Coventry	Newcastle	C	A foul tackle	4
08/Nov	WILLIAMS, P	Coventry	Newcastle	C	A foul tackle	4
22/Nov	HUGHES, C	Wimbledon	Man U	C	A foul tackle	4
22/Nov	PERRY, C	Wimbledon	Man U	C	Deliberate obstruction	4
22/Nov	SCHOLES, P	Man U	Wimbledon	C	A foul tackle	4
24/Nov	EDWORTHY, M	Crystal P	Tottenham	C	A foul tackle	4
24/Nov	VEART, T	Crystal P	Tottenham	C	A foul tackle	4
26/Nov	PETIT, E	Arsenal	Aston Villa	R	Charge under FA rule 26	0
06/Dec	FARRELLY, G	Everton	Leeds U	C	A foul tackle	4
06/Dec	HINCHCLIFFE, A	Everton	Leeds U	C	Shirt pulling	4
06/Dec	RADEHE, L	Leeds U	Everton	C	A foul tackle	4
06/Dec	SPEED, G	Everton	Leeds U	C	A foul tackle	4
15/Dec	COLE, A	Man U	Aston Villa	C	Kicked ball away at free kick	4
15/Dec	GRAYSON, S	Aston Villa	Man U	C	A foul tackle	4
15/Dec	MILOSEVIC, S	Aston Villa	ManU	C	A foul tackle	4
28/Dec	THATCHER, B	Wimbledon	West Ham	S	Violent conduct – elbowing	12
31/Jan	HENDRY, C	Blackburn R	Liverpool	C	A foul tackle	4
21/Feb	DI MATTEO, R	Chelsea	Leicester C	C	A foul tackle	4
21/Feb	HUGHES, M	Chelsea	Leicester C	C	Showing dissent by word	4
21/Feb	IZZET, M	Leicester C	Chelsea	C	Kicked ball away at free kick	4
21/Feb	LENNON, N	Leicester C	Chelsea	C	Showing dissent by action	4
21/Feb	WISE, D	Chelsea	Leicester C	C	A foul tackle	4
07/Mar	RIBEIRO, B	Leeds U	Wolves	C	A foul tackle	4
11/Apr	BERTI, N	Tottenham	Chelsea	C	A foul tackle	4
18/Apr	LOMAS, S	West Ham	Blackburn R	C	Time wasting – delaying restart	4
18/Apr	MCKINLAY, W	Blackburn R	West Ham	C	Shirt pulling	4
18/Apr	SUTTON, S	Blackburn R	West Ham	C	Showing dissent by word	4
10/May	MAY, D	Man U	Barnsley	C	A foul tackle	4
10/May	SHERIDAN, D	Barnsley	Man U	C	A foul tackle	4

62 Cautions 3 Sendings off 2 Reports 67 Offences Total points: 284

The League Table of Premiership Referee Performances, Season 1997/8

	Games	Yellow Cards	Red Cards	Fouls	Handballs	Offsides	Points	Average/game
Willard	21	93	8	637	19	139	1122	53.4
Reed	19	84	2	543	33	169	1009	53.1
Poll	22	86	10	532	28	168	1046	47.5
Barber	22	90	7	484	24	147	967	43.9
Dunn	16	52	2	389	14	127	698	43.6
Elleray	19	64	5	463	22	122	829	43.6
Rennie	19	79	5	400	21	128	816	42.9
Riley	20	67	4	448	34	150	857	42.8
Winter	20	79	2	425	24	150	848	42.4
Jones	21	57	2	518	28	161	890	42.3
Barry	20	68	2	467	18	140	837	41.8
Burge	19	48	4	452	20	149	789	41.5
Durkin	19	61	4	404	17	154	782	41.1
Ashby	19	56	2	400	23	158	755	39.7
Lodge	21	54	3	458	20	162	820	39
Gallacher	19	50	3	366	15	137	686	36.1
Alcock	20	59	1	360	19	146	708	35.4
Wilkie	23	73	2	398	18	160	807	35
Bodenham	21	65	1	310	11	155	677	32.2

Data supplied by Carling Opta

BROUGHT TO BOOK

early codes for the game of football

CAMBRIDGE 1848

1. This Club shall be called University Foot Ball Club.
2. At the commencement of play, the ball shall be kicked off from the middle of the ground; after every goal there shall be a kick-off in the same way or manner.
3. After a goal, the losing side shall kick off; the sides changing goals unless a previous arrangement be made to the contrary.
4. The ball is out when it has passed the line of the flag-post on either side of the ground, in which case it shall be thrown in straight.
5. The ball is "behind" when it has passed the goal on either side of it.
6. When the ball is behind, it shall be brought forward at the place where it left the ground not more than ten paces, and kicked off.
7. Goal is when the ball is kicked through the flag-posts and under the string.
8. When a player catches the ball directly from the foot, he may kick it as he can without running with it. In no other case may the ball be touched with the hands, except to stop it.
9. If the ball has passed a player and has come from the direction of his own goal, he may not touch it till the other side have kicked it, unless there are more than three of the other side before him. No player is allowed to loiter between the ball and the adversaries' goal.
10. In no case is holding a player, pushing with the hands or tripping up allowed. Any player may prevent another from getting to the ball by any means consistent with this rule.
11. Every match shall be decided by a majority of goals.

SHEFFIELD 1857

1. The kick from the middle must be a place kick.
2. Kick Out must not be more than 25 yards out of goal.
3. Fair Catch is a catch from any player provided the ball has not touched the ground or has not been thrown from touch and is entitled to a free-kick.
4. Charging is fair in case of a place kick (with the exception of a kick off as

soon as a player offers to kick) but he may always draw back unless he has actually touched the ball with his foot.
5. Pushing with the hands is allowed but no hacking or tripping up is fair under any circumstances whatever.
6. No player may be held or pulled over.
7. It is not lawful to take the ball off the ground (except in touch) for any purpose whatever.
8. The ball may be pushed or hit with the hand, but holding the ball except in the case of a free kick is altogether disallowed.
9. A goal must be kicked but not from touch nor by a free kick from a catch.
10. A ball in touch is dead, consequently the side that touches it down must bring it to the edge of the touch it straight out from touch.
11. Each player must provide himself with a red and dark blue, flannel cap, one colour to be worn by each side.

UPPINGHAM SCHOOL 1862
1. A goal is scored whenever the ball is forced through the goal and under the bar, except it be thrown by the hand.
2. Hands may be used only to stop a ball and place it on ground before the feet.
3. Kicks must be aimed only at the ball.
4. A player may not kick the ball whilst in the air.
5. No tripping up or heel kicking allowed.
6. Whenever a ball is kicked beyond the side flags, it must be returned by the player who kicked it, from the spot it passed the flag-line in a straight line towards the middle of the ground.
7. When a ball is kicked behind the line of goal, it shall be kicked off from that line by one of the side whose goal it is.
8. No player may stand within six paces of the kicker when he is kicking off.
9. A player is out of play immediately he is in front of the ball and must return behind the ball as soon as possible. If the ball is kicked by his own side past a player, he may not touch it, or advance, until one of the other side has first kicked it, or one of his own side, having followed it up, has been able, when in front of him, to kick it.
10. No charging is allowed when a player is out of play – i.e. immediately the ball is behind him.

THE FOOTBALL ASSOCIATION 1863
1. The maximum length of the ground shall be 200 yards, the maximum breadth shall be 100 yards, the length and breadth shall be marked off with flags; and the goal shall be defined by two upright posts, eight yards apart, without any tape or bar across them.

2. A toss for goals shall take place, and the game shall be commenced by a place kick from the centre of the ground by the side losing the toss for goals; the other side shall not approach within 10 yards of the ball until it is kicked off.
3. After a goal is won, the losing side shall be entitled to kick off, and the two sides shall change goals after each goal won.
4. A goal shall be won when the ball passes between the goal-posts or over the space between the goal posts (at whatever height), not being thrown, knocked on, or carried.
5. When the ball is in touch, the first player who touches it shall throw it from the point on the boundary line where it left the ground in a direction at right angles with the boundary line, and the ball shall not be in play until it has touched the ground.
6. When a player has kicked the ball, any one of the same side who is nearer to the opponent's goal line is out of play and may not touch the ball himself, nor in any way whatever prevent any other player from doing so, until he is in play; but no player is out of play when the ball is kicked off from behind the goal line.
7. In case the ball goes behind the goal line, if a player on the side to whom the goal belongs first touches the ball, one of his side shall be entitled to a free kick from the goal line at the point opposite the place where the ball shall be touched. If a player of the opposite side first touches the ball, one of his side shall be entitled to a free kick at the goal only from a point 15 yards outside the goal line, opposite the place where the ball is touched, the opposing side standing within their goal line until he has had his kick.
8. If a player makes a fair catch, he shall be entitled to a free kick, providing he claims it by making a mark with his heel at once; and in order to take such a kick he may go back as far as he pleases, and no player on the opposite side shall advance beyond his mark until he has kicked.
9. No player shall run with the ball.
10. Neither tripping nor hacking shall be allowed, and no player shall use his hands to hold or push his adversary.
11. A player shall not be allowed to throw the ball or pass it to another with his hands.
12. No player shall be allowed to take the ball from the ground with his hands under any pretext whatever while it is in play.
13. No player shall be allowed to wear projecting nails, iron plates, or gutta percha on the soles or heels of his shoes.

WHO REFS THE REFS

the assessment system

The assessment system came into force in 1970. Referees were largely in favour of it because, previously, the practice was simply for club officials to mark the referee out of ten and this could obviously produce biased marking depending on the result of the match. Generally assessors (only Premiership markers are given the title 'observer', though they carry out the same duties) are experienced ex-referees. In the past, however, referees occasionally complained upon discovering that men who had never refereed in the football league were sometimes chosen to 'assess' them.

In the early days, there were a ludicrous number of criteria (30 in all) for judging referees – assessors were asked to tick alongside trifling comments such as 'Your whistle should be blown harder' or 'Smarten up your appearance'. In 1972, the Football League brought the categories down to six: application of laws and control; positioning and fitness; advantage, stoppages and signals; co-operation with linesmen; general remarks; summing up.

The current system is for observers to report on every Premiership match and assessors to 'mark' one in three Football League games. Referees performances are divided into six sections: Personality; Attitude and perception; Discipline control; Tactical attitude; Physical condition; Interpretation of laws. A mark out of ten is given and general observation made. Premiership referees receive a copy of the report and a match video by the Thursday after a game.

Officials of both clubs (secretary and manager) also assess referees, but are not asked to give marks out of ten.

A REFEREEING CHRONOLOGY

the major changes and innovations

c.1847 – Umpires known to be enlisted for matches
1848 – Cambridge Rules drawn up
c.1849 – Referees known to be enlisted for matches
1857 – Sheffield Rules
1862 – Uppingham rules
1863 – FA formed
1866 – Tape or string used for first time as 'crossbar'. 31 March – Alcock first player ruled offside in FA match
1869 – Goal kicks introduced
1870 – Goalkeepers introduced
1872 – Circumference of ball fixed. Corner kicks introduced; first England v Scotland international (0-0, Partick)
1874 – Shinguards introduced; cross-bars replace tape and stick
1877 – Game limited to 90 minutes
1878 – First use of whistle (allegedly)
1882 – Two handed throw-in introduced
1883 – All home Associations adopt uniform rulebook
1888 – Football league formed
1890 – Goal nets used for the first time
1891 – Penalty kick introduced; suggested by the Irish FA
1891 – Referee and linesmen replace umpires
1893 – Referees Association formed
1894 – Number of official Laws reaches the modern number (17); referee allowed to give free-kicks and penalties without appeal
1896 – First Referees Chart published. Extra time introduced for replayed cup ties
1902 – Modern penalty box markings introduced, with fixed penalty spot
1937 – Semi-circle added to penalty box markings to allow penalty taker more room for his run up
1904 – Formation of FIFA

1905 – Goalkeeper ordered to stay on his line for penalty kick
1912 – Goalkeeper not allowed to handle ball outside penalty area
1913 – Opposing players to stand at least 10 yards from free kick
1920 – Players can no longer be given offside from a throw-in
1924 – Visiting teams obliged to change in the event of a colour clash
1924 – Goal may be scored direct from corner; Stanley Rous develops the diagonal run system of refereeing
1929 – FA Council introduce classification system for referees
1929 – Goalkeepers have to stand still on their lines for penalty kicks
1930 – First World Cup. First man sent off
1935 – Experiment with two referees at the Hawthorns
1938 – Uniform scale of payment for referees instituted. Refs to get 3 guineas for a league game
1939 – Numbering of players shirts made compulsory
1956 – Floodlighting used for the first time at a league match (Fratton Park)
1970 – Red and yellow cards introduced at World Cup in Mexico
1970 – Match assessors introduced
1974 – FIFA's fitness test introduced
1990 – Professional foul outlawed
1991 – Professional foul ruling extended to deliberate handball
1992 – Goalkeeper banned from picking up a kicked pass-back
1996/7 – The linesman becomes the Referee's Assistant
1997 – Player permitted to score directly from kick off; goalkeeper allowed to move along line for penalty kick
1998 – Tackle from behind outlawed
1998 – Electronic scoreboard introduced in World Cup to show injury time; assistant referees' flags are equipped with buzzers to aid communication with referees.
1998 – The Premier League unveils proposals to make referees professional beginning in 1999 and to make use of video replays (but for goal-line incidents only).
2005 – Rennie becomes first million pound official/ sin bins criticised/ magic eye scrapped; agents call for winter break for their clients and demand increased payment for Super League appointments…

INDEX

Aberdeen, v Rangers (1995) 117-118
AC Milan v
  Leeds United (ECWC final 1973) 109
  Levsky Spartak (UEFA Cup 1978) 114-115
accountability 188
age limits, FIFA 155
Alcock, Charles W 25, 31, 32, 34-36, 39
  first offside ruling 25
Anderlecht
  UEFA ban overruled 120
  v Nottingham Forest (UEFA Cup 1984) 97, 120
Angelis, Señor de 78
appeals
  fouls 14-15, 26, 38, 42, 44
  post-match 34-35
appointments, FA Management Committee 47-48
Arceo, Brito 122-123
Argentina
  Caswell, Isaac, crusade 81-84
  club matches
    Boca Juniors v
      Gimnasia y Esgrima (1933) 80-81
      Racing (1938) 83
      River Plate (1955) 86
      Western Railway (1910) 77
    Estudientes v, River Plate (1932) 78
    FC Oeste v, Newell's Old Boys (1972) 108-109
    Huracan v
      Racing (1932) 78
      Velez Sarsfield(1950) 89
  corruption 81
  v
    France (World Cup 1930) 49-50
    Holland (World Cup 1978) 66
    Uruguay (1958) 89
    Uruguay (World Cup final 1930) 51
    USA (World Cup 1930) 50-51
Arsenal
  Brazil tour (1949) 91
  v Chelsea (1998) 186
assaults
  by referees 126-127
  Eastern Europe 120-121, 122
  England 139-140, 142, 144, 183, 184
  Italy 123-124
  Scotland 124-125
  South America 77-78, 121
  World Cup 1930 49-50
Association of Football League Referees and Linesmen 145, 163-4, 168
Association of Premier and Football League Match Officials 131, 205
Aston Villa, v Stoke on Trent Bridge (1891) 29
Australia, v Chile (World Cup 1974) 64-65
Baert, Louis 52, 56
Baglione, Duccio 113
Baines, Steve 135-136
Baker, Danny 211-212
ball size 27
Barcelona
  referees' attitude to 96-97, 98-100
  retribution (pig) 123
  see also Spain, club matches
Bardi, Giovanni 5
Barlassini, Rinaldo 53-54
Barnsley, v Liverpool (1998) 184
Barrick, Jack 91-92
Barry, Neale 184
Barton, Dr AW 41
bias
  Argentina 81
  Barcelona/Real Madrid 96-97, 98-100
  Italy 110-113
  possible, Scotland 115-119
  see also bribery
biographies 59-60
Blackburn Rovers, v Queen's Park [Glasgow] (FA Cup Final 1884) 27
Blatter, Sepp 68, 154-155, 208
Bond, John 170
Borussia Dortmund, v Inter Milan (European Cup 1964) 111
Bouchardeau 67
Braddish, Dave 132, 147-148
Braithwaite, Colin 139
Braithwaite, Lisa 139
Brazil
  club matches, Corinthians v São Paulo (1997) 125
  club rivalries 76
  v
    Czechoslovakia (World Cup 1938) 54-55
    Exeter City (1914) 75
    Hungary (World Cup 1954) 60, 62-63
    Sweden (World Cup 1974) 171-172
bribery 97, 102, 109-110, 113-115, 120
British referees, World Cup debut 49
Bruzzone, (Senor) 78
Buenos Aires
  club rivalries 76-79
  v Scotland (1923) 75-76
Bustamante, Hugo 126
Calcio Storico 5-7
Cambridge, rules of football 20
Cameroons, v Chile (World Cup 1998) 67
Capdeville, George 51
captains, as referees 9-10, 16
Cardiff, v Chelsea (FA Cup 1927) 30
Carlisle, v Grimsby Town (1998) 184
Caswell, Isaac 81-84
Celtic
  and referees 115-118
  v Rangers (1997) 117
Challenge Cup, FA *see* FA Cup
Charterhouse School, game rules 10-11
Chebotaryov, Yury 120-121
Chelsea v
  Arsenal (1998) 186
  Capital (1929) 80
  Cardiff (FA Cup 1927) 30
  Leicester City (FA Cup 1996) 181-182
Cheltenham College, game rules 18
Chile v
  Australia (World Cup 1974) 64-65
  Cameroons (World Cup 1998) 67
  Italy (World Cup 1998) 67
Christoforu, Georgina 141
Clark, JH, Cup final (1873) 30
Clegg, JC (Sir Charles) 33
Colombia
  club matches
    America v Independiente Medellin (1990) 106
    Armenia Quindio v Independiente Sante Fe (1990) 107
  corruption 106-107
committees, as referees 16, 18, 19
communication skills 148, 202
Cooper, Keith
  motivation 131-132, 146
  recruitment 145, 146
  rewards 134-135, 176

skills 148
Corinthians, The 73-4, 76, 79
v Fluminese (1910) 74
Courtney, George 152
Coventry City, v Sheffield Wednesday (1970) 166
Cristophe, Henri 56
Crocker, Ted 164, 200
Cruyff, Johan 98
Czechoslovakia, v Brazil (World Cup 1938) 54-55
Dallas, Hugh 68
Danson, Paul 187-188, 205
Darlington, v Solihull Borough (FA Cup 1997) 119-120
Dasent, JR 30
Dauden Ibanez, Arturo 94
Davidson, Bob 64, 65
Davila, Megia 95
death-threats 78, 86
Denoncourt, Sonya 208
Diaz Vega, Manuel 98-99
discretion, reduction in 186, 212
diving 95, 99, 206
Don, Philip 69, 136-137, 150, 207
Dunn, Steve 152-153, 172
Durkin, Paul 91, 141, 142, 206
Ecuador, v Peru (S American Ch'ship 1957) 87-88
Egypt, v Hungary (World Cup 1934) 53-54
Elleray, David 25, 133-134, 143, 188
Ellis, Arthur 58, 59, 60-61, 63
England v
Scotland (1880) 28-29
The Rest (1933) 41
USA (World Cup 1950) 58
English League, formation 35, 36, 40
Eton College, wall game 11, 13-14
Exeter City v
Brazil Select XI (1914) 75
Racing (1914) 77-78
FA, v West Bromwich Albion (1933) 41
FA Cup
Final, refereeing record 33
inception 23, 25
pre-1900 24, 27, 29, 30-33
Fandos, Manuel 107
Faulkener, Gerry 170
Fédération Internationale de Football Association *see* FIFA
Ferguson, Alex 119
Ferrarini, Divinio 113-114
Fewings, Janet 128
FIFA (Fédération Internationale de Football Association)
age limits 155
dehumanising policy 177
founded 45
rulings 68, 149-150, 185, 190
selection policy 56-57, 67, 69
South American membership 56
see also World Cup
fitness 152-155, 199
Fluminese, v Corinthians, The (1910) 74
Football Association (FA)
defence of referees 34
defers to FIFA 162
Director of Refereeing 186
formation 21-22, 23-24
internal organisation 164
referee appointments 47-48
Referees Committee 164, 165, 172
video replay trial 213-214
see also FA Cup; FIFA, Rulings; laws, FA
France v, Argentina (World Cup1930) 49-50
Franchi, Dr Artemio 66
free kicks 26, 38, 44
Gallagher, Dermot 186-189, 202
Gascoigne, Paul 118, 149, 189-190
Glanville, Brian 110
goal-kicks, introduction of 26
goalkeepers
introduction of 26
rules 27-28, 30, 45
goalposts, early 19, 27
Godoi, Oscar Roberto de 125
Gonella, Sergio 66
Gonzalez, Mejuto 95-96
Gordon, John 114-115
grading system 48, 138-139, 205
Great Britain, v Rest of Europe (1947) 49
Greece
club matches, Panathinaikos v, AEK Athens (1962) 109
referees 103, 109-110
Griffiths, Mervyn 58
Grimsby Town, v Carlisle (1998) 184
Guruceta, Emilio 96-97
Hamilton, (Mr) 28
Handley, Jimmy 41
harassment
by crowd 42, 52, 82
by players 83
Hardaker, Alan 166, 167-168
Harrow School
Cock House Trophy 12, 35
game rules 9, 11-12, 15-16
Hasley, Mark 183
Hibernian
Marabou Stork Nightmares 118-119
v
Leeds United (Fairs Cup 1967) 115
Rangers (1995) 190
Higgs, David 139
Hill, Gordon 150-152
Hill, Jimmy 33-34, 181
Holland v
Argentina (World Cup 1978) 66
Sweden (World Cup 1974) 65
Hrysanis, Nikos 103
Hungary v
Brazil (World Cup 1954) 60, 62-63
Egypt (World Cup 1934) 53-54
Italy (World Cup final 1938) 51
Iley, Stuart 126-127
incitement 190
Inglis, Harry 143
Inter Milan
v
Borussia Dortmund (European Cup 1964) 111
Liverpool (European Cup 1965) 110
Malmo (European Cup 1968) 110-111
see also Italy, club matches
international representation 45, 47, 55
Italy
assaults 123-124
club matches
Bar Acquario v Bar Miki (1979) 124
FC Bastardo v Virtus La Castellana (1997) 123
Inter Milan v Juventus (1998) 112-113
Livorno v Montevarchi (1997) 113-114
Napoli v Palermo (1969) 124
Palermo v Ternana (1997) 124
training officials 196-197
v
Chile (World Cup 1998) 67
Hungary (World Cup final 1938) 51
Spain (World Cup 1934) 52
Johnston, Mick 128
Kelly, Graham 33, 213
Kent, v Surrey (1868) 24
kidnapping 106-107
Kilmarnock, v Rangers (1998) 116
King, Howard 125-126
King, Jeff 94, 98, 105
Kingscott, A 33
Kinnaird, Lord Arthur 31-32, 34
Kirkham, Wayne 142-143
Kirkpatrick, Roger 151
Langenus, Jean 50-51, 52, 55,

56
language
bad 143-144
translation problems 53-54
Laws of Association Football 44-45
laws, FA
Alcock, Charles W 26-27, 32, 34-35
application 188, 189
formulation 23-28, 29-32, 36-38, 39-40
pre-FA 20-2, 23
recent changes 205-206
referees 43-45
see also FIFA rulings; rules of football (early); school game rules
Leafe, Reg 58
Leake, Tony 132
Leeds United v
AC Milan (ECWC final 1973) 109
Hibernian (Fairs Cup 1967) 115
Middlesbrough (1998) 149
Legg, Andy 146
Leicester City, v Chelsea (FA Cup 1996) 181-182
Lennon, Neil 182
Levsky Spartak, v AC Milan (UEFA Cup 1978) 114-115
linesmen
established 37-38, 39-40
excluded from refereeing 67
replacement of 41
linesmen/referee team 170-171
Liverpool v
Arsenal (1972) 33
Barnsley (1998) 184
Inter Milan (European Cup 1965) 110
West Ham (League Cup Final 1981) 163
Lopez Nieto, Antonio 102
McCartney, David 114-115
McCluskey, Jim 117
McGilvray, Jim 189-190
McMaster, Jim 132-133
McMillan, Gordon 41
Mafia 106
Malmo v, Inter Milan (European Cup 1968) 110-111
man management 148
Manchester City, v Manchester United (1974) 161-162
Manchester United v
Manchester City (1974) 161-162
Southampton (FA Cup Final1976) 160
Marabou Stork Nightmares, Welsh, Irvine 118-119
Marindin, Major Francis, FA Cup finals 27, 31, 33, 34
Martin, Edward 183
match fixing
Colombia 107
Italy 110-111
Paraguay 108
media
influence 177-178
positive use of 202
S America 87-88, 90-91
Mendibl, Ortiz de 110-111
Mercet, Rene 52
Middlesbrough, v Leeds United (1998) 149
Milford, Roger 176
Millichip, Bert 163
Mitchell, Bobby 58
Moreno, Bryan 121
motivation 131-134, 137-138, 139, 151
murder, referees 106
Mussolini, Benito 51-52, 53
mutiny 145
Namdar, Jafar 64
neutral referees 55-56
Newcastle United, v Stevenage (FA Cup 1997) 210-211
non-league matches
Highland Laddie v Spennymoor Voltigeur (1995) 41
Maidenhead v Old Etonians (1875) 35
Newport Pagnell Athletic v Wicken Sport 126-127
Old Rose v Hucknall Chequers (1994) 142-143
Portsmouth RN v Thatcham Town 127
Southampton Arms v Hurstbourne British Legion (1998) 128
Nottingham, v Sheffield (1865) 24
Nottingham County, v Stoke on Trent Bridge (FA Cup 1890-1) 29
Nottingham Forest v
Anderlecht (UEFA Cup 1984) 120
Anderlect (UEFA Cup 1984) 97
Nunez Manrique, Jose 97-98
offside 25, 213, 215
Ortega, Alvaro 106
other sports, treatment of officials 191-192, 201-202
Owen, Michael 153, 184
Oxford University, v Wanderers (FA Cup Final 1873) 30-31
Pallister, Gary 150
Paraguay, club matches, Sol De America v Olimpia (1989/90) 108
Partick Thistle, v Rangers (1995/6) 189-190
Partridge, Pat 33, 134, 151, 200-201
Passion of the People, Mason, Tony 72-73, 75
Pawsey, Phil 127-128
payments, official 43, 61, 65-66, 198-200
Payne, Reg 165-166
Pellidid, Constantine 110
penalty box, introduced 45
penalty kicks 29-30, 38, 44, 116-117
Peru
club matches, Atletico Chalaco v Nacional Iquitos (1978) 126
v
Ecuador (S American Ch'ship 1957) 87-88
Romania (World Cup1930) 50
Pes Perez, Donato 107
Pickford, W 43
pitch invasions 184, 185
players, former, as referees 136-137
Poll, Graham 202
Portsmouth, v Sheffield United (1998) 183
Premiership Referees' Officer, Don, Philip 69, 150
professionalism 198-200
Queen's Park [Glasgow] v
Blackburn Rovers (FA Cup Final 1884) 27
Wanderers (1875) 28
Ramos Marcos, Joaquin 101
Rangers
and referees 115-119
v
Aberdeen (1995) 117-118
Celtic (1997) 117
Hibernian (1995) 190
Kilmarnock (1998) 116
Partick Thistle (1995/6) 189-190
Reader, George 58, 59
Real Madrid 96-97, 98-100, 105
see also Spain, club matches
recruitment rate 138, 145
red cards
FIFA enforcement 190
introduced 55
tackling from behind 68-69
Redondo, (Senor) 99
Reed, Mike 170, 182, 199, 213
Referees Association 136, 144, 187, 197-198
formation 31, 43
Referees Chart
1896 15, 43-44
see also Laws of Association

Football
Rego, Almeida 49-50
resignation rate 145
Richards, Phil 183
Ridden, Ken 186
Rio, Jose Miguel del 122
Robinson, Paul 119-120
Robson, Bobby, Barcelona coach 94-96, 97-98
Rolfe, Martin 140
Romania
club matches, Sportul Illescu v Universtatea Craiova (1997) 122
v, Peru (World Cup1930) 50
Ronaldo 112
Rossi, Paulo 111-112
Rous, Sir Stanley 45, 162
Rowbotham, John 117
Rugby School, game rules 8, 10
Russia, club matches, Dynamo Moscow v Spartak Vladikavkaz (1996) 120-121
Scotland v
Buenos Aires (1923) 75-76
England (1880) 28-29
Scottish Cup 36
Scottish League, formation (1890) 36
Seal, Colin 188
sending off 89-90, 100, 206-207
Sernzacqua, Emanuele 114
sexual favours 125-126
Shardella, Antonio 124
Shearer, Alan 182, 210
Sheffield
rules of football 20, 23
v Nottingham (1865) 24
Sheffield United, v Portsmouth (1998) 183
Sheffield Wednesday, v Coventry City (1970) 166
Sims, Jim 170
Sky Sports 178-179
Smith, Arthur, Referees Association 136, 187, 197, 205
Smith, Dougie 190
Soccer Referee's Manual, Ager, David 144, 146-147
Solihull Borough, v Darlington (FA Cup 1997) 119-120
South America
British referees in 81-92
football introduced 71-72
passion for football 72-73, 76-77, 78-81, 86-89
referees 57, 71-72, 78-79, 84-85
Southampton
Argentine tour (1904) 74
v, Manchester United (FA Cup Final 1976) 160
Spain
Barcelona
v
Real Madrid (1998) 99-100
(Spanish Cup final 1970) 97
Real Sociedad (1997) 97-98
Real Zaragoza (1996) 95-96
FC Lovio v Santa Cruz (1997) 122
v
Italy (World Cup 1934) 52
Uruguay (World Cup 1950) 59
Spanish referees 93-94, 96-97, 100-102
Association 100-101
Speake, Dick 165
Stair, A 30
Stevenage, v Newcastle United (FA Cup 1997) 210-211
Stiles, Nobby 147
Stoke on Trent Bridge v
Aston Villa (1891) 29
Notts County (FA Cup 1890-1) 29
strikes 100-103, 109
Strocchia, Felice 113
Surrey, v Kent (1868) 24
Sweden v
Brazil (World Cup 1974) 171-172
Holland (World Cup 1974) 65
Sylvester, Melvin 128
Symes, David 118-119

tackling from behind 68, 176
Tait, Bobby 116
Taylor, Jack 64, 65
technology
effects of 178-179, 212-213
use of 196, 208-209, 213-214, 215
television
trial by 178-179, 180-181
tyranny of replays 180-181, 211-212
use of replays 209-211, 213-215
ten yard rule 206
Tesanic 111
The Final Whistle, Ellis, Arthur 60
Thomas, Clive
attempted bribing of 115
early career 159
match incidents 24, 163, 166
matches 160, 161-162, 166
media coverage 167, 168
personality 150, 157-160
retirement 172-173
stood-up by FA 163-165, 167-169
World Cups 64, 65, 171-172
throw-ins, early 28
Tiffin, Russell 184
Toms, Wendy 207
training officials, Italy 196-197
Turner, Bob 86, 87-88
two referees, experiments 41
UEFA (Union of European Football Associations)
Anderlecht ban overruled 120
fitness tests 154
Ukraine, club matches, Metallurg Mariupol v Vorskla Poltava (1997) 121
umpires 13-16, 17-20, 25, 30-31, 36-37
powers of 26, 41-42, 43-44
Union of European Football Associations *see* UEFA
Uppingham School, rules of football 21
Uruguay v
Argentina
(1958) 89
(World Cup final 1930) 51
Spain (World Cup 1950) 59
USA, v England (World Cup 1950) 58
Vagner, Laszlo 67
Vautot, Michel 154
Vianna, Mario 62
violence
by referees 126-127
off pitch 103, 120-125
on pitch 55, 72, 80, 89, 140, 142, 183, 184
tolerance of 89-90
Wanderers
v
Oxford University (FA Cup Final 1873) 30-31, 32
Queen's Park [Glasgow] (1875) 28
Waters, Phil 145-146
whistles, introduced 38
Willard, Gary 150, 184
Willis, Peter 148
Wimbledon, v Wrexham (FA Cup 1998) 172
Winchester College, games rules 11, 14
Winsemann, Werner 65
women officials 128-129, 141, 207-208
Wood, E 41
World Cup 47-48, 53, 55-56
1930 Uruguay 48-51
1934 Italy 51-53
1938 France 51, 54-55
1950 Brazil 58-59
1954 Switzerland60 62
1974 Germany 64-66, 171
1978 Argentina 66-67, 171
1998 France 66, 67-68
Wrexham, v Wimbledon (FA Cup 1998) 172
Young, Andy 127
Zamrano, Pino